To the memory of
JOHN HENDERSON PRITCHARD, D.D., 1873–1932
JANE DUBOIS PRITCHARD, 1880–1932

Preface

AMERICAN LITERARY and critical theory is intensely interesting in itself. Without developing novel critical ideas, it has consistently borrowed and adapted principles from other literatures until it has become original in the best sense of the word—a new creation to fit novel situations. As the United States has developed, its growing literary principles have illustrated its developing culture, not only in letters but in politics, social institutions, aesthetics, and to some extent in religion.

It is strange that a continuous account of these principles is lacking. This deficiency, it is my hope in some measure to supply by indicating the trends and noting some of the minor writers as well as the major figures who have discussed letters in America. For these minor writers, literary periodicals have furnished much of the material. Their mass of comparatively unconsidered, often anonymous expression supplements the major writers by showing what the literary rank-and-file were thinking. When their essays are read with the works of better-known authors, one sees also that contemporary critics have American roots which have generally remained unnoticed. American forces have molded our critical theory from the very beginning.

Such a study as this surveys the field. It does not, after the method of George Saintsbury, exhaustively enumerate and discuss those who have contributed to our literary culture, but tries to present significant figures and representatives of the various groups. Many detailed studies await the student in this area. Among others, the development of thinking in literary centers like Philadelphia, Baltimore, and Charleston will reward the investigator. The present writer is now studying pre-Civil War literary activities in New York. The relations of American literary and aesthetic theory also merit careful study.

Research connected with this book was supported in part by a grant from the Penrose Fund of the American Philosophical Society; by a Rockefeller grant administered by the University of Oklahoma; and by grants from the Faculty Research Fund of the University of Oklahoma. These grants enabled me to collect materials in the libraries of Cornell and Harvard universities; to the staffs of these libraries I express my deep appreciation for their assistance. The Bizzell Memorial Library of the University of Oklahoma has been a constant help. I wish to thank my colleagues for their aid: John M. Raines for critically reading the early draft of the manuscript; Victor A. Elconin for detailed criticism of a later draft; Stanley K. Coffman for many suggestions; and Joseph H. Marshburn for advice and constant encouragement. My wife helped with my collections, typed the manuscript, and offered valuable suggestions.

John Paul Pritchard

NORMAN, OKLAHOMA
SEPTEMBER II, 1955

Contents

Criticism
IN AMERICA

Chapter 1

The Early Nineteenth-Century
American Cultural Scene

I N 1820, A REVIEWER greeted William Tudor's *Letters on the Eastern States* as evidence of the increased national sentiments in the United States following the War of 1812. Although he admitted that American literature was hampered by many obstacles, he believed that the work of American writers was steadily improving. Literature, he declared, was the surest index to our adolescent culture. Until men like Tudor, however, could devote their major effort to literature instead of merely their leisure hours, he feared that America's literary growing pains would continue.

Obstacles to the development of American letters fell into three overlapping categories: the wide geographical distribution of the people, economic and political difficulties, and the state of culture in the nation as a whole. From its earliest steps toward nationality, the United States had found these conditions reflected and discussed in its literature. Literary theories are intimately related to the conditions of the people among whom they appear; and one must look carefully into the circumstances under which our first literary men worked before he can appreciate their literary and critical thinking.

At the beginning of the nineteenth century, most Americans lived in small, widely scattered settlements or in isolated homes without even the contacts of a rural community. Less than 5 per cent of the population lived in cities of more than eight thousand inhabitants. Most families therefore had to be almost entirely self-sufficient. In smaller communities, bartered services could slightly offset the need for each family to satisfy its own needs by its own labor. Although such labor by its great diversity would tend to breed self-reliance and independence, it was never ending and so exhausting as to leave scant energy for less immediately pressing pursuits. Sunday, the day of rest, was in many parts of the country hedged about with religious restrictions; where this was not the case, the relaxation that suggested itself to hard-laboring people was rarely cultural.

For various causes presently to appear, the efforts of the government to promote nationwide education were in many instances but slightly successful. Literary culture, if not all culture, must rest upon the three *R*'s. But while gradually the greater part of the citizens became rudimentarily literate, many of these advanced little beyond reading and writing. The church, in many hamlets almost the sole humanizing agency, all too often adopted an obscurantism which left rural folk without cultural opportunity. Although many of the founding fathers in the colonies had been men of culture, the exigencies of frontier life permitted the transmission of only a small part of this culture to their offspring even in more thickly populated areas. The demands first of colonial expansion and later of the forming nation channeled the curiosity and interests of the more alert citizens into practical courses, leaving little surplus time or energy to be devoted to literary or artistic ways. One is almost tempted to admire such traces of the fine arts and letters as appeared rather than to deplore their scarcity.

Politics and economic developments united to check the cultural development of the country. Although the arts and literature stem from the life of a people, men whose best efforts are directed to the creation and development of a way of life are likely to have satisfied their creative desires in these activities. Franklin and Jefferson, who represent the ablest creative minds at the beginning of the century, exhausted their energies—except for Jefferson's architectural creativity—in their public services and in scientific inventions or gadgets.

Political and economic developments conspired to turn men's minds away from concern with their possible transatlantic heritage. Jefferson's Embargo, and previous and subsequent embroilments with England, France, and the Algerine pirates, funneled American energy into the West, away from Europe. Men's thoughts of things

British or Continental, except among the better informed, became increasingly hostile. Such developments as the fabulous Astor fur trade focused ambition even beyond the frontier. Undoubtedly Americans of decades to come would profit culturally from the opening of the West, but its immediate effect was to enhance the already strong materialistic interests of the people and turn their attention away from immediate sources of culture. Moreover, effects produced in the West by settlers from the several sections of the East magnified the differences already existing in the coastal sections. Northern capitalism and manufacturing, drawing raw materials from the Mississippi basin, not only set the capitalistic pattern upon the North; they also by discovering mechanical means to process cotton reestablished Negro slavery in the deep South and squeezed out the philanthropic agrarianism which Virginian thinkers had developed out of eighteenth-century French social theorizing.

Another economic force, mass production, deriving impetus from the genius of such men as Eli Whitney, was already starting to supplant the craftsman by the maker of parts. Although the assembling of rifles from parts made by different hands was a far cry from the assembly line, the nobility of toil by craftsmen which Longfellow found so culturally praiseworthy in Nuremberg was already beginning to be debased in America through piecework. As Longfellow dimly saw, the hand that makes the whole product, be it only a shoe, may belong to a Hans Sachs, whereas the hand that produces only the stock of a rifle is not training its mind to produce any sort of rounded whole.

As the chauvinists kept asserting and the Federalists feared, the culture of the new democracy must obviously be democratic. The concept was new; nobody knew exactly how democracy would affect the idea of culture. Northern businessmen and Southern landed proprietors understandably feared the possibilities in such a development. The adherents of Jefferson who took the reins of government in 1801 shared only in few instances their leader's good will toward education, and were incompetent to develop a democratic theory of culture, which had to wait for the age of Jackson to attempt its formulation. Only a few theorists cherished any constructive ideas for the culture of the new country.

[5]

Over the nation as a whole, then, at the beginning of the century cultural conditions were depressingly weak. In New England, Puritan energy and constructive power had deteriorated into bigotry and fanaticism, having the form of godliness but denying the power thereof. Elsewhere, other varieties of Calvinism—Presbyterian, Baptist, or Reformed—likewise turned their backs upon the arts and literature as worldly. The newer Unitarianism, slowly gaining ground, was rationalistic and on the whole would remain satisfied with the *status quo* for two decades before William Ellery Channing should awaken it.

Education shared the general apathy. The public schools still awaited the activities of James Savage and Horace Mann to rouse public opinion to their support. Boston enjoyed the advantage of an excellent preparatory school conducted by John Sylvester John Gardiner, who brought to America the fine scholarship and classical instruction of London's Dr. Samuel Parr; but good preparatory schools were few. Nor were the colleges beacons of light. Harvard was a pallid copy of the English universities, which, even so, were themselves in the educational doldrums. Decorum was still the order of the day, and new ideas, which would inevitably include dangerous Jacobin notions, were denied admittance. Instruction was, as complaints from many students indicated, superficial, and the instructors had to supplement their stipends by other employment. Though the classical languages still formed the backbone of the curriculum, they were taught as the trappings of the gentleman, with no thought of their genuine practical value as guides for life. Had they been presented as they appeared later to Thoreau, who used them as integral parts of his everyday life, the picture of American education might have been changed. As taught in 1800, they had little to offer an American culture.

Libraries were for the most part negligible. By 1815, Harvard's contained only some twenty thousand books. When Joseph Buckminster returned from Europe in 1807 with a scholarly library of some three thousand well-chosen books, his collection was almost unique in America. The Old World heritage had pretty well lost its significance. Many American families had lived in America for six generations, and only a negligible few had preserved any connection with their mother-country. European education and culture seemed to them alien, an impression which the mainly aristocratic supporters of these traditions were unable to dispel. Many Americans who considered the cultural situation gravely doubted the advisability of transplanting European culture to America and thereby gave support to the 100 per cent Americans with whom they were not generally in sympathy.

But these thoughtful students of the American cultural crisis were equally doubtful of the artistic efficacy of the American scene, the American language, or the American art product. Solyman Brown charged the British with deliberately fostering this doubt in order at the same time to undermine democracy and to unload inferior literary wares upon the United States. Whatever its origin, the notion was widespread that the American air was unfriendly to writers and the national temper, anti-intellectual. In America, everything deteriorates—propaganda that James Fenimore Cooper felt needed painstaking disproof even in the fourth decade of the century. More dangerous, however, was the widespread provincial unreadiness to see value in the local scene and the local treatment of it in comparison with the product of England. Brockden Brown's novels, one American defender declared, though widely read in England, were almost unread in his native land. Publishers' statistics show that even the loudest supporters of American books were not buying them.

The cultural spirit that was soon to combat the materialistic provincialism of the young nation had political and social connections. Though some of these affiliations were not beneficial to the nascent culture, their effect was profound. Of them, the most significant were the new nationalism of the early nineteenth century, the Utopian dream, and the inrush of foreign artistic and social practices.

The hotly contested adoption of the federal Constitution was merely a step in the advance toward a national sentiment. It had to be nourished by pressures from without, as in ancient Greece by dangers shared, and by common interest. Although it was the longest established of American international grievances, the hostility toward England was not the sole outward pressure molding the form of the nation. European nationalism, which burst out vigorously after

Napoleon's downfall, had its counterpart in America, where it displayed many of the restrictive characteristics which Goethe was later to deplore in Europe. In the United States, however, it served also as a unifying force. By slackening the chains of dependence upon Britain, it strengthened American national self-reliance. Meanwhile, the strengthening of the federal government, demonstrated by Washington's handling of the Whiskey Rebellion, systematized by Hamilton and John Marshall, and after the fall of the Federalists carried on by Henry Clay, provided the concept of a nation instead of a congeries of loosely related states. The second war with England and the animosity which it engendered furnished an enduring foreign object against which to unite.

Another strong social force was the American Utopian dream. Bishop Berkeley, in declaring "Westward the star of empire takes its way," had implied a manifest destiny for the New World which the new nation related to its own future. Philip Freneau and Tom Paine had taught the perfectibility of man and the ideal situation of the new land for this improvement. Joel Barlow had proclaimed it in his *Vision of Columbus*. The dream visited many Americans in hours of reverie, as it had visited Samuel Taylor Coleridge and Robert Southey in England; and few thought it a lying dream. In the early years of the new century, Mme de Staël gave the dream new impetus. Her explanation of the melancholy, meditative verse of British poets as consisting of equal parts of gloomy British weather and drab British life was a development of the popular environmentalist theories which naturally found instant favor among Americans, not merely for its implied slur upon Britain, but also because Americans read into it approbation of what they considered their own superior environment. Numerous friendly writers from England and the Continent fostered American assurance of destiny and strengthened the national feeling.

Not a few social ferments were at the same time leavening the American loaf. Even in Boston, tradition was hard put to it to continue its hold upon thinking. Feminist and humanitarian movements were symptoms of the new forces hammering at the door of conservatism. Young sailors returned full of new and sometimes revolutionary notions, as did young men back from the grand tour. By

1820, American students, led by George Ticknor, who were studying in Germany, wrote back sharply adverse criticisms of the instruction and libraries at Harvard. These sailors, socialites, and scholars were well-armed opponents of traditionalism.

Continental ideas were entering America by several avenues. French aid during the Revolution had stirred interest in the French language and customs which subsequent opponents of the French Revolution could not suppress. Later unfriendliness to Napoleon in its turn enhanced the already considerable interest in German science and culture. In 1819, George Ticknor's return from Europe to teach modern languages at Harvard marked a major defeat for the diehards. Longfellow's appointment a decade later to a similar chair at Bowdoin indicates the spread of the innovation.

Although interest in Continental cultures was for a time restricted to the educated few and to select circles in the larger cities, it soon filtered into other levels of society. By 1840, Longfellow's popularization of the Continental Middle Ages had made the mass of Americans aware of central Europe. Many of them began to attend seriously to the problems of self-culture and national culture, and to include European ideas in each process. Scions of the new thinking from Virginia and New England began to leaven the West, and young intellectuals stirred men's minds in Charleston as well as in Boston.

Obvious barriers prevented Americans of the early nineteenth century from thinking of other expressions of culture than literature. Of music they had some slight experience. They were, however, more familiar with books than with *objets d'art*. The plastic arts were almost unknown to them and were moreover in the minds of many tainted with impropriety. All were aware of the proneness of painters and sculptors to depict the nude human body and by so doing to tempt to the mortal sin of concupiscence, against which evangelical Protestantism marshaled all its legions. Washington Allston and Horatio Greenough were unable to wear down this prejudice. Even Emerson, though emancipated by free thinking and foreign travel, thought of the past almost wholly in terms of books. Americans in thinking of books as the expression of culture were facing the facts of their life.

[9]

Three conditions of the early nineteenth century in America directly influenced the course of authorship and critical thinking. The first concerned practical problems of publication. American printers found it more profitable to republish new English books than to print works by American authors. English books not only were more readily bought by the still largely provincial public; they could also usually be had without payment of royalty to their authors. The added profit overcame any scruples of honesty or patriotism. In 1820, only some 30 per cent of the books published in the United States were by American writers; the rest were chiefly British and largely pirated editions. The proportion is obviously no criterion of the comparable merits of British and American books, but indicates merely the source of profit in printing. Some attempt was made by American authors to protect the pecuniary interests of their British friends, as Emerson succeeded in doing for Thomas Carlyle; and complaints at the highhandedness of the publishers were numerous. It indicates no doubt the improved quality of American writing, as well as a shift in the attitude of book buyers, that by 1850 the percentage of American and British books printed in the United States had been almost completely reversed. During the period with which we are now concerned, however, the uphill fight of American authors to get their work published was a major factor affecting the course of American letters.

Periodical publication offered a somewhat brighter picture. Hopeful editors were not deterred from starting magazines by the grim mortality rates. Many periodicals had existed briefly in early colonial and early national times, and the new century had hardly started before a number of new reviews were started. Although most of these were ephemeral, fortunate to outlast the year when they saw the light, a few survived for a considerable time and exerted great influence.

Two of the most noteworthy magazines which survived long enough to display their quality were Joseph Dennie's *Port Folio* in Philadelphia, which ran from 1801 until 1827, surviving its brilliant but crotchety editor's death by two decades; and the *Monthly Anthology* in Boston, conducted for nearly a decade by a club of able young Boston reviewers and critics under the editorship of the

Reverend William Emerson, scholarly and industrious father of a more famous son. The *Anthology* was progenitor of the *North American Review*, the sole survivor from this period into the mid-twentieth century. Other periodicals, like the Philadelphia *Analectic*, though surviving for several years, devoted their pages chiefly to excerpts from foreign periodicals and consequently concern us little except as purveyors of British periodical literature to American readers.

Both the *Port Folio* and the *Anthology* discussed many topics of interest. The contributors to the former were perhaps less conservative than their Boston contemporaries; yet both gave space to advocates of new ideas. Their conservatism has been considerably overestimated, perhaps because they stood in sharp opposition to the more radical Jacobin ideas flowing from the French Revolution. Their contributors were men of classical training who defended their heritage, and the Boston group in particular supported sound though not always orthodox Christianity. They were inevitably influenced by the British reviews, which circulated in the cultural centers. They rarely, however, descended to the mudslinging and vilification which occasionally characterized the transatlantic periodicals. The *Anthology's* courteous treatment of Noah Webster, to whom it conceded space to set forth his ideas about the American language to which the editors were vigorously opposed, stands in favorable contrast to the contemporary treatment which Wordsworth was receiving in Britain. Some of the shorter-lived magazines, like the New York *American Monthly Magazine*, were noticeably less restrained; and it may be that the mildness which Henry Adams later noted of the Americans at the start of the century contributed to the decease of such ephemera.

A second problem much in the minds of early theorists was the American language. Walter Channing, a vivacious professor in the Harvard Medical School, deplored the use in the United States of the English language. A national literature requires a national language; the United States employs the British language; therefore, he argued, the new nation can hope at best to produce a variety of English literature which cannot represent the country. Since he saw no possibility of ridding the nation of this language—although

British writers sarcastically declared that Americans had already done so—he despaired of an American national literature. Conservative writers, like an anonymous scholar in the Baltimore *Portico*, were worried lest Americans abandon the well of English undefiled as regulated by Samuel Johnson. Others wrote spirited defenses of Americanism, claiming, as James Russell Lowell did later, that excepting a few new coinages or obvious Indian borrowings, most so-called Americanisms had been established English usage when the colonists came to America. This concern about the language conditioned both theory and practice in letters.

A third element of the literary situation was the study in Europe of able young men who were interested in improving education in the United States. Shortly after the War of 1812, young Americans began to filter into Göttingen, Berlin, and Heidelberg in search of intensive German scholarship. Their reactions were vigorous. George Ticknor wrote to Harvard bewailing the meager library of 20,000 volumes in contrast to Göttingen's 400,000. He had conferred with Jefferson at Monticello before leaving the United States, and at his request sent him lists of books for the library of the projected University of Virginia. Edward Everett, Joseph Cogswell, George Bancroft, and William Emerson, while studying the German language as a tool to aid their studies, came under the influence of the newer German philosophers; they made both actual and spiritual pilgrimages to Weimar. Several met and conversed with Goethe. Longfellow, visiting Weimar shortly after Goethe's death, already felt the city to be a shrine. Ralph Waldo Emerson also made a tour of the Continent. Under the leadership of William Ellery Channing, these young men of the second Unitarian generation had escaped the self-satisfaction of their fathers as well as the doldrums of decadent Puritanism. Returning to America, they brought new vigor and new ideas to education while at the same time preaching the gospel of romantic liberation. Under such leaders, American culture became filled with new ideas that were inevitably to break the bottles of tradition and battle lustily with the isolationist fear of foreign ideas.

In his history of the Jefferson and Madison administrations, Henry Adams characterizes the Americans of that era by intelligence, rapidity, and mildness. Their intelligence was of necessity directed in the main towards practical matters, but it was accompanied by a restless curiosity that went beyond practical and political needs. The rapidity with which the new country developed its necessary institutions—Adams instances the engineering skill of graduates from the ten-year-old United States Military Academy—was likewise not restricted to practical matters. As the periodical writers were fond of pointing out, though the physical requirements of the country were occupying its best minds for the time, they would produce worthy literature and artistic wares when they could get around to it. Their mildness made them unwilling to remain shackled by rules or systems intolerant of the novel ideas which actuated them to new endeavors. In such a soil, new seedlings of thought would quickly take root and grow.

Chapter 2

The Beginnings: 1800–1837

THE NINETEENTH CENTURY found American literary circles
still untroubled by the romantic unrest already active in
England. Eighteenth-century classicism controlled literary
thinking. A mild insurrection indeed attempted to establish "the
energetick Dryden" as dictator in Pope's stead. A. M. Walter ironically described Pope as "a skilful wrestler, who by oily flexibility
of limb could wind his adversary to the ground, but never could
crush him, like Dryden, by iron force and veteran hardihood of
muscle." The firebrand E. T. Dana joined Walter, complaining that
writers had striven so hard to be faultless that they had neglected
to be natural. Next, both Pope and Dryden, along with Congreve,
on the charge that they had founded a neoclassicism that was French
and not truly English, were demoted by the conservatives in favor
of Shakespeare, Spenser, and Milton, who in terms that sound
almost contemporary were set up as the leaders of the genuine British tradition; and Johnson, Gibbon, and Burke were unseated in
the same attack. Addison's style alone survived as a model to follow.

How far this insurrection within the old guard might have progressed, we shall never know. At this juncture, Scott, Byron, and
Southey invaded the field in the name of romanticism. The supporters of the new movement swarmed into the literary stronghold
and were soon at grips with the defenders of tradition.

The theory of literary models was for a time hard hit. It had

[14]

in fact been under fire ever since Edward Young, reviving an axiom of Longinus, had fifty years before urged English writers not to imitate what Homer had done but to consider how Homer would have performed the task before them. E. T. Dana complained that in reading conventional literature he was "either enveloped in the voluminous curl of the Johnsonian peruke, or pierced through the sensorium by the tart laconism of Lavater." He reminded American writers that "those, who follow, can, necessarily, never come up," and moreover become ridiculous when aping a model. P. Allen added that the substitution of a recent model for an older made no improvement. The copyists were stubborn, however. Reinforced thus by the provincial tendency to imitate some writer from the mother-country, the attention to models lasted well into the century, as Lowell noted in 1848 in his "Fable for Critics."

Opponents of literary apery pronounced specifically upon the diction of writers. J. S. J. Gardiner found our writers fertile of thought and logical in reasoning, but deficient in taste. They were too fond of meretricious ornament, hard words, a Latinized vocabulary, tumid periods. Their metaphors were either confused or clumsy. The antiquary James Savage charged them further with needless multiplication and careless use of words. Bryant added to the list of sins excessive inversion and diffuse style. All these faults were characteristic of failure to write correctly in the eighteenth-century style, though some had carried over into romantic writing. The American language, it was agreed, had after two centuries so thoroughly acclimated itself as to be equally adequate for literary expression with that of England; and reviewers jealously guarded its efficiency.

Perhaps the strongest barrier to an accepted American usage was local prejudice. Harvard writers objected to Noah Webster because no good thing could come out of Yale; Southern writers were even less willing to concede authority to a Yankee. Lacking a generally accepted standard of American diction, writers found themselves in an anomalous situation: defenders of American English through default of an American authority were forced to adhere to a British standard.

Edward Tyrrell Channing probably exerted the greatest influence on literary style. As Boylston professor of rhetoric and oratory at Harvard from 1819 to 1850, he influenced more American writers than any other teacher. Channing stood firm against careless change in the language. English was no doubt capable of improvement; the presumption, however, must stand in support of standard usage until incontrovertible improvement could be shown. Before admitting a new term, he assured himself that the concept to be named was really new and not merely new-appareled. He tried to steer a median course between hidebound conservatism and needless innovation, holding fast to every genuine bit of originality that appeared, to the end that the language might not stagnate but develop sanely into as adequate and artistic a means of expression as possible.

Americans revered poetry and read a surprising amount of it. Consequently, the diction of poetry occupied the attention of critics. When Byron, Scott, and Moore appeared, the conservatives attacked their diction as their most vulnerable point. The poems of Byron and Scott reminded one reviewer of young pheasants, "which are said to be so anxious of being disencumbered of the egg . . . , that they are not unfrequently seen running about with the shells on their backs." Scott's *Lay of the Last Minstrel* and Moore's *Lalla Rookh* were condemned for provincial phrases, "colloquial barbarisms," and "a vehement desire to think and talk as nobody ever thought and talked before." American imitators of the English romantic poets found their nationality no protection for them.

In discussing imagery and diction, these early critics foreshadowed current interests among critics. William Ellery Channing, in commenting upon Milton's ability to make language serve his needs, spoke of his bending it into forms demanded by his subject. Our recent critics, led by T. E. Hulme in England and new critics in America, have made the bending or warping of words a commonplace critical metaphor. Bryant's revival of the poet's traditional function as winnower of the language recurs in T. S. Eliot's pronouncement in 1945 of his present duty as its protector. E. T. Channing's rebuke to Thomas Moore for using tropes that were "mere ornaments and appendages—anything but illustration or a poetical embodying of thought," also presages recent attitudes toward imagery. The New Criticism roots in the early nineteenth century, when classical principles—not, to be sure, identical with the new classicism prophesied by T. E. Hulme—still ruled in literary thought.

Special attention to the critical views of Wordsworth and Coleridge did not appear until Coleridge's *Biographia Literaria* aroused interest. Bryant had earlier been poetically awakened by Wordsworth's poetry, but, excepting one printing of the *Lyrical Ballads*, none of Wordsworth's volumes was reprinted in America before 1824. *Biographia Literaria* drew from the *American Monthly Magazine* the comment that it testified as much to its author's kindness as to his softness of head; and the *Port Folio* praised it merely as a revolt from the "tinsel and bombast of Darwin and Della Crusca," failing to see in it a seminal book for most later criticism.

One of their earliest admirers was Richard Henry Dana, who had read Coleridge's criticisms of Wordsworth almost as soon as the book reached America. He found in them the best criticism of Wordsworth and more "philosophy, subtile analysis, and good taste" than any work in his memory. "In fact, our better criticism owes its birth to that." When the two disagreed, he took Coleridge's side. Writing between 1824 and 1829, other critics censured Wordsworth for that very triviality and meanness which he had admitted to be dangers in his poetry, for failure to avoid low or comic associations which his terms occasionally suggested; and they declared that whenever he successfully purged his language of undesirable elements, his resultant diction was essentially poetical. A later critic wondered why he should find people of superior situation unfit for contemplation. These critics at the same time praised his genuine attainment. F. W. P. Greenwood, using a metaphor revived by Friedrich Schlegel, asserted that whereas other poets had merely lifted corners of the veil covering nature, Wordsworth had drawn it aside to reveal unguessed affinities between nature and the general heart of man. Adequate appreciation of Wordsworth had, however, to await the voice of Emerson.

Few readers except R. H. Dana seem to have immediately read Coleridge's *Biographia Literaria*. As a poet, one reviewer remarked, his reputation which had been founded upon the *Rime of the Ancient Mariner* had barely survived the dismay at *Christabel*; another declared his prestige to have been ruined by *Kubla Khan*. The com-memorative articles following Coleridge's death in 1835 first appar-ently abandoned the estimate of him as a leader deserted by the literary world for failure to exercise his great talents in the orbit marked out for him by nature.

> It is now, less than formerly, the lot of such minds to be criticized by men, "whose intellectual claims to the guardianship of the muses seem, from the greater part, analogous to the physical qualifications, which adapt their oriental brethren for the superintendence of the Harem."

Coleridge's enemies stood accused of sciolism, impudence, and mal-ice, guilty of all the quackery in criticism which Coleridge had alleged against the vilifiers of Southey. By the appearance of Emer-son upon the literary scene, although the solid value embedded in Wordsworth's prefaces remained unnoticed, the values in Cole-ridge's fertile ideas had begun to exert that effect which with slight shifts in intensity has continued to the present.

Judicial criticism, thoroughly entrenched in the journals at the beginning of the century, had erelong to withstand violent assaults. In 1805, complaining of the unprincipled feminine horde of novel readers, J. S. J. Gardiner formulated the judicial critical attitude:

> Now the man of taste will not condemn or approve by wholesale, but will weigh in his critical balance the distinguishing beauties and defects of every author, and assign a satisfactory reason for his censure or his approbation.

His program incorporated traditional criticism as enunciated by English men of letters since Francis Bacon. Nothing impressionistic or transcendental should enter such calculations, which were to be performed with as nearly complete objectivity as the critic could attain. He was the anonymous voice of the magazine.

Many Americans accused reviewers of hiding behind the cloak of the periodical. For the reviewers, the brilliant young clergyman J. S. Buckminster counterattacked. Authors often publish their books anonymously or under a pseudonym; why deny critics the same privilege? Authors demand patriotic support simply because they are Americans. They fail to differentiate between criticism designed to aid them and libelous defamation. The object of criticism is works; only a hypersensitive person would take offense at impersonal criticism. The author by publishing calls attention to his book, and should not presume to dictate the response to it. The next writer to take up the cudgels for the critics was less tactful. Mindful of John Dennis's attack upon Pope, he drew a pointed analogy between the lethal function of the critic and the custom in ancient Greece of exposing puny or imbecile offspring to perish. The reviewer's office in the republic of letters is "as beneficial and necessary, though as odious and unpleasant, as that of an executioner in the civil state." Authors whose sole fault is wasting the time of readers "are enemies of their kind, and merit the thong of chastisement and the knout of criticism . . . Voluntary trifling with the public is criminal; and lenity to the former is cruelty to the latter."

By 1809, however, the *Anthology* began to print statements dissenting from the established codes of judgment. The famous remark of Lucretius, that he was treading byways of the Muses hitherto untraveled by man, appeared often in the rebel contention that genius is always on the scout for novelty and turns aside in disgust from well-trodden ways. The proneness of the traditional critic never to leave the established road nor to allow others to leave it came under hot fire. Pope's paradox, that the man who successfully flouts an old rule has discovered a new one, and his interest in the grace beyond the reach of art, were stolen from the arsenal of the conservatives. One writer was willing to keep the old rules only for works in the conventional literary forms; another demanded that the whole theory of universal rules be scrapped on the ground that no such rules can be discerned. In the United States, where a new democratic nation was taking form, how could old rules be binding upon the new literature that was sure to come?

Against the formidably entrenched traditional critics, independent thinkers employed a strategic irony. A defender of Burns admitted that, like Samuel Johnson in defending Shakespeare's irregularity, he was almost frightened at his own temerity.

> Compared with Burns, Cowper dwindles. . . . I am almost afraid to speak my opinion; the ink hardly moves through my pen; it turns

pale and seems to sicken when I say, that compared with Burns, Cowper shrinks into nothing.

E. T. Channing declared that every time he heard critics discoursing he pitied the whole race of authors. R. H. Dana condemned splenetic critics whose inexcusable egotism prevented their interest in anything abstractly good or great; in America readers should welcome works of art without too careful scrutiny for adherence to previously established rules. James K. Paulding, the New York novelist, censured docile American reviewers for selling out to rank, fashion, and authority. In 1824, John Neal, who had under a pseudonym broken into the sacred columns of *Blackwood's* as a British writer on American letters, admonished critics to be kindly to young authors and wary lest, like the Medes and Persians, they strive to maintain blindly every decree that has once gone forth. And in 1829, Samuel Knapp, a hesitant precursor of Emerson's trumpet call eight years later, asserted that America was now ready to assume a share of literary independence. The younger critics desired to use whatever they could salvage from the old criticism, but at the same time to leave both writers and critics untrammeled by Old World rules and systems.

Of the standard criticism which was salvaged for American use, concepts of taste, genius, and originality were preserved in slightly modified form; theories of artistic imitation and nature were considerably changed; artistic finish and sound scholarship were carried over almost intact.

Taste was generally defined in the Addisonian sense; that is, as capacity to perceive the beauties of an author with pleasure and his deformities with dislike. It was commonly agreed that the popular American taste was not yet competent to judge, and that critics should carefully judge for it until it should ripen. Obviously, Addison's injunction to form one's taste by assiduous reading of accepted critics was no longer fully acceptable; and his further direction to converse constantly with men of polite culture was impracticable for most Americans. The critics were concerned to form the taste of American readers, and therefore had to consider the nature and needs of genius as well as the problems of originality.

Original minds, R. H. Dana noted, are notoriously fond of working in their own way. They must be taken as one finds them, with friendly acceptance of their novelties. Insistence upon conformity to rule silences them, forces their novelties into mannerisms, or dooms them to unsuccessful writing in a style alien to their natures. Something worthwhile may come from allowing free rein to genius. Willard Phillips argued that in literature the end justifies the means; whether *Childe Harold* conformed to any known poetic species was immaterial provided that it was successful.

Soon, however, a note of caution was heard, sounded first because American authors chafed at any adverse comment on their works by a fellow-countryman. Warning them that acceptable poetry comes from genius, taste, and diligence, Bryant in 1818 told American poets not to expect an audience "merely because they are written by an American, and are not decidedly bad." Others joined Bryant in refusing to erect a protective tariff about American literature; it must compete in open market with the transatlantic product. In 1824, William Ellery Channing spoke out for direction of the author's effort into proper channels to avoid wasted effort. For Channing diligence meant, among other things, education. Although institutions of higher learning cannot create genius, they can best aid to unfold it. "For want of them, great minds often slumber or run to waste, whilst a still larger class, who want genius, but possess admirable powers, fail of that culture through which they might enjoy and approach their more gifted brethren." As the eighteenth century had taught, Channing believed taste to be a small spark of that same power by which the artist creates; its possession enables the man of culture to appreciate that art which he lacks the power to create. A few years later, Samuel Knapp asserted that American poets were fast ridding themselves of the ridiculous impression that genius is everything, and information nothing, in making a poet.

In their discussion of originality the theorists showed the greatest emancipation. The traditional concept that originality is achieved by filtration of any object, however trite, through the prism of the artist's personality—an idea fostered by the authority of Horace—was still accepted. Reviewers felt, however, that in American literature the best road to originality lay through observation of the new country. Paulding urged authors to fix their eyes upon the familiar American scene. Borrowing directly from nature would not only destroy the ascendancy of foreign habits of thought; it would also give to the new literature "that air and character of originality which it is sure to acquire, unless it is debased and expatriated by a habit of servile imitation." Yet, as both Bryant and E. T. Channing reminded their readers, originality does not require the unique or strange. As Channing put it: "It is not of the least moment whether a subject be just brought to the notice of men, or be the oldest and commonest; nor yet from what quarter or in what way it comes; for, if an original mind acts at all, it must act up to its character; it must reflect itself upon whatever it studies." These, perhaps the best critical minds of the early nineteenth century in America, recommended combination of the classical concept of originality with the development of the American scene.

The basic principle in creative literature is undoubtedly Aristotle's doctrine of μίμησις, which is best translated as "artistic imitation." Students of criticism are familiar with the sea changes it underwent after the revival of learning in Europe. Although most reviewers showed awareness of Aristotle's *Poetics*, the occasional mention of it in these years indicated far from wide first-hand knowledge of the treatise. Neoclassical perversions of artistic imitation were familiar to them, but they seemed quite ignorant of Aristotle's true meaning. Bryant, for example, vigorously attacked the conception of poetry as imitative and preferred to classify it as suggestive. They quite failed to see how closely Aristotle's doctrine approximated that power which Coleridge designated as the secondary imagination.

For most critics, imitation connoted various degrees of copying models. E. T. Channing wrote scathingly of the imitator as the poet who had sent his wit to school: he is "cautious, constrained, and modelled throughout." Two years later, in 1818, he declared the chief business of American critics to be to save American poetry from being merely a bad imitation of foreign popular authors—a charge echoed by Bryant and Paulding. Bryant vigorously stated the modern declaration of independence:

It is no longer necessary that the narrative poem should be written on the model of an ancient epic; a lyric composition is not relished the more, perhaps not so much, for being Pindaric or Horatian; and it is not required that a satire should remind the reader of Juvenal. It is enough for the age if beautiful diction, glowing imagery, strong emotion, and fine thought are so combined as to give them their fullest effect upon the mind. The end of poetry is then attained, no matter by what system of rules.

In spite of a mild reaction about 1830 against this literary libertinism, Bryant had dealt a mortal wound to the concept of imitation as copying. All that the conservatives could muster was a warning against too sedulous avoidance of what had been successfully done in the past—an extravagant originality which the intelligent critics had never espoused. By the end of the period, E. T. Channing told his Harvard seniors that American writers were successfully combining whatever they could adapt from English authors with treasures from their own coffers, thereby giving their work a vigorously national cast suited to the democratic culture of the land. Though Channing and others may not have realized it, the work which satisfied their recipe was substantially Aristotle's artistic imitation or Coleridge's product of the secondary imagination.

Nature at the beginning of the century was still the source of the rules; the *Portico* (1817) deplored dramas "aimed at the subversion of classical principles, so long established by the voice of nature." Wherever we find dependable taste in man, the power behind his judgment is the power of nature. Another contributor, however, accused tasteless critics of hiding their uncertainty by appealing to nature, which they failed to define. But, he slyly added, their taste rules out the manifold beauties which lie without the supposed uniformity of nature, the irregular, unique particulars; and it insists that we "shut our eyes at the very moment when we are most delighted with vision." Such remarks opened the door to the romantic concept of nature, which had already been forcing entrance through other apertures.

For the last two decades of this period, nature was uniformly interpreted to be the world about us. John G. Palfrey congratulated current writers of fiction for their fidelity to life in all its accidental shadings. R. H. Dana added the romantic preference for nature in the raw. True poets, he wrote, let us out from exactly cut hedges and straight canals into the free and careless sweep of hills and streams as God had made them. E. T. Channing used the lifelike scenes of Walter Scott's *Rob Roy* as a demand for truth to life in novels. Paulding, following the same argument, bade the American writer to focus his attention upon scenes connected with "our pride and our affections," to borrow from nature, not from those who disfigure or burlesque her.

Moralizing critics of course had to adapt the plea for lifelikeness to their own purposes. Alexander Everett objected to Schiller's combining in *The Robbers* a "generous worth" with a penchant for highway robbery. Evidently disbelieving in Robin Hood, he demanded that the union of vices and virtues in fictional characters be such as are found together in real life. To go counter to verisimilitude not only diminishes the effect of the work; it also—and here is the rub—tends to corrupt good morals, which are equivalent to good taste. Virtue is good taste in action. Such an affiliation of romantic realism to sound morality was sure to win the approbation of the cultured New Englander who still, as Lowell later hinted, was prone to confuse New England with the New Jerusalem.

The concept of nature as both outward symbol and inner meaning had also its exponents. F. W. P. Greenwood found Wordsworth's greatest glory in his intimate converse with nature:

> He is her friend, her confidential counsellor, her high priest; and he comes from the inmost temple to reveal to us her mysteries, and unravel those secret influences which we had always felt but hardly understood.

Greenwood's rhapsody did not disclose the essence of this symbolism, and many critics were unready for such interpretation of literature. One Jeremiah, who in 1829 despaired of the prospects for poetry, advocated a return to Pope, whose artifice would be found closer to nature than current poetry. Others, unwilling to yield the ground gained, still preferred that authors report what they actually saw. The swashbuckling John Neal severely condemned James Fenimore

Cooper for lacking courage to record "that, which he has power enough to see, as it is." Cooper made his characters talk too correctly, as if he feared that their solecisms or illogical ideas would be charged against him *in propria persona.*

In spite of frequent mention of the imagination writers developed no considered theory about it. The *Portico* for 1816 declared that poetry is best produced in "an age of unilluminated nature," which alone can provide that "enthusiastick genius" needed to ignore critical restrictions. In other ages, "the mind is tamed by science, and the imagination chilled by judgment." To this essentially romantic statement, whose echo of John Dennis probably made it acceptable to the conservative editors, the *Portico* in 1817 added a mythological parentage for the imagination. Like Aphrodite in Plato's *Symposium,* imagination is of two sorts, earthly and heavenly. Heavenly imagination is the legitimate offspring of Feeling and Fancy; the earthly imagination "is engendered in the intercourse of Phrenzy and Imitation." The former enables the poet to use the most ordinary words without becoming pedestrian or trite; the latter, "reared and nourished in doubt, and darkness, and mist," can express nothing. So runs an early treatment of the imagination, neither commending it fully nor denying it a function in the making of poetry.

Wordsworth's Preface of 1815 and Coleridge's response in *Biographia Literaria* made little impression for nearly a decade. E. T. Channing and Willard Phillips indeed wrote for the *North American Review* articles which show some slight similarity to Coleridge's ideas, but the resemblances are too faint to assure their knowledge. A third contributor in assessing the value of James Hogg's work declared that although learning may not be basic in the production of poetry, the unlettered man's imagination is restricted to the track marked out by his models: "he will rarely wander into any new path." Jared Sparks in 1825 repeated the demand for sanity and delay in poetic labors: the eccentricity and haste of American poets continually drove them into "some new and extravagant conceit, either in language, measure, or sentiment, some high 'imaginings' and adventures of deep thought, that shall astonish and confound, if they do not charm and bear away the reader." The same volume of the *North American Review* which printed Sparks's warning against careless imagination contained an indictment of the age of reason, whose faults, the writer declared, the new freedom of imagination had gone far to eradicate.

Stronger admixture of Coleridge's doctrine appears in Bryant. Shifting the emphasis to the reader, Bryant insisted that he responds most actively when his imagination is titillated by scenes and events out of the ordinary. It then fills in and amplifies the suggested outlines, adding colors and shades to suit the taste of the reader. The poet must direct the reader's imagination into agreeable channels; his aroused emotions will then enhance the initial stimulation. He should also affect the imagination rather than the fancy. Imagination can create a satisfying ideal world for poet and reader, whereas fancy leaves both dissatisfied amid actualities. Bryant tantalizingly stops short of clearly indicating his Coleridgean source. He was, however, a sounder, better informed critic than is generally realized; one may safely assume his knowledge of Coleridge's seminal critical theory.

One of the first clear-cut references to Coleridge's esemplastic theory occurs in 1828 in an essay by R. H. Dana. Declaring that the poet needs more than taste for poetry and capacity for poetic expression, he adds, "He must have a poet's temperament,—that in which all coming from him is first fused, and then, running into the mould of the imagination, is turned out a true form." This statement was followed in 1831 by C. S. Hillard's declaration of the imaginative power exercised in making the agents of the novel. By decomposing and forming anew the human beings observed, the author gives us a great variety of new characters.

In 1837 a critic of Bulwer reinforced the importance of the imaginative fusion by denying it to the British novelist. He gives us a mere inventory of each person: "height of the person and of the forehead, color of the hair, teeth, and the model of the nose, whether Grecian, bottle, or eagle-beaked, and so on. . . . But after all, it is only an aggregation of materials." The creature has no unity. "Forms are not to be conjured up in this way from the vasty deep of the imagination." The imagination has finally rid itself of its earlier equivocal reputation. No longer "sickly and diseased," it is the power described by Coleridge, and is safely launched on the course which it still pursues.

During these first four decades, American critics were beset by limiting prejudices in the public which required the exercise of their ablest diplomacy. Though deep religious conviction and adherence to the Mosaic-Christian moral code had degenerated into ritual in some religious groups, these groups were still formidable. Since they constituted the larger part of the population, they had to be enticed into the ranks of the reading public before American authorship could become profitable. Irving, a shrewd man of business, no doubt had these potential readers in mind when he called his first major work a history and his subsequent stories legends. If they had been labeled fiction, the more rigidly religious would have avoided these lying snares of the devil; but history they presumed to be fact and morally instructive, and legend at least founded upon fact. Having been seduced into opening these books, the public would become interested before it realized its plight; and some at least would succumb to the sweet enticement. To reduce the hostility of such people, as well as for more artistic reasons, literary men had to discuss in detail the nature of poetic truth.

The public expected poetry to teach; too many of the reviewers were clergymen, teachers, or lawyers for the moral end of poetry to be widely disallowed. They were, however, less rigid than has frequently been believed. Many, following a principle later advocated by Henry James, divorced moral from aesthetic judgment. They consistently rated Byron's poetry higher than today while condemning his moral tone far more severely. Bryant, adopting a principle later popularized by Benedetto Croce, conceded to poetry the teaching of "truths which the mind instinctively acknowledges" on account of their axiomatic nature. Such elements of moral truth may be readily combined with human actions to produce imaginative literature. The imagination, he added, aspires after a superhuman beauty and majesty—noted also a few years later by Poe—which bears a likeness, perhaps an affinity, to virtue. Rightly directed, this aspiration may "shape the creations of the mind into perfect forms according to those laws which man learns from observing the works of his Maker." Emerson was soon to assign similar powers to his poet. By such adjustment of the didactic function of literature, Bryant turned the attention of writers and readers to ideal truth.

Akin to this relaxing of the moralizing tendency was a decrease noted in 1829 by Samuel Knapp in the earlier prudishness of the American cultured public:

> The good household dames of other days would have turned shuddering from the sight of Cupids, and Venuses, and Graces, which the maiden of the present day, pure as the stainless snow, will sit before whole hours, engaged in her innocent drawing lessons. The mind, properly disciplined, is capable of sustaining much; as the body in full health can support heat and cold. There are no sickly images while there is a sane mind in a sane body.

Later pressures from Victorian prudery, which was scandalized by Powers's modest Greek Slave, put an end to this shortlived freedom of the eighteen twenties. It did, however, foreshadow the still greater freedom of the twentieth century.

William Ellery Channing in a paper on Milton was moved to clear up the confused thinking of his Unitarian followers. In poetry, he pointed out, even when the letter is falsehood the spirit is often profoundest wisdom. Far from portraying a life which does not exist, the poet "extracts and concentrates, as it were, life's ethereal essence, arrests and condenses its volatile fragrance, and prolongs its more refined but evanescent joys." Since in the minds of the most conservatively religious *Paradise Lost* stood with *Pilgrim's Progress* as comparable to the Bible in forming their beliefs, Channing's choice of Milton was a peculiarly effective defense of his doctrine.

A curious variant from the general preference for didactic poetry was a fairly widespread hostility to the use of Biblical story as literary material. The curse in the last chapter of the Revelation upon him who adds to or takes away from it was supposed to be operative for the entire Bible; and writers who used Biblical events were believed guilty of this sin. Those not affected by this belief declared the tales too threadbare to rouse interest. The matter came to a head with James A. Hillhouse's *Hadad* (1825), which was based upon an episode from the Old Testament. Hillhouse in a preface defended angels and demons as supernatural machinery, citing theological

authority and reminding his readers that Biblical times were receptive of supernatural events, magic, and sorcery. Critics rallied to his
defense, among them Bryant. In what seems now a mock-serious
vein, Bryant reminded readers that Biblical personages were men
like ourselves, that obviously many events in their lives were un-
recorded, and that we are not forbidden to dwell upon what may
have been their emotions in the scenes recorded—a sly hit at the
preachers of the day—nor to imagine unmentioned parts of their
lives. The only restriction upon the author's treatment of them is
that which obtains in all representation of historical characters, harmony with the known facts. However superfluous such argument
may seem to us, for his time it struck a telling blow in the defence
of fiction.

But poetic truth was discussed in other than moral or religious
connections. The strong vein of practical common sense that characterized men able to develop new commonwealths still obtained,
and the poet or novelist who violated probability was sure to find
his venture unsparingly condemned. The *Port Folio* in 1811 severely
censured Robert Southey's *Curse of Kehama* for its improbability.
"The poet's business is to affect us," and he cannot succeed by in-
credible supernatural machinery or by transgressing the limits set
to poetic license. Fifteen years later, Bryant told members of the
New York Athenaeum that the deficiency of modern superstititions
entitled poets to levy on all previous ages for diversity of situation
and incident. Materials must, however, be managed "with sufficient
skill to win the temporary assent of the reader to the probability of
the circumstances related." American writers had to be on their
guard not to exceed the limits of the reader's willing suspension of
disbelief for a season; Coleridge's statement, which Bryant evidently
had in mind, is peculiarly sound advice to a writer whose audience,
for all the credulity ascribed to its female members by critics, contained also a seasoning of hardheaded readers of both sexes.

Coleridge's warning was especially appropriate on account of the
already recognized materialistic trend of America, which supplied
a subject of frequent complaint among writers. As one reviewer
assessed the situation, the United States had reached the first stage
of material prosperity, desire of coarse and gaudy luxuries that

could lead only to sensual depravity. The lack of exterior polish indicated the low cultural stage to which the people had fallen. The country had not yet progressed to a cultural development which would permit success in the imitative arts; and the sole hope of attaining that level lay in some power which would raise men from the desires of sense to the love of beauty and order. He called for an exterior culture that should be representative of an inner spirit.

The cultural situation was made even worse by the diversion of imaginative minds, which might otherwise have been literary, into scientific pursuits. In the early decades of the century, the claim that scientific study also had cultural value would have received short shrift. Bryant, indeed, in the vein of Wordsworth, felt that the interest in science would in the long run benefit literature. The more commonly held view was expressed, however, by the youthful Edgar Allan Poe, who in 1829 compared science to the daughter of time, who has taken over her father's house and has begun to remodel it by throwing out the old mythical, imaginative furniture, preparatory to fitting it with hard, practical facts. Similar lamentations were uttered by many writers, especially by those who relied heavily upon classical machinery; and some critics joined in their plaint.

A more optimistic outlook than Poe's was expressed by William Ellery Channing. He made no separation of philosophy and physical science from imaginative literature, for works of mind and works of matter, as he expressed it, are too intimately related to admit of strict separation. He considered as useful that which relates "not only to the animal man, but to the intellectual, moral, and religious man—useful to a being of spiritual faculties, whose happiness is to be found in their free and harmonious exercise." No undertaking by an original or strong mind is useless, for "it may be that what we call vain speculations may, at no distant period, link themselves with some new facts or theories, and guide a profound thinker to the most important results." Channing's attitude toward knowledge foreshadowed such a mixed group as Whitman, Émile Zola, and practitioners of modern research. Such intelligent linking of literary, imaginative work with the course of the nation's intellectual development was, however, recognized at the time by very few writers.

The moral didacticism of the common American reader presented a stumbling block especially to the progress of the novel. The hardheaded American was on his guard to protect the fancied innocent helplessness of the feminine readers who constituted the bulk of novel readers. The defenders of the novel, going back to its very beginnings, wrote apologies for Henry Fielding. A contributor to the *Portico* declared that the heart is not corrupted by the glowing picture of unchaste action, for mothers daily instruct their daughters by such means. He doubted that the imagination of an artist could conjure up an unheard-of vice to anyone who had arrived at maturity. Evil comes from "the impunity of vice, and vulgarity glossed with the charms of beauty and accomplishment, by an infected fancy." Poetic justice, in which Fielding excelled, prevents his works from vicious effect. Fielding, he added, had to include depictions of evil to convey human character in individuals, which is the material of novelists as general moral topics are the business of the pulpit. Clinching the case for Fielding, he cited Holy Writ, "in which the most obscene, and licentious images abound." Like Irving, Paulding, and their coterie, the author saw in Fielding's work the intent to castigate the age. The majority of literary men, however, trained in the combined moral and literary judgments of Samuel Johnson on novels, remained unconvinced.

By 1820, the novel that was winning praise lavishly presented moral sentiments. A defender of novel writing in the *Port Folio* complained that female authors in particular had developed a pattern of including in each chapter pages on one or other of the moral virtues. No method, he declared, could better counteract the very effect which the good ladies had designed. Like many of later date, he found that Samuel Richardson, by letting his virtuous persons moralize "so regularly, so gloomily, so tediously, and so pedantically," had rendered a Lovelace far more attractive than a Grandison. The novel had to be tailored, however, to fit the supposed innocence of its predominantly female audience.

Catering to the demands for feminine entertainment there appeared, to the consternation of literary men, a number of female novelists. They were described by the *Polyanthus* (1814) in Homeric phrase as Amazons that rival men:

I confess that a female author is a notion that never strikes my mind
with pleasure. A throng of disagreeable ideas ever accompanies it. . . .
I cannot say that, strictly speaking, it means morosity, sluttishness,
ill-nature, and a total renunciation of all the rules of intercourse
established among the polite; but I must acknowledge that these
things are as invariably called up in my mind by the mention of that
word, as if every one of them were actually included in its etymology.

Such ungentle hints multiplied as encroachments increased. Other
reviewers, bowing to the inevitable, tried to mingle tolerance with
commendation. A reviewer of Maria Edgeworth in 1817 commended her works coldly as designed primarily for utility; her
reasoning he found generally correct and her course as consistent
with policy as with virtue. A few only, chiefly writers in the *North
American Review,* admitted women to equal literary rights.

Once the novel had overcome the combined antipathies toward
interloping female authors and toward its introduction of a new literary genre, it was pretty well on its way towards acceptance by all
but the most crusted critics. A reviewer in the 1812 *Polyanthus*
surprised himself by staying awake until he had actually finished
reading a novel. He professed to be more attracted by its moral
lesson that the wages of the rake's progress are remorse and despair
than by its interesting story; but he could not deny that the fortunes
of the protagonist had held his attention as fully as the moral sentences sprinkled over its pages had won his approbation. The novel
may have entered the literary fortress under the guise of a medium
for moral instruction; once within the walls, it began slowly to
develop its art with more freedom.

Almost as troublesome was the American novelist's difficulty in
finding suitable themes. Without denying to him the privilege of
using a foreign story, reviewers made it clear that they preferred the
American scene. The nationalistic feeling approved Cooper's shift
after his first tentative novel, *Precaution,* from the English social
scene to the earlier history of America. Especially deplored was the
attempt, best seen in the novels of Brockden Brown, to import the
Gothic romance to the American setting. Scott and Byron were
blamed for having lured American writers into strange paths, seduced by these "Cynthias of the minute" from the illumination of

the great masters. The modish affectation of the writers was severely satirized. Romance had attracted "every description of literati, and of no description at all, counsellors and clergy, statesmen and ladies, booksellers and beaux, some without brains and some with," to write the claptrap Gothic tale. Whether critical attacks effected the change or not, the Gothic extravaganza soon was relegated to less respectable levels in America.

Choice of suitable American themes was not fixed by the abandonment of the exotic Gothic tale. Irving's ironic locating of a romantic tale in a remote period of American history—"that is to say, thirty years since"—indicates the deficiency of that antiquity which delighted the romanticist. Reviewers nevertheless insisted that American themes were adequate for the artist. William Tudor, the founder and first editor of the *North American Review*, asserted in his first number that America had a rich and various mine of subjects, more than rivalling Scott's, that had hardly been opened. He felt, however, that the writer should dig to levels laid down in colonial days in order to reach a suitable antiquity. Three years later, John Knapp included the Revolutionary period as material for the artist; it compensated for its lack of age by its infinite variety of character, scene, and incident, and made up for its lack of supernatural machinery by its historical grandeur and its passionate patriotism.

An early attempt to introduce realism into American literature came as a byproduct of the attack upon the Gothic novel. E. T. Channing in 1819, after ironically asserting that we lacked the ruined, haunted castles of Gothic tales, declared that our commodious houses and busy streets were ill-suited to the more adventurous kinds of romanticism. The times were ripe for fiction that "makes the fable subservient to the developing of national character, or of the manners, usages, prejudices and condition of particular classes." The New Yorker James K. Paulding supported Channing. We should cease to compete with British Gothic novelists and write "rational fictions" about the United States, which could amply employ the imagination in depicting the early settlers as they actually were.

Romantic adventure, however, kept the lead in popularity. W. H. Gardiner listed three periods of America as especially susceptible of romantic treatment: "the times just succeeding the first settlement—the era of the Indian Wars, which lie scattered along a considerable period—and the revolution." Instead of mining these ores, Gardiner complained, writers were providing deluded readers with "mere *fac similes* of the peculiarities of the country." He charged novelists with pasting American names upon scenes that were in no respect American, peopling them with adventurers from all other parts of the globe, "with a native or two here and there, acting as no American ever acts, and talking a language which, on the other side of the water, may pass for American, simply because it is not English." John Neal praised Cooper's *Lionel Lincoln* because, if not altogether American, it was not altogether British. Cooper had opened a truly American quarry from which erelong the true American novel would be hewn, "a brave, hearty, original work, brimful of descriptive truth; crowded with real American character; alive with American peculiarities; got up after no model, however excellent; woven to no pattern, however beautiful; in imitation of nobody, however great." Similar emphasis upon the virtues of the American scene appears in essays by R. C. Sands, Bryant, and Samuel Knapp.

To Americans before 1820, the Indian did not appear as a romantic character, however transatlantic authors might exploit him. For one thing, the settlers, especially in New England, had ruthlessly destroyed the aborigines, and Americans were even then grossly abusing them as an inferior race. It is embarrassing to glorify a people whom your ancestors had butchered and whom you were even then dispossessing. For another thing, Indian raids were still too fresh in the minds of men still living to permit a veil of romantic coloring to change the facts into ideal conditions. The American, like the European, could look upon the natives of Tahiti as romantic, because remote; but he could not easily share the similar attitude of Europeans towards the Indians. Consequently, the introduction of Indians into romance for some time produced violent disagreement.

The *North American Review* with its characteristic early fairness presented both sides of the controversy. In 1825, a contributor declared that, in spite of the lofty and commanding spirit which must be conceded to the Indian, his range of characteristics is too narrow to supply materials for an extensive lofty work. A year later another contributor declared: "We have long looked upon the character of the North American savage as one admirably calculated for an engine of great power in the hands of some ingenious master of romance, who had a true notion of this part of his subject." Previous representations of the Indian, he bitterly complained, would have served as well for "a chieftain of Timbuctoo, or the solitary hero of the moon."

Cooper's *Red Rover* (1828) provided the springboard for another critic to dive into the troubled Indian question. Approaching his theme obliquely, he declared that the diminished popularity of such Gothic writers as Mrs. Radcliffe and "Monk" Lewis had opened the way for descriptions of everyday, real characters, while the novel had also borrowed from the drama a more natural and extensive dialogue. Under such requirements, he believed, the Indian cut a sorry figure. The novelist who puts "our calm, taciturn son of the desert into the attitudes of civilized life" demanded by the infinite variety of the modern novel must present an Indian chieftain "singularly blessed in some dark-eyed child, whose convenient complexion is made sufficiently white for the whitest hero" to fall in love with; he is made "to talk like Ossian for whole pages, and measure out hexameters, as though he had been practicing for a poetic prize." The sole alternative is to present a monotonous picture of the Indian as he really is, so simple in character, destiny, and surroundings as to lack sustained interest.

This writer despaired of the purely American novel, whether its agents were white or red. The life of the early settlers differed only in kind of montony from that of the Indians. Authors should concede that America belongs to the English school of civilization. Their success is best assured when they represent our character and manners in the romantic and traditional settings of England, which are ours by inheritance as rightfully as they belong to the British. Four decades before Henry James put such a principle to work, this New England critic outlined a procedure not unlike his on principles that strongly resemble those actuating him.

Until time and further information should alter the American attitude towards the Indian, perhaps no more could be said. Whatever arguments the reviewers might adduce, American authors continued to turn out stories with an American setting. Their readers worried little whether the Indians portrayed were authentic or not, and found stories of American customs and manners, served with a romantic sauce, a palatable diet. Stories like Cooper's *The Prairie* and *The Pioneers,* and later *Satanstoe,* with their pictures of white and red men in action, were avidly absorbed by the public. In the next period, greater knowledge of the Indian's life and character was to bear fruit in *Hiawatha,* which finally settled the question of the Indian's fitness for literary representation.

During these four decades, the basic critical attitude of American reviewers was compounded of encouragement to young writers, insistence upon complete freedom to express judgment of them, and defense of them from virulent criticism at home and abroad. The Reverend William Emerson, editor of the *Monthly Anthology,* assaulted in his first volume those perfectionist authoritarians who would strangle the new-born American literature. He was equally indignant at self-assured ignoramuses who assumed the critic's office without either knowledge, judgment, or wit. Others quickly joined William Emerson in the plea for an instructed corps of critics.

Honest critics freely admitted that in the first decades there were few signs of genius to be recognized. When Solyman Brown in *An Essay on American Poetry* attempted to glorify American authors and to charge British competition with nearly all their troubles, William Cullen Bryant's scornful summary of American poets, though severe, was neither unjust nor unique. J. S. J. Gardiner, disagreeing with Joseph Dennie's encomiums upon Franklin's prose style, declared it to be "as free of striking beauties as it is of faults." Irving's *Knickerbocker's History of New York* was the only imaginative American book to receive praise from the *Monthly Anthology,* which termed it "certainly the wittiest our press has produced." The insistence by editors of the *North American Review* that Bryant's "Thanatopsis" could not have been written by an American is ample evidence of the low esteem in which American literary men were held in patriotic but discriminating literary circles.

Bryant spoke for many reviewers when he insisted that no protective critical tariff be erected around the works of American authors; they must produce works of genius, taste, and diligence in competition with the rest of the world. The future poet needs sure guidance. "To show him what we expect of him, it is as necessary to point out the faults of his predecessors, as to commend their excellences." Considering the brevity of settlement in America, the infancy of literary and social institutions, and the scarcity of leisure for attention to the arts, he felt that we had made praiseworthy progress. Another critic challenged Scotland to show a like achievement for her first two hundred years. In spite of these hopeful signs, however, authors were told to face the fact of the slight actual worth of their works in contrast with those produced in England. R. H. Dana warned them in 1819: "It is not yet time to empty our shelves of European lumber to make way for American writers,—there is still room enough for these in the vacancies left. An American library would, we fancy, be rather a sorry and heart-sickening sight to a literary man."

The critics were quite unable to convince American authors that the wounds of critical friends were faithful. J. S. Gardiner's caustic explanation did little to soothe them with its scathing assessment of adulatory criticism.

> So little have the writers of our country been accustomed to the rigour of a critical tribunal, that, to secure a comfortable seat in some of our out-houses belonging to the temple of fame, nothing has hitherto been necessary but the resolution to write, and the folly to publish.

Sharp strictures from Americans are resented as conceited aping of foreign impertinence:

> To point out the faults of a living author, instead of making him grateful, only makes him mad; and he discovers all the fury, which is felt by an antiquated belle, when her little niece unluckily spies a gray hair among the sable glories of her head, and innocently presumes to pull out the intruder.

The increasing virulence of British criticism gradually irritated the most Anglophile American critics to the point where they rallied in support of their literary fellow-citizens against the common foe. Though hostility to England ebbed for a time after 1820, it remained for Poe to revive severe criticism of American authors in America.

[37]

British criticism was during most of these years unfriendly and at times vindictive to American letters. In addition to the condescension habitual toward Americans as provincials, the British resented as a stab in the back the American declaration of war upon them at the crisis of their struggle against Napoleon. Americans, flushed with an exaggerated estimate of their second victory over England and with the overweening nationalism characteristic of a young and vigorous nation, failed to make allowances for British pride and economic exhaustion.

Cool-headed Americans tried after the war to smooth over the difficulties. R. H. Dana in 1817 warned Americans to ignore British slurs upon their authors, in full confidence that they possessed genuine merits which sooner or later would produce a worthy literature. Two years later came Irving's open letter to both English and Americans in *The Sketch-Book*. Irving had the unique advantage of speaking to receptive audiences on both sides of the Atlantic. He warned the British not to alienate a young power whose aid he prophetically asserted might some day insure their very survival. He urged his countrymen to disregard the slights from British periodicals and to disprove them by the very quality of their products; as a practical people, the British could not but recognize actual accomplishment. To both nations he pointed out their common heritage and characteristics which rendered dangerous to both any serious breach between them. Irving's sound arguments were the basis of attempts by Americans to keep on friendly terms with Britain for the next three decades; in 1848 Lowell could find none better.

Unfortunately, Dana's and Irving's temperate counsels could not wholly silence the wrathful Americans. Solyman Brown's vigorous if unpolished verse is a fair sample of their resentment.

> *Whatever foreign critics may advance,*
> *Irish or Scotch, in England or in France,*
> *I heed it not;—we look not there for candour:*
> *But shall Americans retail their slander? ...*
> *Our presses change to execrable sewers,*
> *To catch the loathsome filth of Scotch Reviewers?*

An ironic critic in the 1820 *North American Review* produced one of the ablest mock-serious retorts to the famous charge of the

[38]

Edinburgh Review: Who sleeps on an American blanket or reads an American book? The sly collocation of books and slumber presumably winged the American reply. He regretted that, while our blankets were quite as warm and twice as cheap as the English, we were behind in the production of poetry for the international market. "But we take great pleasure in assuring our brethren abroad, whose confidence and want of information on American concerns stand, if they will believe us, in most ludicrous contrast, that the literary manufacture and literary profession is looking up among us." Changing abruptly to seriousness, he succinctly outlined the American cultural situation. We, as a young country, were blamed that we had not produced a primitive literature characteristic of a young civilization. Our civilization was in fact coeval with England's, for we had been until recently colonies closely tied to her. A more proper question would concern our not having kept pace with England in quality and bulk of literary products. The cause of our lagging in literature was the diversion of our best efforts, first to the establishment of frontier colonies, and latterly to the building of a new nation, both of them tasks to occupy the finest abilities and rightfully taking precedence over every other activity. The British presumption of any natural inferiority in Americans is belied not only by our British heritage but by our production of better books every year, by our steady advance in education, and by the constant elevation of public taste. "If this," he concluded, "does not satisfy our brethren abroad, we are unable to satisfy them."

As Anglo-American political relations subsequently improved or deteriorated, so went also the literary squabble. For some years after 1820, the quarrel died down. By 1836, when trouble arose over the Canadian border, it flared again. An American reviewer of Nathaniel Willis' works charged that for years concern for literary truth had exercised no restraint upon English critics. Like Arnold a generation later, he deplored the influence of British politics upon British reviewing. Even ancient classical authors, he claimed, were judged on party lines: the *London Quarterly* called Aristophanes an enemy of modern democracy and Pindar a Tory. Poe's squib several years later on how to write a *Blackwood* article is a reminder that the quarrel was far from ended during this period.

From the beginning of the century, American writers and reviewers had shared the general confidence in the future of the United States. After 1820, however, they less often spoke of American literature in the present tense, and ceased to ignore the difficulties in the way of its creation. Faintly at first but more clearly as time advanced, they saw the literary future of the country to lie in a democratic literature which should be the expression of a democratic people. Since no such literature had previously existed, and since they were still feeling their way towards the meaning of democracy, they were naturally obliged to grope uncertainly after its literary constituents. Educated according to older standards, they nevertheless felt the inadequacy of previous literary expression for the new nation. Yet aware of previous values, they wished to incorporate as much as possible of the old into the new system without vitiating its democratic spirit.

Thoughtful critics generally adopted an attitude compounded of confidence in the American literary future and solicitude lest the American writer fail to follow the proper path in the use of his unique materials and opportunities. Since the beginning of letters, a similar transplanting of a developed culture and literature to a country wholly barren of their rudiments had not taken place; nor had the added complication of a democratic government been known before. Fully aware of these novel elements in their situation, American critics pondered and discussed the direction which American letters should take.

These critics as a rule declined to go along with the demand already being heard in the early years of the century for a literature whose themes should be exclusively American. Like Goethe, they felt that there were no national frontiers for literature; and in America they were particularly heedful to preserve the transplanted European heritage. Early attempts, like Barlow's *Columbiad*, to present heroic pictures of America's past, demonstrated by their failure that neither theme nor audience was ready for such treatment. A reviewer of Paulding's *The Backwoodsman* (1819) asserted that the American mind was then too deeply engrossed in other interests for extensive works of the imagination to receive much attention. With the actual building of the nation on their minds, the public would hardly feel much interest in imaginative representations of the task. The writer should cheerfully bow to the situation; he should not deplore this necessary and healthful interest in practical politics. The only sensible alternative was to write works which would appeal to the public on other themes, whether American or not.

One concession made by many reviewers to American talent was a tacit agreement to refrain from captious criticism of American works. Without praising inferior work, they nevertheless avoided the example set by Bryant's sarcastic comments on individuals in his retort to Solyman Brown's panegyric of American poets, to take his more encouraging position upon the literary prospects. One editor remarked in 1819 that he saw no reason to satirize the daily output of trashy works, because they would do little harm. In 1822, Edward Everett specifically commended the current crop of poets for work that, considering the time and place, was respectable for its great industry, wide study, and intense application to the best models. Their diffidence in their own powers and willingness to learn he found eminently praiseworthy. It was, he tactfully suggested, in their excessive dependence upon models that their mistake lay; and, as James Huneker remarked of American writers decades later, they were too eager to practice their scales in public. Everett declined, however, to encourage poets unduly: it would harm them, and the deceit would ruin the credit of his reviews. He elected therefore generally to be silent where he could not commend.

The reader who in these early years was interested in literary theory would have had to devote himself to wide perusal of the several periodicals if he hoped to keep abreast of it. In view of the narrow regional circulation of periodicals, American writers in New England were only cursorily informed of literary affairs in New York and far less aware of affairs in Philadelphia, Baltimore, and Charleston. The systematic reader of the *North American Review* from 1815 to 1835 would have met a knowledge of literary matters like that of Emerson in 1837. Few men probably knew the files that well, and no one in America had the over-all picture available to the present delver into the stacks of a long-established American library. American thinking in these four decades, though it made long strides, was regional rather than national. A far wider acquaintance was ushered in with the more vigorously national consciousness and greatly improved communications of the next decade.

The conclusion of this first period of American literary opinion has the nature of a political footnote. Although the literary periodicals, as Vernon Parrington and William Charvat have pointed out, were during the first four decades directed by conservative groups, the new romantic leaven kept working through them and appearing in various revolts. Even the conservatives had within their ranks men who were unsatisfied to stand pat with the past. Actuated by political, religious, or social ferments, men kept breaking away from the conservative ranks. Animosity toward England weakened the otherwise traditionalist attitude of some; dislike of Calvinistic formalism and indifference to social and cultural progress strengthened the innovating tendency of others; and the growing belief that in the United States the era of the common man was to find its most eloquent expression slowly crystallized the concept of a democratic literature which the next two decades were to express. As A. M. Schlesinger, Jr., has noted in *The Age of Jackson*, during the fourth decade intellectuals had flocked to the democratic standard, until by 1838 the *Boston Post* could assert: "with few exceptions, our first literary men belong to the democratic party." New periodicals, like O'Sullivan's *Democratic Review* and Orestes Brownson's *Boston Quarterly Review* walked without conservative leading-strings; a favorite pastime of many liberal magazines was baiting that "old fogy," the *North American Review*.

But the early conservatism had done American literature valuable service. Writers had needed the leading-strings of tradition to help them walk steadily. The romantic excesses characteristic of the new literary movement in England and on the Continent were largely avoided here; we suffered no literary *Sturm und Drang*, and were spared an American Victor Hugo. Rampant American nationalists were restrained from throwing out the learning of antiquity while able minds sifted the materials of the past and carefully considered their adaptability for the new world of letters. Most of the literary leaders who succeeded to the conservative pioneers knew what the past had to offer and were competent to mingle it in the amalgam that was to become a more mature national literature.

Chapter 3

Emerson and His Circle

RALPH WALDO EMERSON was undoubtedly the most influential American thinker of his century. Keenly interested in America's culture, he constantly examined those developments in letters and life that were shaping the new literature. Essentially classical, though not neoclassical, he had digested the ideas of Wordsworth and Coleridge and adapted them to his needs. He kept abreast of literary movements on both sides of the Atlantic, and with them in mind he shaped the beliefs expressed in his essays. As Harry Clark has pointed out, the components of his transcendentalism had been expressed by 1835 in the *North American Review;* much of the literary thinking of the age had also been reviewed in its pages. Emerson would not have denied his debt: the greater the genius, he affirmed, the greater his borrowing. Making what he borrowed his own, he produced a body of works original in the Horatian sense which is basic to classic literary theory.

Of his conception of art, Emerson made repeated statements. Art is man's will mixed with essences unchanged by man, "Nature passed through the alembic of man." He added that a rule of one art holds through all nature; what is characteristic of plastic art cannot be alien to literature. Later, he defined art as the path of the creator, divine or human, to his work, as the inspiration of a just design working through all the details. Again, art is the capacity of the poet to describe adequately through his extraordinary powers of observation and expression. Though nature in some respects is superior to art, the artist can reattach to nature what has been dislocated and is therefore ugly. Moreover, the artificial object, like St. Peter's or the pyramids, may by the power of art be so attached to nature as to become a part of nature.

Art is also the spirit creative; in Aristotelian terms, the reason of the thing without the matter, working by necessity, since in nature nothing is arbitrary or isolated. Hence arises its beauty. Using another Aristotelian principle, Emerson asserted that beauty, which the Stagirite saw consisted in proper size and proper arrangement, is inseparable from fitness. Reverting to Plato as transmitted through Edmund Spenser, he insisted that the beauty resident in an object gives it beauty of appearance: "of the soul the bodie forme doth take." Narrowing the term to fit that art which employs words, he considered art most frequently as conscious expression of thought to a definite end, the thought having first been intuitively discerned as primary knowledge.

The path taken by the creator to his work is always ideal and eternal, as well as instinctive in the writer; it is never a technique devised by man that has solidified into literary law. When the poet is emotionally stirred by a mystically perceived idea, this idea spontaneously presents itself in its own shape. This shape is an organic quality of the idea itself. From such premises Emerson developed his theory of organic form. Although it starts with the Horatian belief that he who is possessed by an idea will have words to express it, the organic theory goes far beyond Horace's idea and practice. Horace prided himself upon having brought classical Greek meters to Rome, and did not seek after new verse forms. Emerson believed that traditional forms, while no doubt valid organic expressions for those poets who first used them and perhaps also for those who later developed them, could not express the concepts of all poets. Each poem has its own form as part of its organism. The theme makes its own meter, which may be a complete innovation in form of expression.

Emerson best illustrated his organic theory by the analogy of crystallization. Just as each mineral in nature has its characteristic crystal, each concept of the poet possesses its own peculiar form.

Concepts cluster in characteristic patterns just as do crystals in nature. Both the individual concepts and their clustering are the work of nature, not of the poet's understanding. During the greater part of the process, the poet may see no order in it. The poetic crystals will, however, if permitted, assume their own order, a divine order that is the work of the inflowing Over-Soul, so that the poem will represent in both form and content the poetic revelation.

Two obvious objections to this theory of the poetic process were met by Emerson. First, how adequate is the poet to express in words the divine form which has been revealed to him? Emerson admitted that he looked in vain for his ideal poet. He insisted, however, that the poet who, after qualifying himself to his best ability as a receiver, listened for the message would progress steadily toward ideal reception and expression of the vision. The charioteer in Plato's *Phaedrus* was constantly in his mind. Secondly, why is any polishing or revision of the revealed poem necessary? Since it proceeds from the Over-Soul, is it not perfect as it stands? To this Emerson had a ready reply. Primary knowledge, or Reason—he used the Kantian terms as he had found them in Coleridge—perceives intuitively the revealed truth. Upon this revelation secondary knowledge, or Understanding, sets to work, not to destroy its natural crystalline structure but to polish the crystals in order to let them emit their maximum of beauty and light. The analogy serves even further. If the poet were to change the crystalline structure by trying to force a poem into some arbitrarily conceived form, he would destroy its beauty as surely as a lapidary who should cut a precious stone into any but the proper form.

Although Emerson, like Wordsworth, avoided the term "imitation" in describing the poet's practice, three clear statements of the Aristotelian mimetic theory occur in his works. In "Poetry and Imagination" he likened the making of poetry to the bee's making honey or to the chemist's combinations: as the bee extracts nectar from mint and marjoram, yet produces from them a new product, honey, or as the chemist mixes hydrogen and oxygen to produce a new product, water, so the poet hears conversations and beholds the face of nature only to make out of them a new and more excellent whole. This chemical analogy, after suffering a sea change in France

[45]

in the hands of Émile Zola, was to reappear in American criticism in the early criticism of T. S. Eliot. The second statement was made in his Journal for 1862. In this he contrasted the representation of nature in the *camera obscura* or photograph with the ideal representation which, by suitable addition and subtraction of details, the painter will present. The painter's work is a new creation, the product of a maker. The third reference is Aristotelian, by way of Francis Bacon, to the poet's attempt "to accommodate the shows of things to the desires of the mind, and to create an ideal world better than the world of experience." Romantic prejudice against neoclassical terms did not blind him to the value of Aristotle's basic literary principle.

This mimetic Aristotelian principle is related to his doctrine of organic form. The poet shows us nature revolving about the axis of the poet's primary knowledge, his revelation; and nature fits his thought as symbolic of the idea that possesses him. His eye can articulate the parts of external nature into a more clearly seen system and see the deeper significance of what he observes. This power is not personal but the effect of the Over-Soul's filling him with divine wisdom. The soul of the real poet follows a progress analogous to that mapped out for the lover by Diotima in Plato's *Symposium*. From love of beautiful objects, he ascends successively to love of their hidden meanings, and to love of general principles; and as he grows in love he passes from spectator to maker. On higher levels he retains his earlier love of objects, now seen as symbols. Perceiving each object as both thing and idea, he is thrilled by every touch of nature; and he finds beautiful inventions because desire makes him naturally delight in creating. Through his new insight he sees poetry and annals as one; poetry being, as Aristotle declared, more philosophical and highly serious than history, he sees the universal in annalistic particulars. The poet seeks beauty, the philosopher, truth; but upon the higher plane they discover with Keats a beauty and truth which are identical.

The poet is complete man, superior in both expression and insight. Echoing Aristotle's *Rhetoric*, Emerson asserted that half the man is his expression. Poetic insight expresses itself in a very high level of vision, imagination, which causes the intellect to be both where and what it sees. The *dramatis personae*, for instance, are real persons to the poet: he listens to their conversation as if they were bodily present. The poet does well to embody his ideas in a historical or traditional theme, provided that he does not avoid the common, everyday event, for this can be as poetic as the wildest exotic adventure. And the poet need not worry about originality. Believing that the Over-Soul mystically inspires the poet with his poem, Emerson was unconcerned about its originality; it was of divine origin. The poet will show traces of his training in his expression. Actually, every thinker is retrospective, and Emerson declared that he was the least original of men; yet, he added, the refraction of ideas through his own personality gave them novelty. The thinker's assimilative power is more valuable, he believed, than his originating power. Even Shakespeare impressed him more by his receptivity than by his so-called originality.

Poetic expression occupied much of Emerson's attention. Holding the traditional conception of the poet as namer or word-maker, he denied that the accepted poetic diction and the true poet's diction were the same. With a catholicity beyond Wordsworth's, his poet admits to his vocabulary all levels of diction. He shows interest in the common profanity of the streets and freely uses forceful colloquialisms. Although his poet will in filing his work and in revision be all that the strictest neoclassicist could desire, his gauges will be organic, not arbitrary or traditional.

Emerson thought literary criticism a beautiful art, characteristic of his age. Instead of relying upon its own powers, his age examined the achievements of its predecessors. These things, he agreed, it ought to do. Criticism was an art to be practiced concurrently with creation, for self-reliance requires self-examination. His critical theory, Miss Vivian Hopkins has recently shown, belongs to a fairly well-developed aesthetic theory. Since opportunity and predilection narrowed his aesthetic experience, with few exceptions, to literature, his judgments are nearly always first of all literary.

"The Poet" denounces the critical whited sepulchres who are only locally cultivated, selfish, and sensual. Men who defer to such criticasters have forgotten that the soul makes the body. The just critic sees in literature the operation of necessary laws, which belong to the Over-Soul, not to the human understanding which produced the neoclassical rules. Poems are corrupt versions of an archetypal text; the critic's business is to make them tally with that archetype. Genius, in critic as in author, consists in acute sensibility to universal law and a high degree of power to recognize and express it when it appears in a new form. The poet, first, and subsequently the critic undergo the mystical experience of the poem; and as a result of his sharing the experience, the critic attempts to rectify any errors which human frailty has made the poet commit. The basic law of criticism for Emerson is that every work is to be interpreted by the same spirit which made it before time was. In slightly modified form, this doctrine was to reappear in Spingarn's creative criticism.

The best critic is therefore a competent constructive artist. With first-hand knowledge, he is ruthless toward that sham poetry which fails to cleanse and strengthen him. But criticism does not consist solely in surgery or weed-pulling. It is a vivifying south wind, not merely an east wind that saps the energy. Though Emerson could on occasion be either, he preferred to be the south wind.

He was forced to admit the seeming futility of criticism, whether literary or social: for all that had been written in judgment, the world appeared not to have advanced a step. Yet, like the foolishness of preaching, he enjoyed it and continued to generalize about it. Its futility, he believed, was caused by its so seldom being constructive: "the critic destroys." Properly practiced, criticism is an art, not a mere knack; it goes behind the actual works of the poet to examine the order of his thoughts and the quality of his mind. By expressing his vision, the critic has attained success in his art.

Besides being indebted to the classical tradition, Emerson was informed in the principal critical writings of his own day. His reading of Goethe led him to value the German, in criticism and in creative work, as the writer of all time. It was, however, to Wordsworth and even more to Coleridge that he owed his greatest debt. No ignorance of other recent critics led him to these two guides. In "Thoughts on Modern Literature" (1840) he outlined the course of German criticism from Wolff's *Prolegomena* through the work of Niebuhr and Heeren; and he listed the philosophical analyses of Schelling, Kant, Fichte, and Hegel, with which he had more than nodding acquaintance. With the achievements of these men before him, he still preferred the two English writers.

Wordsworth's fame, he asserted, was a leading fact in modern literature. His greatness lay not in his poetic talents but in his willingness to let the Over-Soul inform his spirit. This merit he shared with Shakespeare and Milton. It counteracts all Wordsworth's shortcomings as a poet, which Emerson painstakingly noted. By letting the Over-Soul flow into him as he climbed Helvellyn or traced the river Duddon, he defeated the literary cliques and journals and restored his age to literary sanity. Although Wordsworth diminished in stature for Emerson after he had met the poet, he was still conscious of the debt which he and his age owed to Wordsworth.

It was to Coleridge, however, that Emerson looked for critical principles. Besides the Kantian distinction between Reason and Understanding, Emerson owed to him the basis for his organic theory and his notions about the fancy and the imagination. It was Coleridge more than any other modern writer who taught him the art of literary criticism. Although he gradually cooled toward Coleridge after 1836, disappointed no doubt by seeing him as by seeing Wordsworth, the influence of Coleridgean thinking remained strong in him.

In spite of his emphasis upon the mystical sources of criticism, he did not jettison the common-sense practices of his predecessors along with their rules. As T. E. Hulme would have expressed it, his Calvinistic heritage and environment naturally inclined him to classicism in spite of current romantic pressures; and Lowell was correct in seeing one side of him as strongly practical. Ancient writers appeared regularly on his lists of authors the world could not do without. "Plutarch's heroes are my friends and relations." In addition to his awareness of Aristotle's mimetic principle, several familiar ancient critical dicta may be briefly indicated.

Discipline for poets forms a large part of his criticism. Like Horace with modern Coleridgean seasoning, he censured poets who wrote from the fancy, remote from possibly unpleasant experience. Poetry, as Coleridge declared, must first of all be common sense, which is developed by action. Like Horace, he would have his young poet know the uttermost secret of toil and endurance; the Over-Soul enters a man disciplined to receive and express it. God does not let us see ideas until we are prepared to see them. The solid, tasteful, delightful criticism of the English writers was made possible by their thorough grounding in the classics and in mathematics; and he wished young Americans of genius to be similarly prepared to receive the heavenly vision. Without that accuracy which is essential to perception of beauty, they would be unable to grasp any revelation.

Like Horace and his own hired man Thoreau, Emerson pleaded for simplicity in all contemporary writing; it was the simplicity and naturalness of ancient literature which he admired and sought. Like Horace and Wordsworth, he admitted that simplicity may result in meanness and lack of density in meaning, but the risk must be taken. The poet must join simplicity with sincerity, must keep his eye steadfastly fixed upon his subject; if he describes mountains, he must have seen mountains, not pictures. Only the man who is stirred by his subject, not by the mere itch to write, can be the poet; and the critic will readily discern between the two.

His understanding must also revise and correct the expression of the vision. Emerson avoided haste in his own composition. In preparing his first series of essays for the press, he wrestled for weeks to improve them; though these tinkering arts irked him, he performed them faithfully. In editing the *Dial*, he resisted the other editors' desire to print the younger Ellery Channing's poems with all their bad grammar and nonsense; could not the Over-Soul parse and spell? File work may indeed be defilement, he punned, yet these manuscript "inspirations" had to risk revision. The naturalness of Chaucer and Hans Sachs is more desirable than the deplorably slipshod newspaper style in parts of Wordsworth's verse. Finish could, of course, be overdone. When he asked for a poet, he did not want an upholsterer. His classically formed taste demanded a golden mean that would express in poetry organically the message of the Over-Soul. It was the critic's function to aid in finding such a mean.

Undue emphasis upon the ethical in literature vitiates Emerson's criticism. Though he would not, it has been acutely said, praise a bad work solely on the ground of sound moral content, he would rate a truly artistic product according to its moral quality. His concept of literature as a revelation from the Over-Soul made high moral content inevitably concurrent with good artistry; the work of art reflects the goodness of its source. Though upon this plane it is difficult to take issue with him, unfortunately he used conventional morality too as a gauge of quality. Hunt's *Abou Ben Adhem,* he asserted, would outlive all the poetry of the age. At times he penetrated behind the immorality of an author's conduct to its cause and argued that it injured him aesthetically. Byron, because of his pride and selfishness, was incurious of his subjects, did not observe them steadfastly, and consequently his magnificent power of language lacked matter for expression. Such criticism, though of morals, goes far deeper as aesthetic criticism than the usual contemporary invective against Byron's libertinism.

Emerson's deficiency in specific criticism appears more clearly in his treatment of the novel. His inconsistency here seems not to be the result of ignorance, for he had studied carefully the techniques of contemporary novelists, even to classifying novels as novels of action, costume, and circumstance, or novels of character like *Wilhelm Meister.* His youthful enjoyment of Scott did not seriously wane, though he admitted that his work lacked depth and his characters were not warm with life. Bulwer he credited with energy and readiness for novel experiment, qualities which, he added with marked reserve, had each its degree of success. In Bulwer's works all was borrowed, nothing brought from himself. Dickens showed indeed an acute eye for costume in *Oliver Twist;* but since his eye did not penetrate into character, his agents displayed mere manners. *Pickwick Papers* was poor stuff. The social conventions of Jane Austen's novels repelled him; he thought them as sterile of genius, wit, or knowledge of the world as the society they depicted. Perhaps most surprising of all his judgments was his remark that Hawthorne's writings testified by their popularity to the personal quality of the author, because the writings themselves were not good for anything.

It is hardly surprising that he should fail to appreciate fiction. In the back of his mind, no doubt, the old prejudice against fiction as a waster of time fortified his feeling that the Over-Soul had far greater matters to convey to man. As a philosopher, he was more concerned with principles than with individuals; though he could express acute flashes of insight into his contemporaries, these were not the steady glow of enlightenment. One is forced to agree with O. W. Firkins that Emerson's perverse literary judgments disqualify him as a practicing critic. Firkins adequately accounts for the discrepancy between his penetrating theory of literature and his unsatisfactory individual judgments by describing him as a man with passion for literature, and preoccupation with spiritual ends, who was faced by a body of contemporary literature whose ends seldom rose above the mundane level. Quite in the vein of his ministerial predecessors, he saw the whole use of literature as moral, expressive either of universal truth or on a lower level of conventional morality. Firkins failed to add that such an attitude was quite to be expected even from so rebellious a scion of the formerly dominant clergy.

On the current American literary scene, Emerson was a more intelligent commentator. He kept abreast of the periodical literature and criticism and digested many volumes that were brought to his attention both in his Journal and in conversations with friends. He further read widely in literary developments across the Atlantic and used them to enrich his comments on American cultural progress.

Every reader of Emerson is familiar with the eliminative irony in which he characterized the annual Phi Beta Kappa celebration at Harvard as a mere sign of the love of letters in a people too busy to beget from it fair discourses. Twelve years after Bryant had declared that the only obstacle to an American literature would be failure to make use of opportunities, Emerson hinted strongly that this very danger was blocking the growth of our letters. America, he insisted, was in 1837 sufficiently developed to strike out for herself in cultural matters. At Dartmouth College, he declared that we should live now and for ourselves, that we should renounce allegiance to Greece, Rome, the so-called Aristotelian unities, and the *Edinburgh Review*. Throughout his career, he attacked America's subservience to law for thing and to foreign tutelage.

Emerson had, to be sure, no intention of discarding all that the world of Europe had to offer. Though more independent than the critics whose pleas for study of transatlantic culture had preceded his, he agreed with their estimate of its value. Sympathetic as he was to contemporary sentiment for democratic literature, he yet included in his charts for the literary mariner all that America could use from past and contemporary Europe. Readers who assume that his judgment of books in the Phi Beta Kappa address represented his considered opinion forget that as a skilled orator he was suiting his address to his excessively bookish audience and making his point by overemphasis. In this same address he declared the theory of books to be noble; and he did not carelessly scatter adjectives. Three years later he wrote that it could not be a bad year which gave him from the presses editions of Plato and St. Paul, Plutarch, St. Augustine, Spinoza, Chapman, Beaumont and Fletcher, Donne, and Sir Thomas Browne. The works of Shakespeare had for a century and a half been the major cause of the tremendous development in German scientific, religious, and scientific pursuits which had made German scholarship the finest in the world. The modern world, he concluded, could not overstate its debt to the past.

Emerson deplored frequently the slackness of Americans in using their cultural independence. Current literature continued to offer a vast carcass of tradition, while the few books with novel characteristics were unhealthful. Young writers, content to write of subjects they had never seen, were in danger of the French error of adhering to the form while losing the substance, of doing what had already been done. Ignoring college rules, each mind should employ the method and message which came to it together from the Over-Soul. The writer is like Shakespeare, above the canons of criticism, not subject to them like Goethe. The American author must be obedient to the heavenly vision, and the critic must share this vision. So far were they from this freedom that a few years after his Phi Beta Kappa address Emerson felt obliged regretfully to declare that American literature was still in the optative mood of contingent futurity; Americans, he wrote in 1843, should still be grateful for their borrowings from Europe, which would have to contribute to our culture a while longer.

One bar to the poet's realization of his ideal was the current notion that the external imaginative stimuli of alcohol and narcotics were prerequisites to attainment. A deeper cause was inattention to everyday life. Though, compared with Europe, the American scene appeared rather bare, life was nevertheless lived here on a noble plane. The author should pierce the drab shell and show the latent beauty and elevation in his fellow-citizens. The greater the difficulty, Emerson believed with Castelvetro, the greater the artist who overcomes it; writers who treated alien scenes were avoiding the harder yet more rewarding task of penetrating to the heart of American life.

Emerson supported the democratization of literature then actively engaging the attention of forward-looking critics. Prester John and the pirates should be abandoned to make room for Texas, the abolition movement, and educational progress. In America, the audience had added to the gentry in the boxes the commoners in the galleries and the pit. He declined, however, to share the fears of William Ellery Channing that the American readers of literature in the aristocratic tradition would endanger American democracy. Keeping his categories of thought disentangled, he insisted that Americans should exploit whatever they could appropriate of the riches offered by Europe. In this way he effectively showed a way to preserve the best qualities of both schools for the good of the country. Paraphrasing Emerson's remark about Plato, one might almost say that out of Emerson have proceeded illuminating suggestions for almost all the literary matters subsequently discussed by American literary theorists.

Emerson's critical descendants followed two branches. One, which saw his militant Americanism without at first hearing its European overtones, was exemplified in Walt Whitman. The other, though for many years supercilious toward him, developed through James Russell Lowell. From Lowell it descended to the New Humanists and to several of the New Critics. Before considering his later progeny, however, it is necessary to consider three writers more closely related to him in time: Henry David Thoreau, Margaret Fuller, and Orestes Brownson.

HENRY DAVID THOREAU

Although Thoreau was accused of getting up a nose like Emerson's, acquaintance with his work indicates the stubborn independence of Emerson's hired man. His sharing in Emerson's transcendentalism in no way implied the slavish following of a master. Both when they agreed and when they differed, Thoreau stood on his own feet.

Thoreau impatiently brushed aside all attempts to define poetry: poetry is poetry, and there is an end of it. No sooner is a definition proposed than some poet through his work instantly sets aside all its limitations. Poetry is rather all that we do not know; we see it in part through mystical experiences. The more nearly a man records his revelation, the more tolerable will the poem be. From revelation the loftiest wisdom comes, and it is always either rhymed or somehow musically measured. If one could condense the wisdom of mankind within a single volume, it would be poetry without one rhythmless line. From revelation, then, comes poetry, and from revelation alone. The best product of the wit of an entire college is a jingle, a series of regularly recurrent jars.

Thoreau recognized two classes of poets: the one cultivates life, the other art. The former desires food for nourishment, the latter for flavor. He recognized likewise two sorts of writer, both of them great and rare. The greater, the genius or inspired person, is inerrant, not subject to criticism, but rather provides criticism with its laws. The lesser writes by intellect and taste. The poetry of the greater is rare, but when found is sacred, worthy of the same reverence as are the works of nature. Poetry in fact is intimately related to religion and philosophy; in the final stages of civilization, as in the childhood of man, the three will be one. Without poetry, in a prosaic frame of mind, man accomplishes nothing memorable. Facts, seen in their vitally significant form, are actually poetry.

Like Emerson, Thoreau found an organic principle in art. Prose is written *soluta ratione,* loosely organized, in sharp contrast to the precision of poetry. Each poem develops its own peculiar rhythm or measure as the poet works it over; it cannot be arbitrarily poured into any mould the poet wishes. Impulse, intuition, is the best linguist and most naturally finds expression for the idea it has brought. The principal difference between Emerson's and Thoreau's concept of organic form seems to be that for Emerson the form was revealed in the mystical experience in which the poet saw the poem, whereas for Thoreau the form develops as the poet revises and works out his conception. In practice, too, Thoreau found commonly that the poem did not radically depart from the forms already established by custom, whereas Emerson's poem might appear in a quite novel form. In the eyes of both men, however, thought and expression are organically related. Failure to recognize this relation, Thoreau believed, prevented our having just and serene criticism.

From his adherence to an organic principle, one would naturally expect Thoreau to subscribe to the standard romantic belief in the superiority of nature over art. His classical training, however, was too thorough to permit him to support fully this position. Many works of art, he admitted, were inferior to nature, but the fault was that of the artists who failed to attend to nature as it really is. He found Ruskin's *Modern Painters* unsatisfactory because Ruskin had described nature only as Turner had painted it. The truest description is the unmeasured response of the artist to the object; it is a poetic description, in sharp contrast to the merely photographic description of the scientist. In a somewhat ironical reminiscence of Aristotle's mimetic theory, he once drew an analogy from the oak galls in the Concord woods. Is not Art a gall, he asked? God has stung Nature and implanted in her the seed of man. Man, become artist, makes Nature change and grow according to his idea. It is hardly complimentary to make man a parasite and art a parasitic growth; yet, given a combination of romantic and classical theories of the relation between art and nature in a mind as cross-grained as Thoreau's, such an ambiguous notion should not be surprising.

Though he stoutly defended the basic position of the ancient classics in education even for farmers, Thoreau recognized that they had not proved an unmixed blessing for English literature. Probably the ablest Greek student in Concord, he preferred always to read the classics in the original tongues. Some Latin verses, he declared, pleased him more than whole English poems on account of their elegant terseness. He wished that young William Ellery Channing, whose poems troubled him as well as Emerson in editing the *Dial*, could be forced to write Latin as a cure for his "sublimo-slipshod style." The Latin would force him to say something grammatically and to consider the meanings of his words. But, although during his life he bought over four hundred volumes of the classics and read them with avid discernment, he felt that English literature, instead of expressing itself freely, had since the days of Chaucer been essentially a reflection of Greece and Rome. Excessive deference to classical authors had rendered English verse too tame and civilized, though these models had at the same time contributed to it qualities no literature could do without. Thoreau himself succeeded in avoiding the dangerous dominance of the classics while drawing from them essential characteristics for his work and life. Without the classics, an able classical scholar has declared, Thoreau would simply not have been Thoreau.

Like the other transcendental critics, Thoreau felt more interested in the writer than in his work. He had consequently little use for the objectivity of works of genius; it was partly the concealment of the authors' nature by their concentration on classical models that had irked him in English poetry. The poet, he insisted, cannot be wholly objective. Following Carlyle, he professed to see the poet as the actual hero of whatever epic he should write. Even Shakespeare's dramas are but fancies and imaginings, less valuable than the truth about his life would be. To Thoreau as to Pope, the proper study of mankind was man; but Thoreau's humanitarianism saw man from a different angle.

Since he was more concerned with the poet than with his poetry, Thoreau logically held the poet in low esteem when under the sway of inspiration; at such times, his talent was all gone and he himself was no longer a poet. The poet should therefore avoid unreserved abandonment to his inspiration and should delay putting to paper his experience. Like Wordsworth, Thoreau wished him to permit repose of mind to contribute to adequate expression. The *furor poeticus*, he declared, stirs up such a dust that the jewel of genuine worth may be buried in the rubbish. In thus belittling the capacities of the poet under inspiration, he was trying to protect the quality of the resultant poem.

Such reasoning led Thoreau to go even beyond Emerson in his emphasis upon the need for careful revision and finish of literary work. He advocated all the care that the most exacting artist could lavish upon the artifact. Horace's union of filework and delay in publication was echoed in his admonitions to authors. What the lecturer worked on for only a single summer would take his audience but an hour to forget. When a zealous poet insisted that the world stood on tiptoe in expectation of his work, Thoreau retorted that in that case he should waste no time before starting to prune and revise. To a friend despondent at lack of literary acclaim, he wrote asking whether he was really disciplining himself by protracted labor at his art. Did he ever get any corns from pursuit of his goal, or think of hanging himself for failure? The secret of success is to express oneself. E. T. Channing might better have taught this one principle to the Harvard seniors than all the systematic admonitions of his lectures.

As a thrifty Yankee, Thoreau advocated careful consideration of one's predecessors in his craft; it is wasteful to do over what has already been done. The man aware of what has already been said of his subject will proceed farther along the road to knowledge and speak more authoritatively than he who starts from scratch. He warned his readers, however, to consider what has been done as advisory and suggestive, not as a directive. Mere adherence to time-honored principles amused him. He pointed ironically to the end of a day spent on the Concord river as the close of a drama which the great Scene-shifter brought to an end with complete disregard of the unities and utter unconcern whether it turned out to be tragedy, comedy, tragicomedy, or pastoral. Such hoary rules or literary genres had no sway over his mind. He used whatever known principles he found suitable. Blair had his uses, but sometimes "better omit Blair, and take the air."

Thoreau lamented the loss from English poetry of the fresh, wild native strain. Even in the ballad, he complained, the wilderness is not savage but the *good* greenwood, and the closest approach to a "wild" man is Robin Hood. The so-called nature revival, he felt, indicated plenty of love of nature without showing nature itself. Under such deficiencies, he felt, the Anglo-Saxon literary tradition desperately needed America. The new land offered writers wild country, wild men, and thus provided a unique opportunity for American writers to express the natural yearning for the Wild. They should employ whatever the art of the past could teach them to recapture this natural quality which had vanished from the Anglo-Saxon world.

Thoreau reinforced Emerson's literary influence at either end. By putting greater emphasis upon scholarship and finish, and making more consistent use of tradition than his master, he pointed the way to more intelligent use of the past. By closer application to nature than Emerson, and by recognition of what nature in the raw is, he at the same time indicated far more clearly the unique contribution that America could make to the civilized world.

MARGARET FULLER

Of all the Concord circle, Margaret Fuller was undoubtedly the most active practicing critic. Educated to excess by her father, this American Mme. de Staël was better read in Continental literatures than the other Concord scholars. Her admiration for Goethe, fully equal to that felt by James Freeman Clarke and Thoreau, did not wane as did Emerson's. Her attainments as student and critic stand the test of comparison with her American contemporaries, and her literary reputation is in no way the result of her unique position as the American bluestocking.

Miss Fuller, whose mind was scholarly rather than philosophical, was less a transcendentalist than her fellow-writers; she did, however, accept several transcendental doctrines. Like Emerson, she demanded for the world men thinking, not schoolmasters or special pleaders. Adapting the myth of "The American Scholar," she wrote that God, the great Poet-Maker, when He became flesh, was subdivided into poets and critics. Poets are men of genuine vision and spontaneous expression. Nature is the literature and art of the divine mind. In this combination of Plato, Sidney, and Emerson, one readily detects ingredients of Concord transcendentalism.

In other respects Miss Fuller was out of harmony with Concord. The truest kind of poetry, she wrote of both Emerson's and Wordsworth's poems, is not philosophical. The poet should create his own designs, not merely interpret Nature. Nor should he consider himself successful if he attained only fit audience though few;

she shared the current desire for a democratic literature. The democratic principle of the greatest good for the greatest number rendered that pure individuality advocated in Emerson's "Self-Reliance" impracticable. These differences were so fundamental as to relegate her to the fringes of the Concord group, which never quite knew how to consider her.

Miss Fuller wrote extensively of poetry and the poet, of criticism and the critic, of the cultural condition of America and the requirements for improving it. Her attempt to define poetry was carefully worded:

> Poetry—the sublime and beautiful expressed in measured language. It is closely allied with the fine arts. It should sing to the ear, paint to the eye, and exhibit the symmetry of architecture. If perfect, it will satisfy the intellectual and moral faculties no less than the heart and the senses. It works chiefly by simile and melody. It is to prose as the garden to the house. Pleasure is the object of the one, convenience of the other.

A detailed aesthetic is indicated in these brief sentences. Its German affinities from Lessing to her own day are apparent. The Renaissance comparison of poetry to a flower garden, which hints at a variety of possible relations, she developed in considerable detail. Literature, she agreed with Dr. Channing, included not only garden plants but the entire growth of the region. Just as all nature is the literature and art of the divine mind, so lichens and weeds exist in man's literature, lesser species than poetry indeed, but still beautiful. Some of these inferior species, which like Longfellow's poetry have poetic qualities, give delight to the reader; and delight, though not the highest end of poetry, is still a legitimate end.

Like the other transcendentalists, Miss Fuller's interests centered more closely in the poet than in his product. To her, as to Wordsworth, poetry was the spontaneous expression of powerful emotions, but unlike him she believed that the greatest poet approached divinity. This elevation ruled out Byron from her list of great poets. His powerful emotions were diseased, his mood morbid and false, the offspring of a moral malaria; the great poet induces health. The poet was also Emerson's man of beauty, original in both idea and expression. And he eschewed realism. She saw Balzac, the typical realist, combining the man of science with the amateur collector, peeping and botanizing with passionless scrutiny over any specimen, no matter how monstrous. He abandons his unemotional state only to sneer cynically at a specimen while he demonstrates on what foul juices it has fed. He can never ascend to the highest heaven of inventive genius. "No more of him!—We leave him to his suicidal work."

Miss Fuller had been thoroughly grounded in the ancient classics. In particular, she agreed with Horace and Emerson that the artist is a selecting principle. She found the "little thoughts that are always twisting their parasites" over the main purpose of Browning's *Sordello* so beautiful that she could hardly bear to wish them excised; nevertheless, "a higher mastery in the poetic art must give him strength and resolution to reject them." The severe discipline of the classical artist must be the training of the modern poet as well.

She believed the greatest poet to be "a genius of a wild, impassioned, many-sided eagerness, restraining its exuberance by its sense of fitness, taming its extravagance beneath the rule its taste approves, exhibiting the soul within soul, and the force of the will over all that we inherit." Like Thoreau, who believed such a poet to be America's contribution to letters, she saw in this wild energy, with its will to act and will to refrain as Irving Babbitt would have described it, something far superior to the product of abandoned genius undirected by a disciplined taste. She had learned well Coleridge's principle of the reconciliation of opposites. "Art is nature, but nature new-modelled, condensed, and harmonized. We are not merely like mirrors, to reflect our own times to those more distant. The mind has a light of its own, and by it illumines what it recreates." The determinism that was to enter literary theory through Taine would have found her in full disagreement.

Miss Fuller approached the practice of criticism equipped with the best that ancient criticism had to offer, extensive knowledge of English critical tradition, and a wide knowledge of German critical method. From these aids and her own capacities she produced a well-integrated theory of criticism with a detailed application to America.

Critics, in her mind, fell into three classes: the subjective, the apprehensive, and the comprehensive. The subjective, who simply record their reaction to art as it presently affects them, are critics only by courtesy. Making no attempt to discover the author's intent, they measure every work in terms of themselves. The apprehensive group enter into the author's personality, show what his work means, and thus make it better known to us as it really is. They almost become the artist whom they criticize. The comprehensive group include the merits of the apprehensive critics with the capacity to judge the work objectively. Like the neohumanists they possess a standard that is partly within them and partly without. Though lower than the actual maker, they are his needed friends, sharing in some of his creative powers. Like Ruskin's highest order of poets, they sympathize fully with the poet while at the same time they hold level the scales of objective justice.

She noted also two modes of criticism. By one, the critic tests every work according to the highest standards of literary perfection; in it, the work is supremely good or it is nothing. In Coleridgean terms, this mode accepts only the highest works of the imagination while discarding the humbler works of the fancy. The other mode permits the critic to appreciate the humbler plants as well as the prize-winning blooms. It finds beauty in each natural form; all nature is but art, as Pope once wrote, if one will try to discover the method behind it.

Ideal criticism will combine the best elements of both modes. "The highest sense of fulfilled excellence will be found to consist with the largest appreciation of every sign of life. The eye of man is fitted to range all around no less than to be lifted on high." Such a happy combination she believed to be specially suited to the present American era, in which the expansion of the reading public had brought some lowering of literary standards. It raised the exalted standard for all who could rally to it, while at the same time it offered to inferior capacities beauty on levels which they could reach. In this recognition of literary levels of quality, she once more anticipated Babbitt; in spite of their being in opposed literary camps, she saw many problems of the literary thinker in terms similar to his.

Her German studies provided Miss Fuller with a pattern of orderly thought. Her demand that interpretation precede judgment, that one discover what the work is as well as what it is not, is characteristic of the German thinker. She also made use of Goethe's criterion for judgment: "Most men, in judging another man, ask, Did he live up to our standards? But to me it seems desirable to ask rather, Did he live up to his own?" Several decades before Joel Spingarn reminded Americans of its validity, Miss Fuller had presented this principle of just judgment.

So frequently did she bring Continental ideas to her readers' attention that she felt obliged to defend her preference for them. She admitted that in childhood, while mastering foreign languages, she had temporarily almost forgotten her English. What she loved in Continental literature was "the range and force of ideal manifestation in forms of national and individual greatness." The expansive greatness of Latin minds she had not found in the English character; and it was to benefit America, by introducing desirable but not Anglo-Saxon traits, that she had steeped herself in alien literatures. Going beyond Mme de Staël, who had contented herself with pointing out the limits of the British spirit, Miss Fuller wished to supplement the English heritage of America by infusions of other cultures. Only enrichment, she insisted, could accrue to America from this addition, for America in forming her democratic literature must select and combine into it the usable good of other nations.

Like many readers of Goethe, Miss Fuller was intrigued by his cryptic distinction between the classic and the romantic. Without attempting to explain the remark that the classic is healthy and the romantic diseased, which had sorely puzzled Eckermann and was later to disturb Sainte-Beuve and Walter Pater, she carefully divided the narrow and broad meanings of the term "classical." In its narrow sense, she wrote, it implies servile adherence to the critical attitude of which the unities form a part. In the broader sense, the term means "such a simplicity of plan, selection of actors and events, such jealous limitations on time and range of subject, as may concentrate the interest, perfect the illusion, and make the impression most distinct and forcible." In this condensation of Aristotelian and Horatian precept mingled with Coleridge's request for the reader's voluntary suspension of disbelief for a season, Miss Fuller successfully fused romantic theory with the basic principles of genuinely classical criticism. She perceived what many of her contemporaries had not yet discovered: the principles of true ancient classicism are more closely in agreement with the enlightened romanticism of Wordsworth and Coleridge than they ever were with neoclassical regularity.

Miss Fuller's critical practice is best seen in her handling of the American literary situation. Sharing Emerson's conviction that America should be independent in literature, she concurred also in his regretful admission that we should not hastily cut loose from Europe. She denied the name American to books which aped the life and thought of Europe, though she felt that Americans might well practice such writing until they could safely untie their leading-strings. American authors would walk alone as soon as they were able. Since the author is the spokesman of his people, an original, American idea must manifest itself before the author can express it and so become himself American. She expressed uncertainty whether the desire of Americans that the arts become acclimatized to the New World sprang merely from an imitative tendency or from the realization of a genuine need to balance our bustling daily life with an unfolding higher nature. If the latter, as she hoped, were the case, a long naturalizing process would be required before we could claim them as rightfully our own.

Transplanting the literature of Great Britain would not serve our needs. That literature served well enough to express the British racial nature, the monarchical form of government, and the insular focus of her trade. It could not fit our mixed race now; and as America should be enriched with new blood from varied stocks, the difference would increase. Although the mixture in our melting pot had not yet advanced far enough to show even a prospect of what would some day be, she ventured to declare the coming of an American literature and the prerequisites to its attainment. First, of course, the fusion of races must become more nearly complete. Secondly, Americans must prize moral and intellectual freedom no less than political independence. Thirdly, the material exploitation of the country must reach a stage so advanced as to leave men's minds at leisure to turn their energies to the higher yet less pressing departments of man's existence. Though far in the future, such an America did not seem to her a Utopian dream. Meanwhile, she energetically busied herself to promote the literature of her own day.

Certain specific recommendations seemed to her immediately applicable. First, neither the age nor the country favored the writing of drama; she recommended that attempts to compose it be abandoned. Though philosophical poetry did not receive her highest commendation, it expressed the meditative spirit of the age. The normal human need of spectacle and dramatic representation must be satisfied with the opera, the ballet, and the pantomime.

Her second recommendation was that American criticism temper justice with mercy. Though severity in rebuke was sometimes necessary, leniency should be the rule. Since pressing material and political activities prevented Americans from giving due attention to belles-lettres, the critics should accept gratefully whatever humble effort an author might be able to put forth. The author receives no credit nor encouragement unless it comes from the reviewers; and any attempt in the creative direction is better than apathy. Satirists, indeed, were needed to drive the magpies from Parnassus, if songbirds were ever to nest there; but the magpies should be driven out, not slain. She deplored the tactics of Poe, the hatchet man of the critical forces. His swashing blows had done more execution among the children of light than among the forces of darkness; he had cut down many promising poets who needed fostering. The most pressing task of the Muse was to refine our taste; when this should have been accomplished, it would be time to build the lofty rhyme.

A third pressing need was a saving sense of humor. In our situation, the scrutiny of a Cervantes, a Fielding, or a Richter would prove more constructive than the solemnity of a Wordsworth. Humor penetrates to the core of things, assesses their real worth, laughs sympathetically at their faults, and while correcting tries to encourage. It also prevents the critic from taking himself too seriously, a fault which American critics desperately needed to correct. It lies at the base of constructive criticism, and renders impossible destructive judgment like much of Poe's.

She welcomed the new to be tested along with the old:

We are not afraid of new standards and new examples. Only give enough of them, variety enough, and from well-intentioned, generous minds. America can choose what she wants, if she has sufficient range of choice; and if there is any reason, any deep root in the tastes and opinions she holds at present, she will not lightly yield them. . . . Her hope is not in ignorance, but in knowledge.

Her American author would have the free range of a large country; but his would be a freedom disciplined by what he had learned from the past and from other cultures. He would use whatever commended itself from these cultures until the resultant compound, as Whitman was to say shortly after her death, would be transcendent and new.

The most serviceable medium for securing ample criticism, Miss Fuller felt, was an abundance of periodicals devoted to reviews. The reviews themselves should be dissertations on the subjects of the books reviewed, not mere critiques of the books alone. The office of the reviewer, instead of merely pointing out the merits of books, is to furnish the reader a view of a large cluster of objects about the subject. Such an essay will stimulate the reader to take a broader or more careful view of the matter than the book itself, with his own prejudice, might prepare for him. The assemblage in one paper of wide information bearing on the subject, especially in a land where good libraries are scarce, is the surest way to make wide knowledge available.

The reviewer must be neither despot nor special pleader. The self-assured, "infallible" critic, who tells the reader what to think, what not to think, or merely what he thinks, has no share of her world. "Wo to that coterie where some critic sits despotic, intrenched behind the infallible 'We'!" Equally obnoxious was the partisan critic, who advanced one side of an argument to support his own preference; defense is admirable, but evidence must not be colored. If proper reviewers could be secured, periodicals would confer untold benefit upon American letters.

Miss Fuller's untimely death closed abruptly a brilliant critical career which promised great attainments. Truncated as it stands, it testifies to the remarkable breadth of literary and critical view attainable in the first half of the nineteenth century.

[66]

Orestes Brownson

Orestes Augustus Brownson, who for a time loomed large in the literary world, briefly contributed a lurid tint to American letters. As impressive a figure as his name, during his first forty years he was everything by turns and nothing long. His religious wanderings, from Calvinism to Universalism and Unitarianism, to a church of his own, to transcendentalism, and finally to Roman Catholicism, indicate the general pattern of his life—a hit-or-miss pattern, like some old rag carpet. Brownson was no contemplative American scholar. He was man in furious action: preacher, contributor to magazines, editor of magazines, for which he wrote nearly all the articles, debater extraordinary on all subjects and occasions, theorist in politics, economics, and social problems. His collected works fill nineteen bulky volumes. Of the same age as Emerson, he was for some years rated the philosopher's superior in ability.

Though largely self-taught and more journalist than litterateur, Brownson found time amid his multifarious concerns to speak his mind on American letters. A "come-outer" in writing as in religion, he belabored Emerson and other critics who seemed to him to discourage the nascent literature of the United States. In an article aimed at Emerson, he asserted in 1839 that the American scholar must address the whole people, and repudiated the doctrine of "fit audience, though few" as unthinkable for an American author. The democratization of literature that followed hard upon Jackson's presidency appealed to him. A literary American class would be intolerable. In order to reach the masses, the writer must possess attainments not greatly above theirs. The possibility that such a writer might have little to tell the masses did not evidently occur to him. A national literature, he declared, expresses the national life, embodies national ideals as held by the masses. Only one from such masses can embrace these ideals. He will appear from the masses at their demand, not from the aloof transcendentalists or the educated few. The American spirit is utilitarian; physical well-being is a more pressing need than spiritual advantage; and these outer groups can provide no work of art for the American people because they provide no end to which their scholarship might serve as means.

Admitting Emerson's charge that American books are few and trifling, Brownson countered by declaring that American periodicals constituted an excellent popular literature that more than compensated for the deficiency of books. The writers of this popular literature kept before their eyes the concern for the people, for equal rights and social equality. In this insistence upon the rights and future sovereignty of the populace, Brownson anticipated later statements by Karl Marx.

Brownson's critical level is well shown in his pronouncement in 1842 upon contemporary French fiction. It was, he contended, inferior in realism to the current British product. Victor Hugo, whom he considered the best French novelist, superior to Alexandre Dumas, unfortunately revelled in the grotesque and horrible. Though Honoré de Balzac wrote realistically, his work lacked the geniality and inspiration of Irving, Dickens, and Bulwer. George Sand's work was less familiar to him, but his interest was perversely roused by it. "We have found her loudly and generally censured, and have therefore been led to sympathize with her. We have heard her called many hard names, and have therefore presumed, without other evidence, that she must have great and positive merits." Somewhat inconsistently, in view of his ignorance of her works, he added that she possessed great ability, even genius; she was "in many respects the first and best of the authors of modern French literature." He did not, however, rate her above Hugo. His praise of her came from no chivalrous deference to women, as it might have in Poe's reviews; and his lifelong insistence upon the inferiority of woman forced him to set Hugo above her.

This prejudice was clearly stated in a late attack on American fiction, "produced chiefly by women, and therefore weak, sentimental, preventing instead of aiding high national literature." Woman fulfills her intellectual mission in conversation, where the gentle, fitful flashes of her mind show to advantage; she cannot rival the sustained, penetrating light of man's discourse. Even the sparks which she occasionally emits would never appear if they were not struck against the flint of man's reason. "She can aid man, but she can do nothing without him. She was made for him, and in herself is only an inchoate man."

Brownson's conversion to Catholicism cut him off from contact with current American life; thereafter he followed a fanatical sectarian line. Though literature is the expression of a people, American Protestantism, the religion of most American writers, was paganism. All culture should reveal beauty, but only when inspired by the true faith can it approach this ideal. The only hope for American literature was a return of America en masse to Mother Church, for Protestantism and "Catholicity" cannot mix, and good literature is synonymous with Catholic writing. Since America stubbornly refused to return to Rome, he fell out of sympathy with her, and his work ceased to have significance for the developing country.

The weakness and temporary strength of Brownson's critical writing spring from the same root. He was one of the earliest American critics to approach literature from a journalistic point of view. He rode the upsurge of popular sentiment stirred by the Jacksonian democratic literary propagandists and attempted to lower literature to popular levels. As has happened before and since, he could not hold the attention of the very audience he would have served; erelong the thinking readers of America on all cultural levels turned their attention to the idealism of Emerson. Writers and theorists generally followed suit. It was several decades later when the realism which Brownson adumbrated and the popular literature of which he vaguely dreamed began to flourish; and they were in opposite camps when they appeared.

Chapter 4

Edgar Allan Poe

I F EMERSON WAS AN INSPIRATION and philosophical guide to American writers, Poe was undoubtedly the first outstanding personality in criticism. The customary anonymity of able earlier critics diminished their personal reputation, and their involvement in other affairs restricted their critical activity. Though he was unquestionably a patriotic American interested in the progress of his country, Poe focused his attention upon belles-lettres and gave them his undivided interest. His vigorous, caustic judgments were more readily appreciated by his readers than his highly artistic creative work. Although the opinion is hardly accurate, it is natural that writers on American criticism have for years dated its significant beginnings with the career of Poe.

Poe's intensive training in Latin poetry colored his conception of the poet. Horace's *vates sacer* frequently appears in his reviews as "the sacred name of poet." Since poetry is the practical result, expressed in language, of the poetic sentiment existing in certain individuals, *poeta nascitur* is a true statement; the power to compose poetry is inborn in poets. Even when, as in Tom Moore, the power appears only casually, no one can doubt that this *mens divinior* is present. Poe took for granted genius in the poet; and he denied with Horace's vigor and in Horatian phrase the possibility of composing genuine poetry *invita Minerva*.

The power to idealize is an indispensable component of the poet's mind. Poe did not, however, rate it above the poet's knowledge. Rather, the "man of metaphysical acumen" will produce a finer poem, though endowed with only a slight degree of ideality, than the possessor of ideality who lacks the philosophical breadth and depth of mind. The man who combines the two qualities will of course produce poetry superior to that written by the possessor of either alone.

The poet is a conscious artist. Poe could not conceive of thoughts beyond the reach of language. Emerson's claim to transcendental knowledge he denied. He did, indeed, admit that at times, when on the brink of sleep, he had become aware of "a class of fancies, of extraordinary delicacy, which are not thoughts, and to which, *as yet,* I have found it absolutely impossible to adapt language." Though he regarded them as glimpses of the spirit's outer world, he declared when he last mentioned them in 1846 that he had already begun to control them; and he obviously did not consider them beyond the power of language ultimately to express them. How he differentiated these experiences from the mystical revelations claimed by the transcendentalists, whom he despised, does not appear. Perhaps his egotism led him to suppose them to be experiences peculiar to himself.

This conscious artistry included careful attention to details of expression. "It is nonsense," Poe wrote, "to assert that the highest genius would not be benefited by attention to its modes of manifestation—by availing itself of that Natural Art which it too frequently despises. Is it not evident that the more intrinsically valuable the rough diamond, the more gain accrues to it from polish?" By this careful polishing the poet satisfies his mind that he has fully expressed his idea. He is as sure as the mathematician that "such and such apparently arbitrary arrangements of matter constitute and alone constitute the true beauty." Though his conviction lies beyond logical proof, the consensus of his poetic brethren will agree that he has employed the one inevitable expression of his idea, to attain which he will not demur at the intense, sustained effort required to achieve it.

Poe realized that other artists had much in common with the poet. With music he had some acquaintance; of sculpture and painting he had less knowledge; but he shared the interest of other romantic writers in landscape gardening. He had the journalist's acquaintance with most of these arts, gotten up for the reviewing of books about them; but he seems to have added to this hurried study a cultured interest in them. Since he was best acquainted with those arts that imitate in words and a talented performer in them, his artistic theories are naturally most fully concerned with literature.

Notwithstanding his cavalier treatment of Aristotle, Poe realized the value of many artistic principles laid down in the *Poetics*. His final definition of art as "the reproduction of what the Senses perceive in Nature, through the veil of the soul" is substantially Aristotle's doctrine of *mimesis* or artistic imitation. The Aristotelian requirement of organic unity in art was basic to his thinking in spite of its being absorbed into A. W. Schlegel's broader conception, the unity of effect. Schlegel's idea, Poe probably realized, was in part the consequence of Aristotle. He employed many of Aristotle's terms regarding unity: that each part is necessary in the place where the artist has placed it; that the arrangement of events is governed by necessity or at least by plausibility; that it has beginning, middle, and end; and that its size is such as to be readily encompassed by the mind. The work of art is credible in details and as a whole, and more of a unit than events in life appear to be. To secure this effect and to create greater beauty, the poet may employ a strangeness of proportion that is "a happy modification of Nature."

Poe hesitated at first to attempt a definition of poetry. The poetic sentiment, however, he believed to be capable of description: it is "a sense of the beautiful, of the sublime, and of the mystical." One may approach a definition of poetry, he felt, in calling it "the sentiment of Intellectual Happiness here, and the Hope of a Higher Intellectual Happiness hereafter." The stronger his sentiment, the greater the poet. In 1842, he quoted a definition by Rufus Griswold: "The creation of beauty, the manifestation of the real by the ideal, in words that move in metrical array, is poetry." Accepting this as the "*sole true* definition" of poetry, he reduced it to a simple sentence: "Poetry is the rhythmical creation of beauty." The poet yearns, Poe believed with Plato, after "the beauty above, . . . the loveliness to come"; and his soul "thus athirst strives to allay its fervor in futile attempts at creation" in the light of its mystical vision.

From this attempt, however inadequately fulfilled, comes poetry.

On various occasions between 1840 and 1846, Poe discussed that most vexed of romantic questions, the nature of the fancy and the imagination. His starting point was Coleridge's famous distinction of the two in *Biographia Literaria*, a distinction which, Poe asserted, is bound up with the mystical significance of poetry. The concept of mystical meanings in poetry he ascribed to the German critics, ignorant that it had been a staple of medieval criticism before receiving its detailed statement by Dante. The poems which mankind has agreed to call imaginative, he declared, are precisely those which are remarkable for their mystical meaning. He claimed as his own this relating of the mystical, the fanciful, and the imaginative, but did not clarify its relevance to his discussion.

To Coleridge's statement that "the fancy combines, the imagination creates," Poe retorted that the distinction was one without a difference: "The fancy as nearly creates as the imagination; and neither creates in any respect. All novel conceptions are merely unusual combinations." Nor do fancy and imagination differ in degree; no elevation of subject can change fancy into a something else to be called imagination. This disagreement of Poe with Coleridge requires attention; and it is to be regretted that, like Wordsworth on the same topic, Poe contented himself with remarking on the subject in the course of his concern with other matters, without rounding out his position.

In his objection to Coleridge's careful distinction, Poe was more captious than genuinely analytical. In 1836, while still under the spell of Coleridge, Poe had refused the name of poet to the versifier who merely reacts to and records beautiful objects or experiences; that name belonged to the creator, who in his yearning after celestial beauty endeavors to express what eye hath not seen nor ear heard. The mere versifier employs in his work a tolerable acquaintance with the objects of which he writes and a moderate endowment of the ability to compare. Comparison, Poe asserted, is the chief constituent of fancy or the power of combination. The poetic sentiment is ideality, imagination, the creative ability. Quite in harmony with his objection to the fancy is his censure of Thomas Moore's abundant similes: "no poet thus distinguished was ever richly ideal."

He could also think of an imagination which was not creative, which he claimed to find in Longfellow's verse. This, however, may be satisfactorily explained as a somewhat careless use of the term as equivalent to fancy—a freedom which he would not have taken if Coleridge had still directed him after 1840.

By 1845, Poe was ready to consider art as containing four qualities: imagination, fancy, fantasy, and humor; and the greatest of these, the imagination, was the artist or creator. It selects such items as are harmonious and rearranges them into new combinations that produce beauty. The forms that enter into this combination "are themselves still to be considered as atomic"—that is, like Coleridge's "fixities and definites" with which the fancy deals; and the whole partakes of beauty as its parts are beautiful. The whole equals the sum of its parts. Not noticing the impending logical disaster, Poe added that the resultant combination may lack the quality of any component, may possess a quality unlike that of any component, and may even fabricate beauty out of deformed elements. It is, he added, a process analogous to certain chemical compositions—and here he strongly implies acceptance of Coleridge's fusing by the imagination of those very parts which he had just asserted to be "atomic," incapable of alteration. Poe's surprising failure to note this glaring discrepancy between his two statements was no doubt due to his absorption in other matters more immediately germane to his review. His permitting such a contradiction to stand concerning a major topic of romantic theory is telling evidence of the fundamental weakness in his poetics, the lack of a developed aesthetic theory. It shows that he captiously took exception to distinctions much more acutely drawn than his mind could grasp.

However confused his thinking on the relations of the imagination and its "half sister, the Cinderella, Fancy," as he referred to them in 1846, Poe rated the imagination as high as Coleridge. Like Coleridge's primary imagination, it approaches divinity in its power. It is supreme among the mental faculties, and can bring its possessor "to the very verge of the *great secrets*." Perhaps all very profound knowledge has originated from a highly stimulated imagination.

Holding these exalted beliefs about the genesis of poetry, Poe naturally denied *in toto* the current American belief which still accepted Samuel Johnson's statement that the purpose of literature was to instruct while pleasing. Such a belief he labeled tersely "the heresy of the didactic." Poetry, as the rhythmical creation of beauty, is concerned with beauty; taste alone is its basis of judgment. If in the course of its creating beauty the poem should incidentally give moral instruction, well and good. And the pleasure produced by the contemplation of the beautiful—"at once the most intense, the most elevating, and the most pure"—though produced in a realm where morals hold no sway, effects a betterment of being in poet and reader. But the poet who writes in order to give instruction of any kind is a heretic.

Poe's ignorance of literary history, with his consequent tendency to reckon as literature of high quality only the kind that he himself could write, probably accounts for his depreciation of the longer forms of composition. His conception of literature was governed by an amateurish knowledge of psychology, penetrating in spots but as a theory, inadequate. It was further restricted by his acceptance of current romantic beliefs, such as the assumption that of all poetic emotions melancholy is the chief, and of all melancholy situations the death of a young and of course beautiful woman is the most poignant. These beliefs played an important part in his preference among literary themes and forms. And one cannot ignore the strong probability that so egotistical a writer as Poe would color his criticism with his own practice in the kinds of work he criticizes.

The proper practice of criticism, as Poe comprehended it, was "frank, candid, and independent, . . . giving honor only where honor was due, yet evincing the most thorough capacity to appreciate and the most sincere intention to place in the fairest light the real and idiosyncratic merits of the poet." In practice, however, Poe followed a course implied rather than stated here, and with a quite different emphasis. The critic should keep in mind, not the feelings of the author under his scalpel, but the benefit to "the general cause of letters" which will accrue from ruthless removal of diseased tissue. He should be independent and honest, meting out justice to all men without fear, favor, or partiality. Excellence in literature, he held, is self-evident, axiomatic: when it occurs it stands in no need of demonstration or comment. The critic's task then becomes one of correction. "In teaching what perfection *is*, how . . . shall we more rationally proceed than in specifying what it is *not?*" Poe admitted that in the *Southern Literary Messenger* he might have been guilty of "a somewhat overdone causticity"; but his promise to mend his later ways indicated only the avoidance of petulance, with no diminution of rigor in his judgment. Margaret Fuller's denunciation of his practice, already noted, indicates how his criticism was generally judged.

Poe noted explicitly the critic's qualifications. First, he should be "at least a linguist and classical scholar." Poe's genuine respect for the classics was somewhat marred by his parade of his own attainments in Latin while exposing the ludicrous ignorance of many contemporaries, and by his implying a knowledge of German and Hebrew which he did not possess. Secondly, he must have the analytical mind. It is not enough to possess "a keen appreciation of the beautiful and fastidious sense of the deformed"; taste must be enforced by the ability to discover "why either is either." The review which contented itself with excerpting passages from the book under consideration likewise met his rebuke. Thirdly, the reviewer must avoid excessive generalization. Although Poe was no enemy to critical theory—perhaps too much the reverse—he recognized the danger of "delighting more in the dictation or discussion of a principle, than in its particular and methodical application." True method in criticism, he declared, was rarely illustrated in American periodicals. He was convinced that differences in critical opinion were usually the result of improperly applied, commonly accepted principles; and the differences in critical schools themselves were attributable more to unsound or totally lacking method than to wide disagreement on premises. Simple common sense can produce irresistible criticism.

The fourth qualification of the critic is the courage to ignore tradition and to consider anew the capabilities of literature. He did not desire to scrap the past; like the earlier critics in this, at least, he would have his critic the Biblical instructed scribe able to bring out of his storehouse of wisdom things both new and old. Finally, the critic should be himself an artist. Poe had as a youth restricted criticism to the poets themselves; later, he came to doubt the critical

[76]

qualifications of the poet; and by 1846 he had compromised his requirement: the critic must "at least have the poetic sentiment, if not the poetic power—the 'vision,' if not the 'faculty divine.'" In this position he looked back through Wordsworth to Addison's and Pope's emphasis upon taste in the critical reader, and forward to Benedetto Croce.

The true critic tests his principles by practice. "Theory and practice are in so much *one* that the former implies or includes the latter. If the practice fail, it is because the theory is imperfect." Here Poe was following the footsteps of Corneille, who, as Dryden had noted, had advanced the same objection to the Renaissance theorists who had perfected the dramatic rules. The smaller fry of criticism, Poe added, estimate the worth of a book by the number of readers, with "Does it sell?" as their sole criterion. To him, large sales indicated inferior quality. He cynically quoted Horace's remark that the author who wins all votes has mingled the useful with the attractive in his work, but in his own practice he stedfastly refused to cater to popular taste.

Carrying the battle to the "literary titmice," he attacked their scornful assumption that the successful author must contravene established literary principles. Dickens's *Barnaby Rudge* owed its merit to its adherence to "certain well-understood critical principles reduced by genius into practice." Dickens had simply done for the present age what Defoe with *Robinson Crusoe* and Goldsmith with *The Vicar of Wakefield* had done in preceding generations. These three novels, he wrote, prove to the alert critic that those qualities in a masterpiece that continue to please are the result of the author's skilful application of time-tested literary principles. Instead of seeking such principles, the public let itself be deceived by the widespread "quackery" and "puffery" which, Poe declared, ruled everywhere in literary reviews. He waged war to the death with "those organized cliques which, hanging like nightmares upon American literature, manufacture, at the nod of our principal booksellers, a pseudo-public-opinion by wholesale."

Like Goethe, Poe allowed the author to choose his design; he insisted, however, that the critic hold the author to its fullest possible completion, and to the employment of the most advantageous means for its attainment. In reviewing Bulwer's *Zanoni*, for instance, Poe complimented the novelist for its grandeur of design but vigorously objected to the introduction of details and incidents with no bearing upon that design. The author seemed actually to have changed his mind about the novel while in the process of writing it— a cardinal sin in Poe's list of literary lapses. Occasional flashes of merit in a work are alone insufficient to bring it his critical approval. "Poetical merit which is not simply an accident is very sure to be found, more or less, in a state of diffusion throughout a poem."

Poe required the exercise of good taste in what the author presents to the reader. He objected strenuously to the current interpretation of the old adage *de gustibus non est disputandum* as if it meant that any man's taste is as good as any other's. He saw this error as the cause of so many contemporary writers' needlessly harrowing the feelings of their readers. William Gilmore Simms was guilty of "villainously bad taste . . . a certain fondness for the purely disgusting or repulsive, where the intention was or should have been merely the horrible." James Fenimore Cooper's *Wyandotte* seemed to him to kill a number of characters without advancing the plot, but producing a needlessly painful impression. Poe himself occasionally transgressed the very bounds he had set up, but far less often and less extensively than many of his contemporaries.

In his insistence upon the end of poetry as delight or an elevated pleasure, Poe ran foul of Coleridge's curious misquotation of Aristotle's statement concerning poetry and history. Aristotle had stated that poetry is more philosophical and serious than history. Coleridge, his phenomenal memory for once playing him false, recalled the statement as an assertion that poetry is the most philosophical and serious of all writing. In this mistaken form, the statement appeared also in Wordsworth's Preface to the *Lyrical Ballads*. Poe, not troubling to check Coleridge's statement, several times took issue with what he supposed Aristotle to have written. "Aristotle, with singular assurance, has declared poetry to be the most philosophical of all writings, but it required a Wordsworth to pronounce it the most metaphysical." The Lake Poet's insistence upon truth as the object in the poet's eye, Poe declared, is wrong; the end of our existence is happiness. Poetry purveys for us a sense of ethereal beauty which is the

[78]

source of the highest happiness. In this position, while thinking he was confuting Aristotle, Poe was in fact closer to his meaning than were Wordsworth and Coleridge.

The poet's insight, Poe insisted, must produce a new work. Originality developed into a near mania with him. Although he admitted that a poet might unconsciously and quite innocently repeat another's words, when he came upon what seemed to him a literary theft, he seldom gave the culprit the benefit of the doubt. Authors toward whom he felt animosity he suspected of pilfering verses or ideas from his own works. It is perhaps more just to emphasize his considered admission of possibly innocent theft than to give weight to instances when haste in writing or the heat of irritation led him to ignore this alternative. His irritation pre-empted space in his criticism which might better have been devoted to discussion of the mimetic qualities of the subject.

His delight in novelty also led him perhaps to overvalue it. Though he did not permit unbridled search for the new at the expense of beauty or good sense, he heartily welcomed the new and pleasing. He hoped for deviations from the more beaten paths in American literature. In Hawthorne's *Twice-Told Tales*, he rated the author's originality as a trait worth as much for fiction as invention, creation, and imagination. Even more important was it in poetry. The two elements of poetry are first, man's thirst for supernal beauty and, secondly, his attempt to satisfy that thirst by *"novel* combinations, *of those combinations which our predecessors, toiling in chase of the same phantom, have already set in order."* The poet should limit his endeavors to the creation of novel moods of beauty in form, color, sound, and sentiment; he should leave to the prose writer all else. Obviously, he was no revolutionary in these matters, as Whitman was soon to be; he would have the poet follow pretty closely the tradition of the elders. "To originate, is carefully, patiently, and understandingly to combine." The writer who neglects to take advantage of novelty is false to his own interest; though not the most important object he should seek, it is the first.

Poe insisted that the critic should watch three other matters in judging the author's work. First, the proper choice of subject is a *sine qua non* of success. Bulwer in *Zanoni* had chosen for prose a topic demanding dramatic presentation. J. S. French, who wrote a now-forgotten novel *Elkswatawa,* had chosen a story which hinged upon improbability and required the author to keep several threads of narrative spinning concurrently, so that the reader was no sooner engrossed in one detail than he was required to divert his attention to something else. Secondly, selection of episodes and details requires careful attention, especially for their keeping. Rufus Dawes's poem *Geraldine,* for instance, confused Greek mythology with events of the eighteen thirties in America. "Only think of a group of *sirens* singing to sleep a modern 'miniatured' flirt, kicking around in the water with a New York dandy in tight pantaloons!" Thirdly, the author must take care to find a proper beginning. Longfellow's play *The Spanish Student* not only had a prologue prefixed to the action; it unfortunately and inartistically required one. Many a good book, Poe declared, has suffered neglect because it had an inefficient beginning which failed either to attract the reader or properly to set the emotional tone of the work. His conception of a proper beginning he illustrated in the opening sentence of "The Fall of the House of Usher."

But Poe, on account of the faults in many books reviewed, had to criticize even the rudiments of composition, even to correct syntax and punctuation. "A slovenly punctuation," he pointed out, "will mar, in a greater or less degree, the brightest paragraph ever penned." Years later, he added: "for the want of merely a comma, it often occurs that an axiom appears a paradox, or that a sarcasm is converted into a sermonoid."

Diction and style also occupied him. Simms regrettably introduced "pet words" into his writing: "coil," "hug," and "old-time" made monotonously frequent entrance into his pages. Such matters, which the *New Yorker* still censures, Poe included in his reviews. Levels of diction were often the object of his scrutiny. *Sheppard Lee,* a forgotten novel, he praised because "the language is exceedingly unaffected and (what we regard as high praise) exceedingly well adapted to the varying parts." These minutiae formed the preliminary requirements of good writing, and in a literature just beginning to find itself, they loomed peculiarly large.

Similar concern actuated Poe in criticising poems for meter and euphony. Though he rated them among the "minor morals of the Muse," he counted them significant in poetical composition. He condemned the forcing of words into rhythms that violated word accent with all the vigor, though with somewhat less finesse, than did the opponents of Thomas Drant and Gabriel Harvey in Elizabethan England. Words like "áccord" and "résource" were "utter abominations." Equally offensive were such verses as "In clustered stars beneath Spring's footstep meets." "The poet who would bring uninterruptedly together such letters as *t, b, s, p,* and *r* has either no ear at all, or two unusually long ones." The subjects of his reviews all too often provided him with such animadversions upon current prosody.

In spite of his constant carping at the defects of his contemporaries, Poe successfully avoided the pitfall of judging a writer finally by these technical "minor morals." He occasionally passed over even glaring errors which "glare, nevertheless, to no very material ill purpose." They were either readily corrected faults which needed only mention or peccadilloes completely atoned by sterling excellences. Although Poe was more likely to excuse such faults in a poetess than in a poet, it was not only his Southern chivalry that activated him; he could take female writers to task, just as he could point out genuine worth in poets who, like Longfellow, seemed to him to veil their merit behind misconception of the poet's function.

Poe's comments on the American literary scene are illuminating; besides being a literary figure, he was a citizen awake to the characteristics of his age. In the utilitarian arts, he wrote in 1843, "where Necessity impels, Invention, Necessity's well-understood offspring, is ever in attendance." Wherever the reason is allowed a free hand, advancement is constant. In the imitative arts, however, advance occurs only when some technical improvement makes imitation easier. In sculpture and architecture, better tools and more skilled workmanship have caused some progress; in the drama, improved lighting, costuming, and stage machinery have caused the only advance; painting has hardly improved since its beginning. "Where Reason predominated, we advanced; where mere Feeling or Taste was the guide we remained as we were."

The reason for this stagnation of the arts seemed obviously to "repose in old Feeling and antique Taste." When all other arts were developing, stagnation was equivalent to retrogression. To end this stoppage, it seemed logical to him, reason must be grafted upon feeling and taste; reason, by dominating them, would force them to relax their paralyzing grip upon the anchor of the past. Where the past was not paralyzing, he would continue to lay hold of it as a tool for further progress. His cavalier treatment of accepted authorities was the effect of his suspicion that good sense had too often solidified into law that inflexibly ignored whatever useful innovations later ages had added to the store. Though he should proceed warily, the seeker after earlier authorities who influenced Poe's thinking has a fertile field to harvest.

Having had experience with a number of literary centers, Poe was convinced by 1846 that the center of American literary activity was New York. The writers in New York, he said, comprised perhaps one quarter of all those in America; and their influence, though perhaps they were less vociferous than those about Boston, was extensive and more decisive. His insight was to be confirmed shortly after the Civil War by the decision of Edmund Clarence Stedman to settle in New York in spite of his reverence for the Brahmins. By 1880, William Dean Howells, a shrewd literary businessman, had also left Cambridge for Gotham.

Poe shared the general American impatience with British assumption of cultural superiority. Though he was too keenly aware of American deficiencies to have written a declaration of literary independence like Emerson's in "The American Scholar," he was equally eager for American writers to get out of their leading-strings. A year before Emerson's Phi Beta Kappa address, Poe had berated his fellow-authors for their subservience to England. Give the Britons, he wrote, full credit for their magnificent work; but defer only where deference is due. On the other hand, do not arrogate to yourselves credit you do not deserve. Our bumptiousness had in fact reached alarming proportions. "We often find ourselves involved in the gross paradox of liking a stupid book the better, because, sure enough, its stupidity is American." "As a literary people," he wrote a few years later in a fit of disgust, "we are one vast perambulating humbug."

The independence which he demanded that American writers exhibit did not include license to make fools of themselves.

Poe's judgments of his contemporary authors in most cases showed discriminating judgment and are still in many instances valid. He deprecated the tendency of patriotic American sentiment to exalt "the few who were *first* in convincing the mother country that her sons were not all brainless," and urged judgment on more literary criteria. A list he made in 1836 of story-writers ranked them in order of merit as follows: Hawthorne, W. G. Simms, Nathaniel Willis, with one or two unnamed competitors. Ten years later his list of American poets read as follows: Longfellow, Bryant, Halleck, Willis, Sprague, and Dana, with a strong implication that others who had written less were more deserving for poetic merit.

Of the poets, he felt that Bryant, while deserving most of the acclaim he received, fell short of any high rank. Longfellow, with many poetic gifts and fine poetic material, held mistaken notions of the purpose of poetry and vitiated his poems with didacticism. Willis interested Poe chiefly by his play *Tortesa, the Usurer.* It possessed excellent conception of character, was well expressed in suitable language, and had an elevated theme; but its plot was inconsequential and overloaded with extraneous detail. As Poe confided privately to Lowell, "Natty" was no genius. Poetesses generally received courteously restrained criticism from Poe, but he was unsparing of male versifiers who falsely aspired to "the sacred name of poet."

Among the novelists, Poe distributed scant praise. Cooper and Paulding, who derived their popularity principally from their pre-emption of the scene through early arrival, could not compete even with the average American novelist of the 1840's. Simms, by virtue of his invention, vigor, movement, power of exciting interest, and management of his themes, was on the whole the best novelist; his tales were disfigured, however, by his employment of the disgusting and repulsive. The general run of novelists in America, Poe submitted to the same caustic criticism that he meted out to the versifiers.

Poe's highest praise was reserved among prose writers for the short stories of Hawthorne. He used Hawthorne's *Twice-Told Tales* as the occasion for elaborating the proper technique of the short story, which they illustrated. In 1847, he explained Hawthorne's scanty audience partly on the grounds that he was neither wealthy nor a member of any publisher's clique. Hawthorne possessed an order of originality also found in Addison and Irving, the ability to present to the reader thoughts which seem natural to him but have not previously occurred to him. The prevailing quietness of this style, which is almost a monotone, prevents works which display it from ever becoming widely popular with the sensation-loving public. It is also cursed with a strain of allegory which does not appeal to most readers. This originality, though high, is not of the highest quality. Readers acquainted with Poe's egotism will have little hesitation in naming the American writer whose works seem to him to embody the highest strain of originality.

Much as he regretted the deficiencies of the literary product in detail, Poe's estimate of American literary potentiality in 1842 was high. "We have snapped asunder the leading-strings of the British Grandmamma, and, better still, we have survived the first hours of our novel freedom—the first licentious hours of a hobbledehoy braggadocio and swaggerer." His picture of the literary situation differed little from that drawn by Emerson at about the same time, and agreed in the main with that outlined by many of the "Young Americans" in New York.

In criticism, Poe found less to inspire his hope. In 1836, he remarked upon the change in American reviewers from deference to British opinion: American reviewers now set chips upon their literary shoulders and praised extravagantly whatever was American. His attack closely paralleled that made by Bryant eighteen years earlier. In 1842, he violently attacked the publishers' reviewing cliques, characterizing their procedure as blackmail or bribery of the reviewer. The few independent editors of periodicals who accepted books from publishers only with the understanding that an unbiassed criticism would be printed could not counteract the many who were venal. He charged publishers with supporting coteries which manufactured reviews to their order, to be published under the name of the editor who subscribed to this "service," or, in the heavier periodicals, to be printed anonymously.

Poe's character of the quarterly reviewer is worthy of Theophrastus or Joseph Hall:

> A veteran reviewer loves the safety of generalities, and is therefore rarely particular. . . . He has one or two ideas of his own, and is both wary and fussy in giving them out. . . . He is a sworn enemy to all things simple and direct. . . . he either jumps at once into the middle of a subject, or breaks in at a back door, or slides up to it with the gait of a crab. No other approach has an air of sufficient profundity. When fairly into it, however, he becomes dazzled with the scintillations of his own wisdom, and is seldom able to see his way out. Tired of laughing at his antics, or frightened by seeing him flounder, the reader at length shuts him up, with the book.

Though there were worthy exceptions, Poe's picture was far too often accurate.

Poe's most carefully stated survey of the American critical situation was printed in the opening number of the 1842 *Graham's Magazine*. American periodicals were finally beginning to recognize the importance of criticism—which he classified as a science—and to reject the flippant expressions which had long passed current for literary judgment. He censured the tendency toward 100 per cent nationalism: the world at large, no one nation, is the stage for the literary actor. In abandoning the rampantly nationalistic position, however, reviewers were increasingly "abandoning particulars for masses," resorting to generalities. The review, in surveying the book under study, should analyze it and pass judgment upon its peculiar qualities. Resort to generalizations, though it might convey the illusion of profundity to its readers, was at its best not viewing the book, at its worst the merest balderdash. As models for guidance to the American critic, Poe held up the French reviews as a whole; and as specimens of the able reviewer at work he mentioned the *critiques raisonées* of Winckelmann, Novalis, Schelling, Goethe, and the brothers Schlegel. The present generation should not suppose that the laws governing sound literary judgment varied from age to age.

Poe insisted that literary criticism be restricted to comment upon art. It is a book that is under review, and it is tested as literature for its literary qualities. Criticism does not test the validity of the author's idea, which is the proper duty of other disciplines than literature. Literary criticism is the analysis and judgment of art, not of opinion. In his proper area the critic should, as Bulwer had asserted, have "courage to blame boldly, magnanimity to eschew envy, genius to appreciate, learning to compare, an eye for beauty, an ear for music, and a heart for feeling."

With Poe, literary criticism got its start as an American profession. It is unfortunate that his tactlessness alienated writers whose works he reviewed and offended many of his fellow-critics, for he indicated paths that both author and critic might well follow. It is also to be regretted that he lacked a knowledge of literary history; it might have shown him literary problems in clearer perspective. With all his deficiencies and prejudices, his critical practice was valuable to the nascent art of literary criticism. If younger critics could have availed themselves of his practice in the light of Emerson's theorizing, American criticism might have developed both wider and deeper insights at an early stage of its history. It was to be several decades, however, before a national cultural consciousness could prepare the way for a more nearly nationwide criticism.

Chapter 5

Minor Critical Figures: 1837–1855

Emerson's "American Scholar" was symptomatic of the widespread desire for an American literature that had come into being. Critics less in the literary spotlight also urged the problem with great vigor and fiery diatribes. Brownson's efforts to found a liberal periodical were paralleled by the establishment of the *Democratic Review* in 1837 as an organ of the reinvigorated national feeling. This publication was followed shortly by the conservative *Whig Review* as an antidote to extreme liberalism; and numerous magazines appeared on both sides. Gauged by the strength of the opposition they aroused, the new liberals influenced considerably the literary, political, and social scene. The conflicting ideas of these two critical wings provide material for the greater part of this chapter.

Concern for a national literature had abated, but not disappeared, since its outburst in the years following the second war with England. A thoughtful article in the *Southern Review* for 1831 had reminded readers that a free country will not automatically produce a national poetry, that more than mere opportunity is required to create it. In the United States, its progress was further hampered by the Puritan cast in our culture—the writer anticipated Mencken's concept of the wide distribution of Puritanism. Since the Puritan "scorned music with all its harlotry," America had not commemorated the Revolution with a single lyric. (Freneau's war poems were apparently unknown to him.) Enmity toward Britain could only weaken us in all respects, including letters; hostility can never be a constructive state of mind. If we abandon our heritage of British culture, which is our property to use as we will, we confine our interests to our brief period of national existence, a narrow realm indeed. The American writer should use every resource that is properly his. These views were unfortunately too sane to be widely shared in times when demagoguery was fanning the flames of a separatist Americanism.

Although the 1837 *Southern Literary Messenger* declared that Americans can venerate British literature for its antiquity and dignity "without the servile flattery which characterized our early history," the active separatists soon began to express themselves. Mme de Staël's theories about the relation of a nation's climate and society to its literature had been reinforced by the ideas of Sismondi and Friedrich Schlegel and by the nationalistic feeling that mounted high after the overthrow of Napoleon. The resultant sentiment supplemented the natural American self-confidence to produce a vigorous demand for a 100 per cent national literature, with only the haziest notion of what the term implied. Readers of Emerson's Phi Beta Kappa address failed then as now to realize that his doctrine had been specially tailored to fit his Harvard audience and was not a garb designed for all America; and the impetus given to the common man's rights by Jacksonian democratic principles aggravated the not carefully reasoned but natural desire for a distinctly American literature. Thus varied forces contributed to form American nationalism in the 1840's. This sentiment, appealing as it did for various reasons, was found throughout most of the centers of literary activity, from Boston to Charleston.

New York in the person of Evert Duyckinck and Charleston with William Gilmore Simms as spokesman wrote vigorously in defense of an American spirit in our writing. "Our language is English," Simms admitted in the preface to *The Damsel of Darien* (1839), "but such need not be the case with our literature." A year later, Duyckinck declared that no nation lacking a spirit of its own "can ever be truly respected by others, or know rightly how to respect itself." He put aside scornfully the notion, already beginning to be heard before Whitman uttered it, that America was herself a great poem: it was meaningless to assert that a nation lived epic poems unless it also wrote them. Duyckinck's distinction between poetic material and poetry fell, however, on deaf ears. North and South trumpeted to all ears that "the Poet of America is the Genius of her Institutions; and our National Epic is the memory of our origin, and the contemplation of our destiny."

Writers naturally preferred, however, to think of literature as words, not territory nor history; and they took thought how to produce it. Simms in 1844 recommended to the poet to look for inspiration in "the illustration of the national history, or in the development of the national characteristics." Only when allied to these would his poems endure or attract general interest. Although the American writer should use our literary European heritage, his product should be an integral part of the national life. As the *Southern Literary Messenger* (1845) put it, a national literature "must breathe a national spirit, reflect the peculiar habits and character of a people, and derive its ennobling inspiration from the history, institutions, and scenery of its native land." Lack of reliance upon ourselves and our own resources, Rufus Griswold declared in 1847, had made our writers timidly endeavor to follow foreign models; "We have been so fearful of nothing else as an Americanism, in thought or expression." Griswold evidently felt that the prose efforts of American authors were so uncertainly made as to lack the merit that comes from looking into one's heart and then writing.

The contenders for 100 per cent American themes did not find the field uncontested, as Longfellow's persistent use of European themes attests. Longfellow himself found a hesitant champion in a reviewer of his *Belfry of Bruges*. Admitting that half the book was foreign in character, he did not hold with those who would bind an author to America. In Longfellow's work he found a wisdom and strength which could be the gifts only of his native New England; "so," he added, "we will not complain that he is not American, but will rather rejoice in the 'pretty things' which he has brought back to us from his wanderings." The equivocal phrase, "pretty things" hints at a guilty fear that the poet would have better occupied himself with the American scene; yet he does not restrict the poet to homely materials.

Evert Duyckinck, conceding to the writer the liberty to use what themes he would, urged upon him the duty to give first consideration to American subjects. The writer should patriotically write "for the illustration of passing events, and the preservation of what tradition has rescued from the past, and for the exhibition of the manners of the people, and the circumstances which give form and pressure to the time and the spirit of the country." Although such themes are necessarily employed by a national literature, Duyckinck would not have American literature become a species apart from the literature of the world: "we would not narrow, but enlarge, the horizon of letters; we would not restrict the empire of thought, but annex our noble domain to it." As T. S. Eliot later expressed the idea, the author should by his writing contribute his rivulet to the stream of tradition; and, as Eliot further insisted, an author's contribution to this stream is not his idiosyncrasies, but that in which he resembles those authors who have preceded him.

The 1842 *Christian Examiner* revived Walter Channing's assertion that there never could be an American literature that was not provincially British. A young Philadelphian critic, Horace Binney Wallace, countered in 1847 by pointing to "a thousand tokens" which made manifest that a spirit of power animates America; "this creative vigor," he added, "breathing and burning in the bosom of the nation, must find an issue in art as well as in action." Our literary problem was to be genuinely American "without falling into Americanisms," to be original without becoming peculiar. We must express the new by means of the old; far from agreeing with Emerson's concept of organic form, he saw no danger in pouring the new wine into old bottles. Men could not be American by slavish following of even faultless foreign models. Edward Young's doctrine about properly following the ancients found repetition in his attitude.

That Americans were becoming less concerned about British opinion was a source of satisfaction to all but the most conservative. The tone of American response to British critical remarks was well expressed by a writer in the 1848 *Southern Quarterly Review*, who remarked ironically on our "conscientious pedagogue," John Bull. Our enormities in his eyes consisted chiefly in "our mode of eating all things, (but more particularly, eggs) and our style of writing poetry"; the latter "furnishes a perpetual escape-pipe for the spleen of transatlantic writers." Authors who can thus ironically comment on foreign criticism have advanced far toward self-reliance without becoming excessively self-assured.

The reviewer just quoted was more disturbed that some American writers were ambitiously trying to supply the demand of foreign critics for that national literature which they insisted we should immediately produce. Forgetting that the tone of the author's mind determines the nature of his work, they were industriously portraying backwoodsmen and Indians under the supposition that novel materials make a new literature. The book is American only if the author writes from an American state of mind. Five years later, a writer in Charleston added that the American writer should realize that solitary American figures treated by themselves do not constitute adequate literary material: when the author is directed to represent life he is directed to portray society. Man as member of a family, even, is not the same as man in society; and only by representing American social life can the author be truly national. William Gilmore Simms, widening the scope of American materials, insisted that the age, not the country alone, should be the subject of the author's study; the national character of our literature was a secondary matter. A writer in the new *Putnam's Monthly* neatly contrived to turn the implied internationalism in such sentiments to Lowell's account. Without resorting to constant mention of the Alleghenies and the Mississippi, Lowell "infuses into his writings the spirit of our times and our institutions, so unmistakably, that no one could be deceived as to his birth-place."

Such sentiments were anathema to the New York writers, referred to as the "Young Americans," who were in most instances impatient of foreign influence. As Herman Melville declared in 1850: "let America first praise mediocrity even, in her own children, before she praises ... the best excellence in the children of any other land. ... And if any of our authors fail, or seem to fail, then ... let us clap him on the shoulder, and back him against all Europe for the second round." These ultra-patriots were eager to raise the literary protective tariff which Bryant, Poe, Lowell, and Longfellow had devoted their energies to tear down. A provocative article quoted in the first number of *Harper's Magazine* (1850) from the *Dublin University Magazine* did not weaken their position. The writer remarked that democracy, by obliterating differences in social rank, had narrowed the field of human observation, and furthermore did not conduce to the development of elegant tastes. Consequently, he charged, every page written by American authors testifies to the immense debt of Americans to "those sources which the advocates of her claims would endeavor to repudiate." He caustically added that the removal from America of opportunity to aspire to a coronet had not diverted men's energies into pursuit of a laurel wreath. Such words had little effect upon the eager defenders of a purely national literature; and the high point of such sentiment was reached by Walt Whitman in 1855 in the preface to *Leaves of Grass*.

REGIONAL SENTIMENT

Somewhat confusing the nationalist issue was a strong regional feeling. Jay Hubbell has stated that the Southerner's national feeling, in spite of his principal loyalty to his state, steadily increased during the half-century following the Revolution. Frank Luther Mott has also shown the extent that, between 1825 and 1850, region was arrayed against region with sometimes violent enmity. Edd Winfield Parks has noted, too, the narrowing emotional and intellectual horizons of Simms and his circle during this quarter-century. Their wide and varied reading failed to counteract the restricting political, economic, and social forces that culminated a decade later in the Civil War. In the North, a similar though less acrimonious enmity existed between New York and New England. Foreshadowed in Irving's *Legend of Sleepy Hollow* and depicted in Fenimore Cooper's *Satanstoe*, it reached full development in the contemporary New York periodicals.

The opening article of the *Southern Literary Messenger* (1834) had appealed for support of the magazine to Southern pride: "*Shall not one* [literary periodical] be supported in the whole south?" Northerners adopted a patronizing attitude toward Southern letters, doling out here and there a modicum of praise to Southern writers in order to keep the subscriptions from south of the Susquehanna rolling in. "We ought forthwith to buckle on our armour, and assert our mental independence." Southern readers, however, did not buy or read what was written by Southern authors or printed in the South. Even Simms, in spite of his popularity as a novelist, could find no readers except for the books that bore a Northern imprint. His one romance printed in the South did not sell, and all the efforts of himself and his circle could not persuade Charleston readers to patronize Southern authors.

In letters as in politics, Southern animosity was directed primarily against New England. Poe's animadversions are well known. Though Simms and others kept on friendly terms with the New York Young Americans until political feeling overwhelmed their relations, they disowned the New England writers as soon as their abolitionist sentiments became marked. Simms wrote in commendation of Longfellow and Emerson as late as 1845. In 1848, however, his notice of Lowell's *Fable for Critics* was almost unqualified abuse and hostility; shortly thereafter, he denied all imaginative faculty to New England. M. R. Garnett in an address delivered in 1850 on the defects of Northern literature charged its writers with poverty of invention and paralyzing subservience to public opinion. Their work "wants native force, and there is nothing in the texture of thought, which shows that it could have been produced nowhere but on an American loom. . . . I see nothing new, but little that is American, in their elegant narrative, or rich coloring. I see only a systematic and very close imitation of foreign models." The New England writers have become "their" authors, not "ours"; and one wonders what the consistent Southerner could read of American writing if he condemned Northern writers and refused to read works written in the South. "Boston is *par excellence* the very home of literary prejudices," wrote an irate editor of the *Southern Literary Messenger* in 1852, not troubling to sweep his own doorstep.

Though somewhat less vigorous, there existed in New York a similar air of unfriendliness toward New England. Evert Duyckinck worked energetically to form a New York literature that should rival the works produced in the northeastern states. In 1852, George N. Sanders in the *Democratic Review* directed an article on "Fogy

Literature" at New England writers generally and the *North American Review* in particular:

> The present decrepid [*sic*] health of Fogydom, its attenuated figure, dyspeptic system, shattered nerves, neuralgic stupidity, rheumatic inertness, agueish trepidation, chronic dishonesty, and feverish uncertainty, has been superinduced ... by the swallowing of such debilitating literary physics ... English black draughts from an American bottle. Young America does not require such pap. .... It must have fresh, vigorous, wholesome, mother's milk, strong as the blood which flowed in '76, not the green tea of parvenu society, nor British concoctions of chalk and water.

The *North American Review* is "that superanuated [*sic*] dust-box into which old Fogydom expectorates freely." Though haste and fury have marred the writer's metaphors and vitiated his taste, his animosity is incontestably sincere.

The calmness of New England writers under fire no doubt stimulated the attacks from those outside of Canaan. Such notice as appeared of these onslaughts was patronizing, the New Englanders reserving for the privacy of their correspondence most of their stronger comment. In the face of such strong local feelings it is hardly surprising that the advocates of national literature complained frequently that American writers were failing to make use of their opportunities. Part of what they attributed to laziness may have been the result of misdirected regional effort.

NATIONAL LITERARY SUBJECTS

To the great majority who were still hoping for a national literature, the further problem was posed of its proper subjects. Since America was a democracy, and since the proponents of the new literature were devoted to the common man, they felt constrained to write about him. But both traditional and romantic tastes preferred tales of greatly renowned or noble agents. Realization that the writer cannot wholly ignore the taste of the times deflected authors to the historical novel or romance, and to speculation upon the prospects for the great American epic. When Sylvester Judd's realistic novel

Margaret appeared, only Lowell and a few others knew what to make of it. The rest were not yet able to recognize an attempt to produce the very literature for which many of them were clamoring. And yet a young American critic could declare that the trump of martial glory could no longer rouse and thrill our spirits. Cornelius Mathews's *Poems on Man, in His Various Aspects under the American Republic* received their unstinted approbation, its democratic-sounding title blinding them to its mediocrity.

Defenders of the historical tale, sensitive to the strictures of the democratic reviewers and aware of their popularity with the public, insisted that their work was suited to the democracy. It was based on truth, which its writers carefully sought in history. "Its illustrations are those general traits of character and those every-day occurrences of life, which, though so deeply rooted in our nature as to be renewed in every age, are yet so flexible and subtle in their details, that they adapt themselves to and mingle with the leading characteristics of each." The author of the historical tale, declared the *North American Review*, undertakes at once to give a correct picture of human nature and to depict accurately the times of which he writes.

To this somewhat pedantic position William Gilmore Simms stood vigorously opposed. History seemed to him to be valuable chiefly as provider of materials for the purposes of art. Ignoring the demand for a literature expressive of the people, he defined the territory of romance as beginning where history leaves off; too many facts interfere with the imagination. In America, the romancer's chief problem was to find periods in which the historical accounts were sufficiently vague in detail to admit of the author's throwing over them the veil of the imagination. Lacking a medieval period before the invention of printing had disseminated knowledge, we lacked also the lengendary stage of culture which the romancer finds so fruitful; "and the audacity of invention is paralyzed on the threshold."

Getting down to specific problems, Simms suggested that we might follow Thomas Campbell's example in "The Battle of the Baltic"; we might, as Campbell showed Nelson, present our great but too well-known personages at a single moment of action, as "a graceful abstraction, the ideal of a hero, rather than *the* hero whom we know." Such historical presentation would serve our purposes even better in prose fiction and be more widely popular. Simms, an admirer of James Fenimore Cooper, perhaps had in mind the brief glimpses of Paul Jones which we see in *The Pilot,* where the historical figure begins to assume the height of a folk hero. "Something, even now, might be done with our Brigadiers of the Revolution"; and he outlined with some detail how Benedict Arnold could be properly shown by the romancer.

Simms's argument anticipates recent theory about the artistic process. It derives from Coleridge's concept of the secondary imagination at work together with the fancy, and adds to it the New Critic's emphasis upon the relation between artist and image. "A happy thought, an inspired fancy, brings out to his mind the form and the colour in the mass, and teaches him to throw off the incumbrance, and in what way to relieve from its impediments, the exquisite ideal that his imagination has pictured in the rock."

There was, of course, opposition to the use of the American theme in literature. Rufus Griswold had listed among suitable themes American scenery, the Revolution, and "dark conjectures concerning the ruined cities of central America." Philip Pendleton Cooke (1846) demolished all three subjects: no man can write a good poem of descriptions; our colonization and Revolution, being unenchanted by time, possess no alluring possibilities; and the fullest imaginative exertion cannot repeople the wholly unknown Mayan world with living men and women. "Poets must be let alone in the choice of their subjects. Force them to be patriotic—and voila Barlow's *Columbiad!*" Stung by foreign carping at American matters, a writer in the 1854 *Putnam's* exclaimed at the silly minds who assumed that the land which had produced a Washington could not furnish themes for the greatest writer. "Genius will find themes, if themes can find genius," he asserted, and he added pointedly, "and there's the rub." Like Bryant thirty years earlier, he was convinced that the fault for our failure to produce masterpieces lay in ourselves, not in our themes.

During these years, the desire was increasing among literary men for a literature that would represent actual life in America. In 1847, Horace Wallace declared that everything in American life from its beginnings to the news in the morning paper was suitable for literary treatment. In 1846, the *Southern Literary Quarterly*, after admitting that to many readers the descriptions in Sylvester Judd's *Margaret* would seem caricature and not reality, spoke out vigorously in its defense: "Our author speaks out plainly, and writes things down with a literal exactness. . . . He practices no hypocrisy and no concealment." Judd's moral purpose guided his selection of materials and elevated him to the society of "the few really good writers in this same department, where Carlyle and Dickens are the best and most successful examples." In 1853 the *New York Quarterly*, rashly risking a critical prophecy, declared that Judd "has done for New England life what Chaucer did for Old England, and Homer for Greece, and after days will count the work as worthy as theirs." These early proponents of realism, however, were still voices crying in the wilderness.

"Democratic" Literature

The characteristic hostility toward England was frequently expressed during this period. The northeastern boundary with Canada, the Oregon question, and England's machinations with the prospective Republic of Texas, provided incidents to whet American animosity. Fortunately, cool heads on both sides negotiated friendly settlements of the boundaries, and the annexation of Texas put an end to British overtures to that state. The periodicals naturally aired these matters thoroughly, and the normal desire for a truly democratic literature, with its corresponding opponents, was further roused by the political disturbances. William A. Jones, whom Poe considered one of the ablest critics of the day, sounded the note for the nationalistic Young Americans in a series of articles in the 1842–43 *Democratic Review*. All poetry, he declared, is political, an outpouring of the Spirits of Freedom and Humanity. His position was frequently repeated: *Harper's*, for instance, in 1851 ascribed a humanitarian message to Wordsworth, and *Putnam's* in 1855 classed Tennyson as a humanitarian thinker.

True poetry, Jones continued, cannot flourish under a despotism;

if poetry does not eulogize freedom, the Law of Truth, the Law of Right, and reverence of the Beautiful, it becomes "a mere heap of fables and false devices." Though it may exist under a monarchy—he did not discount the value of British poetry—pure democracy is "the only atmosphere in which the plant of genius may expand and grow." Under a democracy poetry will relate to life and will become "Poetry for the People." Literary men today must express "what we popularly describe as the Spirit of the Age," which is democratic and humanitarian. It will number among its themes "the necessity and dignity of labor," "the native nobility of an honest and brave heart," and "the brotherhood and equality of man." The new poet is "the Poet of the People and the Poet of the Poor."

Besides expressing itself in democratic literature—"America is all poetry," the *Southern Quarterly Review* had recently declared—the United States was manifestly destined to spread its gospel to other lands. In stating this principle, Rufus Griswold gave the doctrine of national influence upon literature a new twist. Rapidly improving communications are reversing the effect of the Tower of Babel, so as to realize Goethe's idea of a world literature. Its consummation is still, however, far distant, for all distinctions of rank, privilege, and freedom of judgment must first be broken down. In this process, our literature furnishes the vital principle; and though we borrow from the older nations in making our own literature, we make everything subservient to recognition of the freedom and dignity of man. Griswold, a clergyman, wrote in missionary zeal; but the spirit of the age in the United States was prepared to spread the gospel of democracy—a gospel still preached forty years later by Lowell as minister to England.

Against such doctrines, which seemed to them subversive of all sound principle, the conservatives fulminated. E. W. Johnson wrote in the 1845 *Whig Review* that the speciously captivating catchword, "the Spirit of the Age," labeled disorganization and decay literature, politics, and religion. America was not yet furnished with "causes, external to literature, which acting upon it, can, unless very slowly, displace that which we inherit and give us a new one." Writing in 1847 of Herman Melville's *Omoo*, G. W. Peck longed for the good old days when "the 'one progressive principle,' Democracy" had not subverted sound religion and philosophy. Two years later, H. N. Hudson published the theogony of the new spirit: "a peculiar, half-ridiculous, half-terrible madness sprung from the marriage of a spurious democracy with a bastard transcendentalism." The *Whig Review* was forced, however, to admit that "literature has gone over to the people"; the defection of most of the better-known authors to the liberals had forced this admission.

Literature for the people included, wrote Rufus Griswold, books of every description: not only belles-lettres but science, philosophy, history, and law. With such a comprehensive notion of literature, reviewers of imaginative works were naturally concerned about their effect upon readers. "The moralist, the historian, and the poet," said the 1842 *Democratic Review*, "the three intellectual characters who include all others, are essentially democratic . . . . pure ethics is *democracy moralized.*" Democratic literature was thus tied up with morality. Like William Ellery Channing, these New York liberals could not conceive of literature that, like pure mathematics, should never be of use to anybody. The conservatives were equally concerned with the practical uses of literature and thereby failed to realize that literature is anything but national in its boundaries, that above all nations is humanity, and that the classification of literature as democratic or monarchical is hot ice, and wondrous-strange snow.

With this concern for the morals of their readers, reviewers strove to inculcate a sound appreciation of uprightness. As in the previous periods, Fielding's "indecency and licentiousness of too many passages" was excused by a careful direction to consider the end and note the poetic justice meted out to his characters. Bulwer, lacking the merits of Fielding while showing his vices, fared badly for his evil tenor. The poems of Béranger were likewise condemned for their tendency "to overthrow the whole structure of the national religion, by bringing to bear upon it the force of ridicule." Such godless poems should be withheld from the unprotected lower classes; those better informed would be little affected by them. Charles Lamb's defense of the Restoration drama was severely censured. "His ridicule of the moral precision of our age, in relation to that most licentious school of writers, falls harmless to the ground. The age is right, only that it does not go far enough in its reprobation of dissolute literature; and Lamb is wrong, utterly wrong." The horrified comments of Macaulay were far better suited to the age than were Lamb's.

Didacticism sometimes mingled unexpectedly with competent literary judgment, as the review by George Holmes of Sue's *The Wandering Jew* shows. Writing in the 1846 *Southern Quarterly Review*, Holmes noted Sue's considerable merit, but he also poured out furious invective over the immorality he detected in the work. His long diatribe included "exposing noxious sophistry, reprehending vile immorality, chastising loathsome obscenity, and reprobating an insidious attack upon all that conduces to the well being of society, and tends to secure and elevate human virtue." Pausing after this resounding period, he commended the undoubted genius of the author, only to add: "genius, which, however, only augments the deep moral turpitude of the man, who, wilfully oblivious of all the claims of decency, propriety, and rectitude, seeks for opportunities to gratify his prurient itching to prostitute his highest gifts to the basest uses." After venomously ranging himself for eight pages on the side of the angels, his sense of literary art asserting itself, he praised the rare talent for analyzing character, the invention, and the ordering of the action by the *dramatis personae* into a unified whole. Beneath his function as custodian of public morals, Holmes was also a sound judge according to the best knowledge of his day. Such men as he, when they had ceased to look upon the public as helpless prey of literary wolves, would form the nucleus of a sound critical body if nothing should intervene to prevent it.

Novel reading was one of the most vexing problems of the period. As the *Southern Literary Messenger* remarked, "the day has passed when works of fiction could be dismissed with a contemptuous sneer." Die-hard conservatives insisted that novel reading was a vice with effects comparable to those of alcohol upon the nervous system or of opium upon the body. Scott had created a public of outlaws and freebooters; Hugo and Bulwer were even more deleterious. The *Democratic Review* pictures a Bible Society agent laboring with an aged addict to novels. "What will he do with his passion beyond the grave? Can he throw aside God's truth, and have fiction in heaven?

Can he have it in hell? though more fitting there than in any other department of eternity!"

Friends of the novel expressed concern as to how its moral effect should be brought about. Fiction should follow poetry and elevate and ennoble its readers; critics cited Wordsworth's wish to be considered as a teacher, or as nothing. Writing merely for money roused their contempt. "With Scott, literature was a great money-making machine. With Byron, it was the trunk of a mad elephant, through which he squirted out his spite at man, his enmity at God, and his rage at even his own shadow." Scott's purpose was ignored; Byron was the man who longed to teach evil, not the satirist. The spotless purity of Wordsworth, "who uttered nothing base," was the model to emulate. The *Confessions* of the madman Rousseau were "undoubtedly the most shameless volumes ever composed." Even Irving was censured because, though he did no evil, "in pleasing always he has foregone the possibility of pleasing ever in the highest degree."

The excessively didactic reviewers did not have the field to themselves. W. A. Jones declared bluntly: "Most tale-writers are altogether too didactic." Though the book should always have a moral tendency, Jones denied that it should directly teach any "peculiar system of morality or religion" or "have a palpable moral aim." He cited Coleridge and Hazlitt in support of his position. Simms, too, declared that didactic imaginative literature never can possess individuality; being equally characteristic of all countries, it will arouse little enthusiasm in any.

Advocates of moralizing literature, however, were stronger. Revoking the custom of separating an author's personal life from his work, *Harper's* (1851) asserted that the poet's gift has a moral purpose which his life must match. "If he desecrate his powers, he is a traitor to their original purpose, and shall share in the condemnation of that servant who 'was beaten with many stripes.' " The wiser critics, it added, pursuing their moral duty, were measuring the poet's life and works by the same standard. Victorian morality was a severe detriment to American letters. Lowell remarked dryly that a man's being hanged for his faith is no surety for the quality of his verses; but *Harper's* advocated the converse of this proposition.

Acceptance of the moralizing principle was doubtless hastened by the enormous increase in the reading public, among whom women and the young predominated. Reviewers felt it their responsibility to shield these lambs from winds of evil doctrine. In this endeavor they abandoned the saner attitude toward literature which the preceding generation had assumed.

The popularizing of literature which resulted from the desire to serve or exploit this new audience aroused the fear that literary quality was waning. The *Southern Literary Messenger* (1838) insisted that authors who distort or exaggerate cannot expect lasting popularity. "Bold, new, odd devices of language" cannot substitute for elegance, harmony, delicacy, polish, and propriety, "nor can the slipshod, uncombed, unwashed muse of Don Juan, with all the genius, wit and caustic satire she displays, ever throw Childe Harold, or Pope's Rape of the Lock, or his Moral Essays into the shade." Another writer added that readers who fed on no stronger fare than popular provender would never mature beyond "the diet of the nursery." A third feared that cheap writing, whether imported from "the gutters and stews of all Europe" or locally produced, was "playing the very mischief with our country." Bluntly heading an article "The Inferiority of American Literature," the 1853 *Messenger* minced no words. "We have not, in this, kept pace with our other improvements." We did not lack genius. "Palsied be the tongue which would utter the foul aspersion!" We praise our mediocrity excessively; "we are our own idolaters! Our own land is, indeed, but the whole earth is not full of our fame." Our brief existence provides no excuse; Hesiod earned literary fame while his people were still barbarous. "American genius needs but to be aroused!"

Newspapers, then as now, received part of the blame for the low quality of our work. The newspaper publisher set standards by his willingness to buy. Instead of trying to educate taste, he catered to its whims. Simms believed that we had never as a nation taken stock of our literary resources. A third writer declared that our hard practical pursuits, which our writers shared, strengthened the judgment at the expense of the imagination; in prose our authors might excel, but not in poetry or imaginative writing. A fourth placed our weakness in our diffidence; imitation, "vampyre-like, clings to the energies of our woodland worshippers. We are rather tame and quiet,—too fearful of strong and vigorous flights,—preferring to whiz off, like a barn-door fowl, instead of indulging in eagles' soaring, to the skies of inspiration and sublimity." This last writer yearned that Longfellow "would tune his lyre . . . to sing of Titania" and make the prairies "teem with the gambols of other Pucks and Ariels." One can only feel relief that Longfellow, who claimed that he seldom read the reviews, was not seized with the desire to follow the writer's suggestion.

AMERICAN AUTHORSHIP

The American author also posed a problem for the theorist. Gulian Verplanck in 1836 reminded his readers that the best authors from Shakespeare to Scott had followed pursuits as varied as those required of the American writer. More commonly, however, the lack of livelihood in literature was deplored. A writer in 1848 declared that one could expect only light and fugitive literature in a land where Bryant edited a newspaper, Halleck was a clerk, and Longfellow a college professor. The demand was, he added, only for such literature as could be produced by part-time writers, something to appeal to the tired business man or the exhausted professional man. Writers for such an audience, the 1847 *New Englander* complained, had to strain after piquancy while ignoring sound learning.

Part of the trouble with authorship, many critics agreed, lay in the continued encroachment of women into the field. Since these were now firmly entrenched, the masculine critics decided upon a policy of containment. The 1838 *Western Messenger* recommended that authoresses confine themselves to a field especially suited to them: "all productions, whether poetic, fictitious, or didactic, that concern the affections, the social nature and the social world." Here they can also purify domestic life: "They rule over manners, and manners rule over morals. It is for the women to say what the men shall be." The 1841 *Southern Literary Messenger* would further restrict their efforts to prose. In an open letter to young women, an author pleaded: "My dear girl, there is nothing, not positively dishonorable, that I would not as lief see you, as a poetess. Of all unstained characters, *that* is among the least respectable." He dangled before her all manner of feminine accomplishments: sewing, cooking, nursing the sick, managing the household; he even permitted her to ride a trotting horse, to walk, "to dance like a fay, and sing not in the squalling style." If she must write, let it be good sense expressed in neat and attractive prose. As for magazine poetry, "it is, in truth, a sheer dissipation; and a most hurtful one. Avoid it, I beseech you."

Not only were the women undeterred from all branches of literary activity; there were soon deserters to their cause from the encircling masculine forces. Francis P. Greenwood declared it a fortunate thing for any country that women should share in writing its literature; their influence was sure to be powerful, and likely to be good. In spite of the tendency of a few women—was he thinking of Margaret Fuller?—to hold high discourse at all times, to ask silly questions and give as silly replies, and to neglect their household duties for quill-pushing, the greater number were worthy members of the profession. Horace Wallace in 1848 found women to be substantial contributors to all levels of fiction, to criticism, to political writing, and to useful and elegant composition alike.

The defenders of female authors were, it is true, soon put down by their opponents. A writer in the 1852 *Southern Quarterly Review* denied to women the power of philosophical or abstract reasoning, and recommended that they confine their efforts to the attempt to "light in our souls a sympathy for wretchedness, marshal up the better promptings of our nature, and teach us the conquest of lust and cold-heartedness." Five years later, an ungallant contributor to the *Southern Literary Messenger*, addressing female writers as "dear Aunts," adjured them: "Do put a little more metal in your poetry . . . If you have nothing to say, do not write 'Poetry.' No: knit stockings—knit stockings in all such cases." But while the men were stirring up their verbal tempest, the women were going their serene way, writing in whatever field they entered with a success equal to the men's.

THEORY OF THE NOVEL

Though poetry on the whole received its share of attention, the novel, as the most widely read genre of the times, was the center of the literary scene. A reviewer of Cooper's novels in 1838 declared the novel to be one of the highest products of genius. The novelist, in showing "character and passion, acting in their peculiar scenes and producing their characteristic effects," embraces the poet, the philosopher, and the dramatist. In constructing his plot, he must exercise all the skill required by Aristotle of the dramatist; and he must convey to his readers the firm illusion of reality. Having recently become respectable, the novel was riding the crest of popularity not only for its own merits but also for its novelty.

The chief practitioner of fiction during these years was unquestionably William Gilmore Simms. Like Aristotle, he rated action as first in importance, characterization second. The most important gift of the writer, however, he declared to be the power of intuition, which contributes fully as much to the artist as ratiocination. The plot, however derived, must be reasonably credible; Mary Shelley's *Frankenstein* was an ingenious work, but it was marred by "extreme violation of natural laws." Fiction was to Simms "probable truth under intenser conditions than ordinary."

Simms attempted to distinguish between the novel and the romance. The novel, as represented by Richardson and Fielding, deals with domestic life and familiar events. The modern romance is "the substitute which the people of the present day offer for the ancient epic." It is therefore loftier in origin than the novel, for it approximates the poem. Instead of restricting itself to the probable, it "grasps at the possible"; it places its agents in novel situations and exercises the author's ingenuity in extricating them. It employs what is commonly believed, as Aristotle said of the epic, rather than what we know to be true. His differentiation, however, was not generally followed; a writer in the 1854 *Putnam's* expressed the general idea in describing the novel as ranging over the entire field of the real and ideal and touching at every point of man's consciousness. Another writer in *Putnam's* declared the novel and the poem to differ

[105]

only in the novelist's abandonment of verse and elevated style in favor of a ruder but more flexible and copious style better adapted to express the greater expanse of emotion and action which he must treat. "The novelist is essentially a poet." Simms's unsuccessful dichotomy of novel and romance indicates that there was a growing sense of the need to analyze the novel more carefully than it had previously occurred to theorists to do. Criticism was beginning to look up when authors and critics became concerned about the purposes of the literary genres and their advantages and disadvantages as well as their interrelations.

Outside New England, the transcendental thinkers met almost uniform hostility. Daniel Whitaker admitted that *The Dial* was a work of great interest but characterized by eccentric opinions far in advance of the times. To him the Transcendentalists were "hostile to existing institutions, and prevailing systems in morals, in philosophy and religion." An age concerned to develop a distinctly American literature and favoring historical fiction would not readily welcome an obviously foreign philosophy. A Southern writer remarked on the frequency of new revelations, chiefly from "the East, from whence the wise men proverbially come," of which the latter-day mystery seemed "a sort of bastard Germanism" which "has sadly addled some weak heads in and about the precincts of Boston." This reviewer had hit upon the German sources of the new philosophy, which Robert Pleasants Hall in 1841 also accurately ascribed to their Kantian origin. "I do not expect," he wrote in the preface to his *Poems*, "to please the followers of Kant. . . . I shall be satisfied if my poems are admired and understood by those who are not slaves of German transcendentalism, but the children of nature."

New York critics were as unsympathetic to Transcendentalism as those in the South. W. A. Jones could find no precise doctrines in it, as he had anticipated would be the case in a movement which referred everything to the original soul. Like other critics, Jones placed Emerson far above his fellows, praising his sentences and rich declamations while censuring his lack of continuity. Less thoughtful reviewers condemned the whole movement and the country which gave it birth. "From traffic to treason," one irate reviewer declared in the 1847 *Democratic Review*, "nothing is safe against Yankee versatility." He added bitterly that in any promising situation you would find that a Yankee had already snapped up all the bargains and subsequently clinched control by setting up a newspaper. Even in hell you would infallibly find a Yankee, getting new ideas for "new patent cooking-stoves and hot air furnaces." Emerson was the most respectable among them; the motley following in his train seemed merely to suffer the dyspepsia naturally consequent to New England boiled dinners. The great American writer will not come from New England:

> The great men of this country are to appear beside the mighty rivers and amidst the fruitful fields of the west. Thence too will come to us the poets of immortal fame; great, world-embracing souls, who shall weave all things into their strains, and paint as in fire all forms of passion, opening up for man the blessedness of Paradise and the glories of the New Golden Age.

CRITICAL THEORY

The age devoted much attention to the theory of literature and criticism. The critic's judicial and interpretive functions were clearly recognized. Philip Pendleton Cooke had stated them in 1835: "The legitimate aim of criticism ... is to point out the proper path towards excellence. A true critic effects this by gently and courteously exposing error, and lauding beauties where beauties are to be found." Poe's subsequent cutting and slashing had no place in his mind. The 1838 *Democratic Review* contributed the idea that the critic bridges the gap between the understanding of the auditor and the intuition of the utterer; he is a literary paraclete. The 1840 *Knickerbocker* had claimed for him the same station in the realm of taste that the clergyman occupied in religion. "His business is to teach the truth, to denounce falsehood, to enkindle lofty sentiment, and glorious aspirations; to apply the standard of the immutable laws of nature to the productions of art."

John Stafford has noted four attitudes taken by the critics of this period: the judicial, the prescriptive, the interpretive, and the impressionistic. Their methods he separates into the formal or "neoclassical," Aristotelian way of criticizing and the ideological or "Romantic," Platonic criticism. Of the New York Young Americans, W. A. Jones stood out by reason of his catholic inclusiveness. The critic should possess thorough knowledge of the subjects, periods, characters, books of which he treats; he should have mastered the genuine spirit of the age; he should be just, yet generous and sincere; he should know rules, but possess a "fit spirit to guide in the adaptation of them"; and he should himself have skill and experience in writing. Add to these wide general knowledge, judgment, and tact, and you combine the best of eighteenth-century criticism with a governed liberty seldom achieved.

Other regions produced critics who approximated in part the standard set by Jones. The 1846 *Southern Literary Quarterly* declared that critics make too much of rigid rules and too little of flexible and universal principles. "Genius takes a variety of forms, and submits reluctantly to the restraints of arbitrary law." Amory Mayo in the 1847 *Massachusetts Quarterly Review* fell into line with his assertion that "any theory of the Art is incomplete which shuts the door against the future." Simms corroborated the recommendation to consider the future with a description of literature which anticipates T. S. Eliot's concept of the stream of tradition into which each artist pours his slender current. And the 1853 *Putnam's* emphasized the need for clearly stated guidance of public opinion. The critic should evoke from the reader the remark, "just what I thought," which indicates that his "half-formed notions have been expressed for him, and extorts such approbation from those whose opinions he may be making rather than expressing."

Against this liberal attitude the conservative critics fought a game but losing battle. Their attempts to blacken their opponents as subversive of morals, sound religion, and the American polity had failed. Their treatment of Catherine Sedgwick's novels indicates their method. The 1839 *New York Review* objected to "a tinge of Radicalism" in her recent books, "an appearance of quiet taking-for-granted that ultrademocratic sentiments are the only philanthropic ones." If the common people become instructed in the rights of liberty as well as the duties, they will develop "the licentious spirit of *Liberty above Law*, begetting discontent with established and necessary distinctions and subordinations, and hatred towards the richer classes." Miss Sedgwick was accused of giving advice to servants that would set them above their position; she should remember that the faults in the employer-employee relation are not "wholly or chiefly on the side of the employers." The appeal to fear was, however, ineffective, and the conservatives temporarily were halted.

The level of criticism during this period dissatisfied many critics. Edward S. Gould berated the American tendency to count all its literary geese as swans; nine out of ten current reviews of American books were commendatory. Gould had heard repeatedly of the American Addison and the American Goldsmith; and he looked forward apprehensively to the time when the appearance, according to the reviewers, of the American Milton or Shakespeare should conclude all progress from sheer lack of competition. His reasons for the actual low estate of American criticism, as reported by Frank Luther Mott, were six: first the complimentary copies received from authors instead of from publishers; secondly, kindly handling of authors who were personal friends of the reviewer; thirdly, courtesy extended to colleagues who ventured into authorship; fourthly, fear of alienating from the reviewer the author's admirers; fifthly, a mistaken hope of promoting American literature by puffing it; and, lastly, sheer laziness. Another reason implied in Gould's article is the servile acceptance of British models. On this last head, the 1835 *Knickerbocker* had wished that one of our critics would "pluck up sufficient courage to question the orthodoxy of a bull of the pope of London or Edinburgh"; and the 1844 *North American Review* ironically complained: "If the *Quarterly Review* or *Blackwood's Magazine* speaks well of an American production, we think that we can praise it ourselves." The reader of such censure soon realizes that Poe's voice was far from alone in the literary wilderness proclaiming the generation of vipers.

Numerous additional causes were adduced for the unsatisfactory state of American criticism. The reviewer had to vie in the ordinary periodical with the "thousand novelties of the day," hence came the incitement to write something piquant or sparkling, caustic or exaggerated, instead of sober analysis and judgment. A second cause was the anonymity of the reviewer, who all too often became a stern inquisitor instead of a judge. Another saw in the wider circulation of books a third peril for criticism. Realizing that the contents of the book were known to the majority of his readers, the reviewer was no longer justified in summarizing the contents or citing large excerpts. The fact that he now had wider scope and greater freedom to discuss the book had not eased the situation for the average critic, who found himself at a loss what to do with the additional space; the greater amount of original work involved in a review appalled all but the most industrious.

Perhaps the greatest obstacle to good criticism was the widespread belief that criticism was an inferior sort of writing, and that any man who possessed creative gifts should not waste his time on criticism. Horace Wallace severely condemned Poe's interest in criticism: "A man who can produce such a work as 'The Raven,' ought to feel that it was his office to afford subjects, and not models, to criticism." W. A. Jones, too, ranked the critic below the poet in invention, fancy and imagination, and love of the beautiful. The lower estimate of criticism undoubtedly led some with critical power to misdirect their efforts into creative work; as a result, criticism was abandoned to less able and occasionally slipshod practitioners.

The conviction was growing more prominent in the critics' minds as the period drew to a close that technical skill of expression, though not negligible, should be secondary to matter. "Critics in the progressive nineteenth century should be concerned with ideas, opinions, and the like"; men spoke scathingly of the "quasi literati" who still prided themselves on their imitation of Addison and Gibbon. "The taste of the age is now changed, and shrewd men discover that to be possessed of ideas is the first requisite; the next, to express them as clearly and correctly as possible." In poetry, the liberal literary sets believed, the time was at hand to strike out for a new freedom of writing and thinking about literature; and the more conservative thinkers, though unconvinced, had been abandoned by the most influential writers and were perforce silent.

Lack of space prevents discussion of judgments upon individual authors. Generally admired were Sir Walter Scott, James Fenimore Cooper (with some reservations among people whom his political and social comments had alienated), Dickens, Tennyson, Keats,

Shelley, Bryant, Longfellow, and Hawthorne. Those generally condemned included Byron, Bulwer, Carlyle, and Martin Tupper. Mixed reactions were aroused by Wordsworth, Coleridge, Hazlitt, Robert Browning, Emerson, Margaret Fuller, Irving, Lowell, Melville, and Poe. Where local bias was not aroused, observation was generally acute and judgment based upon carefully thought out application of principles.

The period was brought to a close with the culminating expression of liberal victory, Whitman's *Leaves of Grass*. Outside of New England, the conservatives were almost entirely subdued; and though they held their ground east of the Hudson, they were challenged even in their own stronghold.

Chapter 6

Walt Whitman

THE IDEAS of the New York Young Americans, the liberal seekers for democratic literature, found their fruition in the poetry and theoretical writing of Walt Whitman. Deriving its ideas from the French philosophers of the Enlightenment, reinforced by the inspiring words of Emerson, his work carried the theories of his contemporaries in New York to the highest development they were to reach in America.

Whitman, it is true, once described himself as "a hell of a critic," and was deplorably ignorant of literary history; he knew no language but English. Nevertheless, the New Humanist Norman Foerster rated him as one of America's most important critics, the last commanding personality in American romantic criticism. Foerster gave him this high position for his theory of literature, classifying him as a critic for the same reason that Wordsworth receives this stamp: both tried to relate literature to contemporary life, and both illustrated their theories of poetry, which they expressed in awkwardly stated prefaces, in their poems.

Somewhat unexpectedly in a man who believes firmly in the critic's need of literary scholarship, Foerster asserted that despite his deficiencies Whitman was well equipped for his task by his independence of thought, massive emotional and imaginative endowment, accurately tuned physical senses, intense moral earnestness, susceptibility to currents of thought, and desire to lead his fellows to a more abun-

[112]

dant life. On the debit side, Foerster listed his lack of humor, common sense, and reasoning power; and he doubted that Whitman's knowledge of the past contributed much strength to his critical work. Although these are formidable defects, especially in the eyes of a New Humanist, Foerster declared that the man who combined such strong qualities with utter fearlessness was inevitably a potent influence upon the literary thinking of his times. Praise from a New Humanist for a man with Whitman's deficiencies is praise indeed.

Among Whitman's literary principles, the first in significance for his criticism is his admonition to write *sub specie aeternitatis*, to say only what will be alive centuries in the future. At the same time, of course, what the poet says must be appropriate for America in the present. After listing the famous poetic subjects of bygone years: Catullus's sparrow, Ovid's parrot, Anacreon's love songs, Homer's siege of Troy, and Tasso's siege of Jerusalem, he commented: "What have these themes to do with America?" Admitting their beauty and even their permanence, he aimed at typically American themes: "the robust, large, manly character—the perfect woman—the illustriousness of sex."

Whitman desired in poems a unity similar to Emerson's conception of organic unity. The work is to be a unit in the same sense as the earth, the human body, or a perfect musical composition. Like Emerson, he belittled the distinction between works of art and works of nature. If poetic expressions take form as naturally as lilacs and roses, chestnuts and pears, they will each exude a natural perfume of their own. The resultant form will be simple, Whitman thought, for the author will speak "with the perfect rectitude and insousiance [*sic*] of the movements of animals." Such a literary form, however, as Gay Allen correctly observes, will be far from simple; it will rather be unrestrained, untrammeled by convention, with an end result unfortunately difficult of communication. In Whitman's mind, simplicity probably included avoidance of current romantic errors: "Nothing can make up for excess, or for the lack of definiteness." As he later told Horace Traubel, he had known only one sculptor who contented himself with the sight of what was there without changing it to conform to some preconceived notion of what ought to be there. His *Leaves of Grass*, he promised, no matter how often they should be revised, would present actual life. "All beauty comes from beautiful blood and a beautiful brain," and the only proper ornamentation is organically part of the whole.

Quite in keeping with such premises, the artist swears not to meddle with his art, to erect no veil of elegance or originality; "What I tell I tell for precisely what it is. . . . What I experience or portray shall go from my composition without a shred of my composition." The artist is a transmitter of truth. "You shall stand by my side and look in the mirror with me." He called the *Leaves* a photograph: "Nothing is poetized, no divergence, nothing for beauty's sake, no euphemism, no rhyme." He could express only what was in him, and what was in him came from contact with real things, not from the pictures of things. He must not even quote or refer to the works of other writers. By strictly observing these directions, his poet would produce a truly original work, free from the insincere copyist traits that were vitiating nineteenth-century poetry.

Whitman accepted Shelley's assertion that the poet is a law-giver. Poets should "hold up high to eyes of land and race the eternal antiseptic models, and dauntlessly confront greed, injustice, and all forms of that wiliness and tyranny whose roots never die." They are primarily social and religious reformers; literature is not an end in itself, but a means toward the poet's great end. A few first-class poets, "philosophs," and authors have practically established the religion, education, law, and sociology of the hitherto civilized world; new poets have the same never ending task. To gain this end, however, Whitman did not moralize as many of his contemporaries did; his poet knows the soul and simply addresses himself to it, neither pointing the moral to clarify it nor adorning the tale to attract readers. The hopes of the Enlightenment were still burning within him.

Although as a true romantic Whitman rated the emotions above the understanding, he was too practical to allow them to rove uncontrolled. Like Emerson, he believed primary knowledge to be intuitively perceived, but he thought more highly of the secondary, rational knowledge than did his master. "I call it one of the chief acts of art, and the greatest trick of literary genius (which is a higher sanity of insanity), to hold the reins firmly, and to preserve the mastery in its wildest escapades." The poet, never denying himself to the strangest emotional moods, should never let himself be carried away by them; he should always know "when and wherein to limit and prune them." The personage able to perform this feat is for Whitman as for Emerson the seer, the complete man, differing from other men not in kind but in degree, especially excelling in observation and expression.

Whitman's poet "does not stop for regulation—he is the president of regulation." Writers should not trouble themselves to conform to laws; "a great poet is followed by laws—they conform to him." He uses freely his power to destroy or remold; he possesses also the power to attack, but seldom uses it, preferring to demonstrate by his product the superiority of his work over what he opposes. Without realizing it, Whitman had in his conception of the poet come close to that of the classical Greeks and Greco-Romans, a conception which had been concealed under the legalistic influence of Roman law upon the authoritarian medieval Church and culture and under subsequent regulation as well.

To these statements which were applicable to western civilization generally, Whitman added a number of penetrating remarks about the American situation. His first Preface had undertaken to clarify the relation of America to the past. The often quoted statements that America does not repel the past or its products but accepts them as a heritage for her own use—commonplace from the American periodicals—and that the American poets, being representatives of the "race of races," enclose old and new, were supplemented in later articles. In "Shakspere—The Future," the new poetry is credited with taking advantage of the housecleaning conducted by science of "old stock-fables and superstitions" to make room for its ampler verse. The democratic spirit is preparing a world in which the true poets may appear. Their poems will be "not the satin and patchouly of to-day, not the glorification of the butcheries and wars of the past, not any fight between Deity on one side and somebody else on the other. . . . Entirely different and hitherto unknown classes of men, being authoritatively called for in imaginative literature, will certainly appear." Since the poet mirrors his people, a literary law of supply and demand will operate in America as it has formerly operated elsewhere, but on a higher level of both man and poetry. The American writer derives from all civilizations and literatures to bring forth a distinctly American product, which will incorporate all their values; ultimately it will evolve a fusion of them in a greater society and a greater literary expression than the world has yet seen. "If we are not to hospitably receive and complete the inaugurations of the old civilizations, and change their small scale to the largest, broadest scale, what on earth are we for?" Such statements, which in the mouths of men of lesser vision were bombast, in Whitman expressed a considered belief.

Whitman attempted to draw in outline this democratic poet of the future. Among the details of an early statement is an assertion that he will strive to destroy social and other barriers, to show the iniquity of partial and unjust laws, to make men love their fellows, to cast down the mighty from their seats and exalt them of low degree. Such a writer, he felt at one time, had appeared in Charles Dickens, and these qualities loom large in the poet described in the Preface to *Leaves of Grass*. Not many years later, he had decided definitely that his writer could only be an American, not one brought up in "that vast abnormal ward or hysterical sickchamber which in many respects Europe, with all its glories, would seem to be." That "almost indescribably august form, the People" is to be shown in "the divine mirror, Literature." Within a couple of generations, he prophesied in 1891, the United States will be populated by a hundred million people who will need "a sane, sweet, autochthonous national poetry." This the coming American poet will provide.

Further information about this democratic poet is expressed in Whitman's scattered directions for poets. As is often the case, the suggestion "how to write" may be translated into "how *I* write." Whitman admitted that he possibly escaped the overemphasis of so many writers upon style because he was himself thoroughly obsessed by the idea. Convinced that each poem finds its own form, he avoided "at all times the temptation to patch up and reform, preferring to let each version or whatever go out substantially as it was first suggested." He took great pains at the time to express whatever came to him; and presumably his later revisions were justified by further insight. His revisions were done after his own judgment. "I am doing my job in my own way: it don't suit them: they growl, curse, ridicule: but what is left for Walt Whitman to do but complete the job in the most workmanlike fashion he knows?" And finally, he insisted that his poems were "altogether subjective"; his realization that the great classical epics and Shakespeare's plays were objective in no respect moved him from the plan he had matured for his "transcendent and new" American poem.

As Whitman clearly indicated, he was concerned less with complete expression of a thought than with its suggestion to the reader; he would set up a co-operation between them through which the reader might achieve his own poetic experience. The various titles given to the "Song of Myself" indicate that, like other romantic poets, he professed to express the experience of the race in himself. As he declared, he devoutly wished to show men the path between reality and their own souls, which they were losing in an America almost wholly given over to material interests and ruled by law for thing.

Whitman was alert to the deficiencies not only in the current crop of poets but in contemporary America as well; though it was "a poem in our eyes," it was not the poem that he mystically perceived it might become. A year before his death, he frankly posed the question: "American National Literature—is there distinctively any such thing, or can there ever be?" He had long recognized the strong Old World competition, where mighty accumulations made American attainment seem puny. American writers were understandably daunted by what they saw abroad, and were prone to doubt whether they could offer anything distinctly American that would be of value. "In most of these fields," Whitman admitted in 1874, "while our brain in the United States is intelligent and receptive enough, Europe leads, and we still follow, receive, imitate." In 1891, he listed American excesses in authorship as "subordination of spirit, an absence of the concrete and of real patriotism, an excess of that modern esthetic contagion a queer friend of mine calls the *beauty disease*." Quoting Baudelaire, he added that the frantic greed for the beautiful, like Vergil's *auri sacra fames*, causes all the balances of truth and justice to disappear. In art for art's sake, which he despised, all Whitman's conception of the poet's task was ignored.

To correct American faults, Whitman offered several suggestions. America could not legislate what she needed, for her needs were spiritual. Fundamental requirements for an American literature, he declared, were "Patriotism, Nationality, Ensemble, or the ideas of these, and the uncompromising genesis and saturation of these. Not the mere bawling and braggadocio of them, but the radical emotion-facts, the fervor and perennial fructifying spirit at fountainhead." Like his earlier contemporaries in New York, he emphatically denied that the American literatus could come from New England. There the standards were "constipated, narrow, and non-philosophic"; the pioneers whom he had pictured in their westward march were part of the nationwide spirit, the Ensemble, which would produce him. Such a poet would be completely democratic, freed from the feudalism of the past even in the lesser degree in which it had penetrated our Eastern shores. For an immediate treatment of the American malaise, however, he reflected the conclusion reached by Emerson in 1842: "Meantime, we can perhaps do no better than to saturate ourselves with, and continue to give imitations, yet awhile, of that past and those lands we spring from." While we are still developing our national sense, we should be learning what the older races have to offer; meanwhile, we should be gradually pouring our original contribution into our product until, at the ripe time, we should present to the world the acme of literary success. Like Matthew Arnold, whom he otherwise detested, he felt that his own age was dwelling between two worlds, one aristocratic but dead, the other democratic but undergoing a difficult birth. That the new democracy would see the light, he did not doubt.

Though Whitman contributed more to criticism through his theories than by his actual judgments, his judgments are often interesting. Maurice Johnson acutely detected in his critical practice a basic double standard: one concerned with artistic excellence, the other with the democratic purpose of the book criticized. When he rarely found both qualities in the same work, he praised it without reservation. Johnson listed as Whitman's tests for great literature its restraint, originality, purpose, optimism, universality, concern with Nature, concern with contemporary life, and emphasis upon democracy. These qualities, Johnson added, were sought for in his criticism as well as demanded in his prefaces.

According to Horace Traubel, Whitman had repeatedly tried to read Arnold's books, but found them simply boring. "Arnold always gives you the notion that he hates to touch the dirt—the dirt is so dirty!" His fastidiousness prevented his understanding people or sharing in the democratic spirit. Arnold "brings into the world what the world already has a surfeit of: is rich hefted, lousy, reeking with delicacy, refinement, elegance, prettiness, propriety, criticism, analysis: all of them things which threaten to overwhelm us." His criticism, since it deals with art merely, Whitman found worthless. The unfairness and inaccuracy of his strictures upon Arnold lead one to doubt that he had read enough of Arnold to form a competent opinion.

Remarks on three other critical figures are enlightening. Dr. Johnson, he complained, lacked veracity, smelled too much of the lamp, never cared to meet men and learn from them, "does anything to score a point . . . is not concerned for truth but to make an impression." He is a relic of a bygone age. Ursa Major evidently ruffled the good gray poet. Wordsworth, though poetically endowed, was likewise too aloof from his kind; moreover, he used his art to secure legacies and comfortable political preferment at the sacrifice of his democratic principles. The student of Wordsworth will readily discern in this garbled statement the reaction of a man who has lost his own political appointment and has only hearsay knowledge of the facts in Wordsworth's case. Coleridge, too, he reprehended for having abandoned his revolutionary principles. He was nonetheless a true poet; and his *Biographia Literaria*, Whitman declared in an early review, "will reach the deepest thoughts of the 'choice few' among readers who can appreciate the fascinating subtleties of Coleridge."

Whitman was more appreciative than is usually believed of the well-known American poets of his day. In 1846, before he had nailed up his revolutionary theses, he had written of Longfellow that "the country is not half just to this eloquent writer; an honor

[119]

and glory as he is to the American name—and deserving to stand on the same platform with Bryant and Wordsworth." Thirty-five years later, Longfellow was still above all the contemporary writers of Europe save one for his "rich color, graceful forms and incidents—all that makes life beautiful and love refined." At this time he paired Bryant with Aeschylus for his handling of the highest universal truths. Whatever the well-informed student of comparative literature may think of his judgment, his admiration for the American writers is unquestionable.

As the culmination of the liberal New York movement in letters and the spokesman of the enlightened nationalists in American literary theory, Whitman has been an important force in our development. Seen against the background of the Young Americans, he assumes a more clearly defined position in our literary evolution. He went beyond his contemporaries in New York in realizing that the ideal America was still only *in posse;* and his vision of the literature of democracy encompassed an America which might still fulfill the dreams of eighteenth-century philosophers by including, as his unadmired contemporary had said, the best that is known and thought in the world.

Chapter 7

The Brahmins

THOUGH CONCORD AND CAMBRIDGE are only some dozen miles apart, in literature and philosophy they were widely sundered. Though they shared the literary revival of the first half-century and were alike interested in social and cultural progress, in methods and aims they differed extensively. Cambridge romanticism had been grafted upon the eighteenth-century stock; German and Oriental transcendentalism found few followers. The students who heard E. T. Channing at Harvard developed concepts of great importance to American letters; but those who lingered around Harvard tended to become literary conservatives. Since the work of most of them appeared in unsigned periodical articles, they did not in most cases emerge as clear-cut personalities. Two who did emerge exercised deep and wide influence: Oliver Wendell Holmes and James Russell Lowell. With their followers, they constitute what Holmes might have called the Brahmin literary contingent.

OLIVER WENDELL HOLMES

Some critics are originating minds; others preserve, adapt, and publish what earlier critics have discovered and developed. Of the latter group the Autocrat was a distinguished member. He preserved into the mid-nineteenth-century many qualities associated with the neoclassicists, but was at the same time, by virtue partly of his medical training, a skilled adapter of literary principles to the age of science. In literature and medicine he distinguished himself as a revolutionary conservative, far from the last to lay the disproved old aside and occasionally in the radical van. Though his medical specialty was anatomy, he was also concerned with preventive medicine and psychology; and when he turned his attention to literature, all three of his medical interests followed him.

Holmes came rather late into the critical field. Prior to his preparation for giving the Lowell Institute lectures on the English poets in 1852, Miss Eleanor Tilton brings evidence to prove, his reading about poetry had been slight. Justice Holmes could remember few volumes of poetry in his father's library when he was a boy. To prepare for these lectures, however, Oliver Wendell Holmes read Jeffrey's criticism in the files of the *Edinburgh Review* and studied carefully the critical works of Coleridge, the brothers Schlegel, William Hazlitt, and Leigh Hunt. He had also been thoroughly grounded in Latin, and freely used tags from Horace's *Ars Poetica*. By 1857–58, when he wrote *The Autocrat of the Breakfast-Table*, he had become familiar with a considerable range of poetry and criticism.

As has been indicated, Holmes's three medical concerns carried over into his literary interests: he was deeply concerned with the construction of the poem, he gave lavishly of his time to warn young writers of literary pitfalls, and he thought long and deeply on the qualities that make up the author. His conclusions on all three heads bear the stamp of his early classical training, but the time-tested classical dicta are often reinforced by modern scientific knowledge and presented by means of metaphors drawn from medicine or mechanics or zoology. Romantic ideas appear sometimes in strange guise. The notion that the child and the poet have much in common, for instance, appears in Holmes's writing in the statement that the fontanelle in poets' heads never completely closes. Holmes was fond of restating older principles in up-to-the-minute terms as a test of their truth.

Holmes did not subscribe to the Wordsworthian definition of poetry. When the poet writes, he is under the spell of no recollected emotion; except in rare instances, the *furor poeticus* has completely passed and he is engaged in "a cold-blooded, haggard, anxious, worrying hunt after rhymes which can be made serviceable, after images which will be effective, after phrases which are sonorous." It is true that much of his verse had been occasional, produced to order, and that when he made the statement just quoted he was overwhelmed by demands that he criticize manuscripts and volumes that hopeful writers showered upon him. There is no evidence, however, that he had felt the urgency to write which poets consistently have declared that they feel. In fact, he found verse a chafing restraint to expression. Rhythm seemed to him to be a tether, rhyme a ball and chain. Unless the long line of poets who disagree with him are all mistaken, one is forced to the conclusion that these admissions remove him from the ranks of poets, and classify him in the main as a skilled songster.

The poet, Holmes believed, did at the time of the poem's inception experience an emotion and receive some kind of inspiration from without. Without subscribing to Emerson's extreme doctrine, he declared that "the creative faculty is not voluntary at all, but automatic; we can only put the mind into the proper attitude, and wait for the wind, that blows where it listeth, to breathe over it. Thus the true state of creative genius is allied to reverie, or dreaming." Emersonian too is his insistence that the poet sincerely express his message: "Don't be consistent, but be simply true."

A topic of interest—in view of the current differentiation between poet and scientist—is Holmes's view of their difference. As the Professor, Holmes's alter ego in one phase, remarked to his other personification, the Poet, the latter handles his goods much more expensively than the former. The Poet must hoist his wares into the upper levels of the mind and imaginatively rework them, before offering them to the public, after the manner prescribed by Coleridge; whereas the Professor has merely to take in his materials at ground level, reorganize them, and issue them without expending costly foot-pounds of energy. The scientific man, Holmes says elsewhere in words anticipative of John Crowe Ransom, "connects objects in sequences and series, and in so doing is guided by the collective resemblances. His aim is to classify and index all that he sees and contemplates so as to show the relations which unite, and learn the laws which govern, the subjects of his study." The poet, on the other hand, "links the most remote objects together by the slender filament of wit, the flowery chain of fancy, or the living pulsating cord of imagination, always guided by his instinct for the beautiful." He does not, however, continue in Ransom's Kantian vein that considers poetry as a form of knowledge, but considers the object that started the poem rather as a point of departure than as a subject for intense contemplation.

As his literary career proceeded, Holmes added to the critics whom he had read for the Lowell Institute lectures other significant writers. He showed acquaintance with Buffon's *Discours sur le Style,* and with Sainte-Beuve, Ruskin, and Arnold. He knew all of Emerson's works. He expressed admiration for Lowell's literary essays, and read the numbers of several literary periodicals as they appeared. Undoubtedly the literary conversations which he held with Lowell, Whipple, Longfellow, Charles Sumner, James T. Fields, Howells, and other luminaries of the time played a great though indeterminable part in forming his ideas. The ideas presented through these media were received by a mind steeped in the ancient classics and in the neoclassical writers; and the resultant combination, as has already been indicated, could only be basically conventional except where Holmes's scientific knowledge and awareness of his times modified it.

Holmes's medical knowledge had taught him to be slow to dogmatize, and he carried over this attitude into his judgment of current American writing. He censured the tendency of the country to call its literary geese swans; he deplored the local reputation attached to mediocre poets, the neglect of artistic finish, and the inattention to construction. He saw the handicap upon poets in a land where everyone, poets included, was so frequently transplanted that he could not set his roots deep into the soil of any one spot; such migratory tendencies, he feared, made America in some respects inferior for literary purposes to the long-dwelt-in Old World. Whatever the causes, American literature had reached, he felt, in most instances only a high level of mediocrity.

[124]

One should not hastily assume, however, that the diagnosis of America's literary health by Holmes was also a condemnation of it; he was simply recording the facts of the case. He expected the patient to effect the cure himself, and he did not prescribe a rigid regimen to be followed by all patients. The poet was free to choose his own meters, his themes, and his vocabulary, though Holmes on his part reserved the right to dislike his product. Though he liked Whitman's virility and audacity, Whitman's work as a whole repelled him; the eighteenth century held him too strongly for him to enjoy radical departures from previously accepted standards. In like manner, the romantic influences among which he had grown up and the conventions of his native society made Zola and Flaubert and their tame American imitators distasteful to his latter years. The French novelists saw only the swampy, malarious patches of the literary soil; they were unwisely invading the province where the man of science seeks the truth, and were trying to use it for literary effects. The scientist must look at detail, whether it later prove significant or not; the literary man should concern himself with truth, which is not merely the sum of all the data.

These are binding strictures upon current literary developments. Holmes declined, however, to deny value to anything merely because it went counter to his principles. He compared young America to a three-year-old colt whose saddle and bridle have just been taken off. "The first thing he wants to do is to *roll*. He is a droll object, sprawling in the grass with his four hoofs in the air; but he likes it, and it won't harm us. So let him roll,—let him roll!"

Holmes, without contributing new ideas, conveyed to literate America an awareness of literature that no other writer had yet been able to convey. Like Horace, he talked men into sense without method. Readers who would never have intentionally perused a critical treatise were presented with literary principles embedded in the mass of current comment served up in his papers monthly by the *Atlantic Monthly*. Though the tone of his writing on literature was on the whole conservative, it was sane; and it provided a valuable balance wheel to the American literary machine whose boilers were being stoked with some highly inflammable novelties.

James Russell Lowell

James Russell Lowell, whom Foerster labels our most distinguished critic, remarked once that he had been half meant for a genius. He possessed most of the qualifications for literary success. He loved men so vehemently that he sometimes hesitated to judge his friends' writing. He loved nature as deeply, though not so mystically, as Thoreau. He enjoyed life with all of Browning's gusto. America was to him a passion, and his native Bay State its quintessence. Henry James eulogized him as the "healthiest of highly cultivated geniuses. . . . He looms . . . very large and ripe and sane." To James as a Harvard student, his classes had represented whatever Old World culture there was in Cambridge. Though to his neighbors after his diplomatic sojourn abroad he seemed to have become Anglicized, to his European acquaintance he was unmistakably American, in all things a staunch defender of the United States. Privately, he suffered occasional fits of despondency; in the public eye he appeared as an "essentially masculine, robust, and optimistic" personality.

To these qualities were added a vivid imagination, a love of language, and a passion for books. One friend classified him as "man reading." W. C. Brownell, a critic little given to hyperbole, wrote of him: "He read everything except the inept and negligible; and everything, ancient and modern, in its own tongue." Following occasional periods of apparent idleness, he would read intensively, twelve to sixteen hours daily, for weeks on end; he declared that he never wrote a critical essay without reading or rereading the entire works of the author. By careful training in research he overcame a constitutional aversion to detailed labor, and specialized in the precise field of romance philology. To all this scholarship he added something of a mystical capacity—not transcendental, however, for though he came to admire Emerson and his work he was never of the Concord school.

The principal cause of his being only half a genius lay undoubtedly in his mercurial temperament. In the course of his seventy-two years he was by turns lawyer, lecturer, journalist, editor, abolitionist campaigner, poet, critic, college professor, diplomat, and politician. No Yankee ever had more talents and interests, but not even a Yankee could pursue any one of them successfully while also engaged in the others. All were worthy, most of them interested him, but they were simply too numerous. The Alexandrian Greeks spoke of Callimachus, a similar polymath, as "the Great Beta" because he followed too many pursuits in literature ever to excel in any; and Lowell's career is in essentials parallel to that of Callimachus. His many talents made him a valuable, distinguished citizen, but prevented his attaining the heights.

In literary criticism he made his most significant literary contribution; his poetry, in which he had hoped to excel, is with few exceptions no longer easily readable. It is the work of a skillful practitioner, a master of prosody and poetic language, but the rhetoric too often drives out the poetry. His poetic theory indicates what he strove to produce and what he thought poetry should be; some parts of it may indicate also why he failed of success in it.

Lowell's concept of the poet was compounded of a romantic base with heavy admixture of classical principles, with a heritage from New England Puritanism. This last element appears especially in the assumption, which he made with some reservations, that the great poet is also a good man. Objective poets like Shakespeare, he admitted, might be pitiful fellows in personal conduct without weakening their work. Subjective poets are more likely to vitiate their work by defects of character. Dante's Divina Commedia, for example, could not have been composed by an author who lacked Dante's essential strength, for it is a record of the poet himself. Dryden gave Lowell more trouble. He lashed Dryden's serving "as a link-boy to the stews" with Puritan fervor; yet he found in Dryden a manly man of singularly open soul who by confessing his errors and seeking to mend his literary ways went far toward redeeming himself. He maintained consistently the greatness of Goethe without mentioning any moral obliquity.

Sincerity, indeed, was the redeeming feature in a writer. His Puritanism contributed the declaration that a man can conclusively demonstrate his sincerity only by giving himself for a principle; and his classical training brought his assertion almost in Horace's words that the man who attempts to stir our feelings must first show some small reality in his own. Even the magic of words must be accompanied by genuine feeling: "the secret of force in writing lies not so much in the pedigree of nouns and adjectives and verbs, as in having something that you believe in to say, and making the parts of speech vividly conscious of it." While the poet must be sincere, sincerity does not alone produce poetry. That a man is hanged for his faith does not make his verses poetry; painful evidence of this sad fact had been presented in Sternhold and Hopkins and in many a verse by the martyrs.

Coupled with the poet's sincerity in Lowell's mind was the creative imagination. His discussion of this faculty owed much to Coleridge and, as Leon Howard has shown, to Dugald Stewart, the Scottish rhetorician and philosopher. Analysis of this idea is rendered difficult by his chronic carelessness in the use of critical terms. Imagination is the shaping faculty; it bears the same relation to fancy that the lightning does to the aurora borealis. Again, he wrote of the imagination as being "fused into a molten unity with its material," as if it were not only the force which produces the fusion but also an element entering into the combination. His poetic imagination was often at work suggesting new images while he was engaged in criticism, and he used the new image instead of the standard term. His concept of the imagination was very like Coleridge's.

In his use of the term "secondary imagination," however, Lowell deviated from Coleridge. By this term Lowell meant, not the power which fuses elements into the new creation, but the power which interprets the poet's conceptions in words. Here, probably, his overmastering linguistic interests contributed to his innovation. This power "may be either creative or pictorial, may body forth the thought or merely image it forth. With Shakespeare, for example, imagination seems immanent in his very consciousness; with Milton, in his memory." Though the power of the poetic maker is implied in these words, the intent of the passage in which they appear puts the greater emphasis upon language.

Like other romantic critics, Lowell attributed to the imagination the chief function in the making of poetry. "It cheats us with a semblance of creative power that seems almost divine, and exhilarates us by a momentary enlargement of the boundaries of our conscious being, as if we had been brought into some nearer relationship with elemental forces." It is, however, only one of "two great factors of human character and springs of human action"; the other is the understanding. Lesser yet necessary components are originality, sense, and eloquence.

Originality, closely allied to imagination, was a question "not of form, but of substance, not of cleverness, but of imaginative power." What you see in life determines what you make out of it; and the expression of what you see is original. Effort to be original ends in becoming merely peculiar like Wordsworth, who "never quite saw the difference between the eccentric and the original." By suffusing what he sees with his own personality, the writer becomes original. Absolute originality is unattainable and might be undesirable if attained. In the parliament of the present, every man represents a constituency of the past; or, reversing the figure, the intellectual ancestry of a great poet will unexpectedly flash out even after a gap of generations. And just as the poet is old yet new, so his office is to show how much variety, freshness, and opportunity resides in the obvious and familiar.

Lowell's concept of originality is but one indication of his classical interests. At times, as when under the medieval spell of the cathedral at Chartres, the Grecian perfectness glutted him; normally, he gave to classical literary theory the strongest support it had received from any American critic since Legaré. Plato and Aristotle are "mountain-ranges forever modifying the temperature, the currents, and the atmosphere of thought"; Plato affords the loftiest vantage point for human speculation, while Aristotle has on most points said the last word that general observation can supply. Though he realized the defects in the pedantic German classical instruction at Harvard—"Many a boy has hated, and rightly hated, Homer and Horace the pedagogues and grammarians, who would have loved Homer and Horace the poets, had he been allowed to make their acquaintance"—President Eliot's moves to abandon a classically centered curriculum caused him poignant grief.

For literature, Lowell insisted in the midst of a panegyric on the Elizabethans, "the Greeks must furnish us with our standard of comparisons. Their stamp is upon all the allowed measures and weights of aesthetic criticism." Like Edward Young, he taught the right imitation of classic models. "The model is not there to be copied merely, but that the study of it may lead us insensibly to the same processes of thought by which its purity of outline and harmony of parts were attained." It shows us a strength consistent with repose, an abundant simplicity, a force that is also grace, and expression of a thought that may at once be deep and limpid. In so writing, he struck a body blow at the 100 per cent American writers and those followers of the "sublimo-slipshod" style who practiced a romantically vague unintelligibility. For Lowell, there was no culture which did not set one foot firmly upon a classical foundation.

One lesson which the classical tradition especially impressed upon him was the art of selection, Pater's "tact of omission." The *limae labor, et mora,* file-work and delay, emphasized by Horace in his *Ars Poetica,* was a common principle of his judgment. Wordsworth wrote too often to always write well. "An author should consider how largely the art of writing consists in knowing what to leave in the inkstand." Henry James profited from an artistic sense "which controls, corrects, and discontents." As he summed up the matter, "the poet with the real eye in his head does not give us everything, but only the *best* of everything. He selects, he combines, or else gives what is characteristic only."

Upon a man of pronounced traditional and romantic interests like Lowell, the impact of the new scientific thought was almost terrifying. His scientific interests had never been great. The stimulation of zoological and botanical studies at Harvard by his friend Agassiz, whose scientific position he approved, did not prepare him for the shattering impact of the Darwinian theory, and his personal admiration for Charles Darwin could not overcome his dislike of it. He wrote to Mrs. W. E. Darwin that he hated science as a savage does writing, because he feared it would hurt him somehow. Science seemed to him "the most obstinately prosy material," probably because it dealt not with truth but with that matter of fact which suffocated the Muse. Even in his friend Agassiz, whose mind he revered, he feared that "science had barred the gate that lets in dream." Though he did not share the theologically conservative warfare against science, undoubtedly his Puritan background helped to condition his mind against the new evolution.

Most of the traditional ideal concepts of poetry appear in Lowell's writing. He had also a shrewdly practical, Yankee side; he realized that the poet in order to communicate his poems to others must go where they are; he cannot compel their attention. Other things being equal, he believed that the best authors are those who make themselves most easily readable. To be interesting is the first duty of every artistic product—a principle from his journalistic experience which he carried over into literature. Interest derives from a combination of originality, eloquence, sense, and imagination; and the greatest of these is imagination. Lowell wisely did not offer any recipe for their mixture, for the poet, if he is truly a poet, will know the proportions.

Though Lowell never published any formal definition of poetry, Richard Henry Stoddard recorded in his *Recollections* a conversation in which Lowell discussed the matter. Asked by Lowell how he would define poetry, Stoddard replied with the Coleridgean statement that it is something that cannot be so well expressed in prose as in verse. Lowell added to this Coleridge's further statement that poetry is the best words in the best order. When pressed by Stoddard to state his own definition, he responded: "Poetry, as I understand it, is the recognition of something new and true in thought or feeling, the conception of some heroic action, the creation of something beautiful and pathetic." He added that real poetry "authenticates itself, and so absolutely that it seems not to have been written but always to have been." Emerson's belief that "poetry was all written before time was," which René Wellek has recently expanded, appears here. One should not emphasize what he never saw fit to incorporate into his collected works; the ideas expressed can, however, all be supported by reference to Lowell's works.

Joseph J. Reilly, an unfriendly witness as a rule but here substantially correct, summarized Lowell's concept of poetry from his works: "Poetry is the expression of beauty, but that beauty must be the medium for such ideas as make truth and nobility dearer to men." The first clause is a romantic commonplace, formulated in its best-known statement by Poe; the second, though at first glance the outcropping of Puritan heritage, is essentially the effect of the Platonic union of the good with the beautiful. Leon Howard, a patronizing but accurate witness, sees in Lowell's early attitude towards poetry the influence of Wordsworth's definition of it as the spontaneous overflow of powerful feelings, a statement which Lowell took too literally. Such attempts to show Lowell's conception of poetry actually go little beyond mention of some of the characteristic and obvious sources of poetry. If he had meant to give us a statement, he would have done so.

In one detail, Lowell interestingly anticipated recent poetic theory. "My notion of a true lyric," he wrote to Charles Eliot Norton, "is that the meaning should float steadfast in the centre of every stanza, while the vapory emotions (protean in form as you will) float up to it and over it, and wreath it with an opal halo which seems their own, but is truly its own work. The shades of emotion over, there floats the meaning, clear and sole and sharp-cut, in its own luminous integrity." Here eighty years before the relations of poetic texture and structure were discussed by John Crowe Ransom and Allen Tate, Lowell adumbrated the approach to lyric poetry which these well-known New Critics have amplified.

Lowell was naturally impressed by the statement in Horace's *Ars Poetica* that poets should teach or give pleasure or, if they would be widely read, do both. As abolitionist and youthful apostle of reform, he at first gravitated toward the idea of poetry as a didactic instrument. In 1843, he wrote that poetry should "reduce to the essence of a single line the vague philosophy which is floating in all men's minds, and so render it portable and useful and ready to the hand." Gnomic verses stud his earlier poems. By 1860, he could remark of Whittier's *Home Ballads and Poems*, "To put a moral at the end of a ballad is like sticking a cork on the end of a sword"; from a weapon it is degraded to a foil. The death of his earnest and brilliant first wife had helped to weaken the hold that didacticism had upon him.

By the end of the Civil War he "had learned that the first requisite of good writing is to have an earnest and definite purpose, whether aesthetic or moral." A few years later, he asserted that "to be delightful is to be classic," and "the first duty of the Muse is to be delightful." In a lyric, "The Origin of Didactic Poetry," he refers to "didactic bards and poppies" as the strongest narcotics; at its end Minerva hints to the poet,

> Put all your beauty in your rhymes,
> Your morals in your living.

Lowell's conclusion of the whole matter was reached in 1869: "As one slowly grows able to think for himself, he begins to be partial towards the fellows who merely entertain." Lowell had in mind an aesthetic pleasure produced by the fellows who entertain, and an enlargement of personality. The few great poets, he wrote, give "a right direction and safe outlet to their [*i.e.*, men's] passions through the imagination, while insensibly helping them toward balance of character and serenity of judgment by stimulating their sense of proportion, form, and the nice adjustment of means to ends." The old didacticism is here raised to something truly artistic.

Life in what he called its bread-and-butter associations seemed to Lowell unsuitable material for literature. He tried his best to speak well of the novels of Henry James and William Dean Howells, but Howells' "truthful treatment of material" seemed to him merely factual. Perhaps his dislike of details contributed to his antipathy to their work. In 1848 he had written to Briggs: "It fags me to deal with particulars. . . . I can interest myself in general ideas (such as include the particulars), but weary of their application to the present." The Reverend Homer Wilbur remarked in the *Biglow Papers* in a strong Aristotelian vein flavored with St. Paul: "There is . . . a truth of fiction more veracious than the truth of fact, as that of the Poet, which represents to us things and events as they ought to be, rather than servilely copies them as they are imperfectly imaged in the crooked and smoky glass of our mundane affairs." Lowell, who was throughout his life actuated by this Aristotelian belief with its Platonic overtones, complained that Dryden, born to see things as they might be, too often elected to see them as they are, to serve God in a prose translation. Fielding, too, often missed the distinction between truth and exactitude. Our ancestors, Lowell remarked, had a science that was poetry; with us, poetry is becoming science.

In an uncollected essay on D'Israeli, Lowell defined criticism as "the unbiased application of certain well-defined and self-existent principles of judgment." These principles are not fixed in their mode of application; criticism "must accommodate itself to the material supplied to them by the time and by the national character and traditions." In other words, the environmental theories of literature which had been popularized by Mme de Staël affect the critic's use of his yardstick. Lowell was by this combination of critical views able consistently to use traditional criticism in evaluating the American literary situation. Contemporary and later students who have failed to note his flexible yet unbiased method have done him injustice.

It follows logically that a poet may be measured absolutely as well as relatively. He may be judged by a purely aesthetic standard, or "relatively to his position in the literary history of his country and the conditions of his generation." As a rule, Lowell concerned himself with figures of proven merit whom he could gauge absolutely: Dante, Chaucer, Spenser, and Shakespeare underwent his scrutiny on aesthetic principles. Dryden and Pope received judgment by both standards, aesthetically and in relation to their times. The few American authors to whom he devoted detailed study were judged almost wholly on the basis of their position in American letters. Lowell never looked for the great American poet or novelist who should rival the established figures, but consistently examined American writers in relation to their milieu. Irving is not the American Addison, nor Bryant the American Wordsworth. His essay on Thoreau, wrongheaded as it is in many ways, treats of him as the Concord writer and product of New England.

Since Lowell acknowledged self-existent literary criteria, several students of his criticism have manifested surprise that he could also write: "the higher wisdom of criticism lies in the capacity to admire." It is true that he seldom cut and slashed as Poe consistently did. "It is the best rule for happiness in life, as well as for soundness of judgment in aesthetics," he wrote to his daughter Mabel on her first trip abroad, "to find out why a thing is good rather than why it is bad." He was averse to cutting up anything unless some good purpose was served.

Some critics of Lowell who have assumed that Lowell's preference of the admiring attitude in the critic was his basis of criticism have assumed him to be a mere impressionist. What Lowell had in mind, it seems probable, is admiration of the grace beyond the reach of art, the *je ne sais quoi*, which the critic can enjoy while realizing his inability to explain it. Appreciation is the basis of that interpretation which must always precede judgment. Lowell's essays uniformly include extensive selections which Lowell has tastefully collected for his readers' appreciation as aids in forming their judgment. Though he follows in this an earlier American custom, he does not use his selections to substitute for his own careful evaluation, but to support it and to show what the author has done.

The charge that Lowell was an impressionistic critic must first dispose of his insistence upon design as the chief criterion of the great author. The impressionist's attention is focused upon matters which Lowell believed to be significant but of less import than design. The essays on Chaucer, Shakespeare, the Old English dramatists, and Carlyle teem with demands that criticism cleave to the teleological argument; and Lowell's published letters also insist upon the vital necessity of design in literature. The man who judges by impressions will, except in relatively brief works, commonly make his decision on his reaction to parts of the work; but Lowell insists, "a great writer does not reveal himself here and there, but everywhere."

Foerster's contention that Lowell's literary criteria are distinct and impressive is amply supported by the evidence of his own words. Critics like J. J. Reilly have failed to see that his knowledge that the author can snatch a grace beyond the reach of art is no more his whole critical belief than it was Pope's.

As one would expect of a man whose critical essays dealt usually with the masters, Lowell liked the test of time as stated by Longinus and adapted from Vincent of Lerins. He was in fact so dependent upon the *quod semper, quod ubique, quod ab omnibus* that he was sometimes fallible in his estimation of contemporary writers. In harmony with the test of Vincent as far as it was applicable, he was more inclined than Wordsworth and Poe to "argue from popularity a certain amount of real value," though he admitted that it might not be the sort of value that leads to enduring fame. In his youth, as editor of the short-lived *Pioneer,* Lowell had declared that while the artist must use the tools of others, "the skill must be of his own toilsome winning, and he must not, like Goethe's magician's apprentice, let the tools become his masters." The conservatism which increased in him with age and wider knowledge led him to a less cavalier attitude toward authority.

From a hidebound conservatism he was rescued by the combination of Plato's and Spenser's idealism which drifted from Concord to Elmwood. "It is the essence of poetry that it should be unconventional, that the soul of it should subordinate the outward parts; while the artificial method proceeds from a principle the reverse of this, making the spirit lackey the form." The form of real poetry is not a garment, he declared, but a body. The true poet, as Dante shows in his *Vita Nuova,* may develop by self-culture and force of will until his imagination is as much a part of his being and as much under his control as his own body. Since it is by nature that he is a genius, he will of necessity be natural in his writing. Since taste is a lower degree of the poet's genius, it must never presume to "correct those profound instincts out of whose judgments the highest principles of aesthetics have been formulated." The critic must recognize the sovereignty of the poet's genius. He may, however, do good service in preserving the *keeping*—fidelity to the facts of history, avoidance of anachronisms, and co-ordination of character—in the poet's work, as Lowell did conspicuously for Pope and Carlyle. But, having recognized the presence of genius in the artist, he must bow to its principles and not presume to put it into any strait jacket of convention.

As a specialist in philology, Lowell also felt that a large part of the critic's duty lay in examining the poet's language. His essay on Spenser was occupied with diction to such a degree that he felt obligated to defend this emphasis. "Apart from its importance in his case as showing the way to the poets who were just then learning the accidence of their art, and leaving them a material to work in already mellowed to their hands, it should be remembered that it is subtle perfection of phrase and that happy coalescence of music and meaning, where each reinforces the other, that define a man as a poet and make all ears converts and partisans." Ovid, he declared, could have done greater service to mankind by writing a treatise on the language of the Getae than by the lachrymose poems he composed in exile. This concern with language as the lumber of which the poetic structure is built appears in his studies of Chaucer and the Elizabethan dramatists, in his praise of Dryden's influence upon English prose, in his careful distinction between slang and colloquial expressions, and in his eager support of the *New English Dictionary*.

As a young man, Lowell had egotistically thought of himself as the first poet to express the American idea. He had made himself acquainted with his country, though unfortunately not with all parts of it, in his abolitionist lecturing and in his work as editor as well as by careful study of political problems. He was versed in, though not subservient to, the popular German criticism of his day, knew the literary currents in France, Italy, and England, and had studied abroad. As professor of modern languages at Harvard, he was at the center of one of the principal sources of literary effort in America. He could speak with authority for New England, which was still the center of American culture, and the new literary developments in New York, to which after the Civil War the literary center was moving. Such a critic's survey of his country's literary condition is of inestimable significance.

Though no Anglophile till late in life, Lowell was far too well informed to accept the clamor for a distinctly American literature. He felt that neither Europe nor America possessed by itself all literary advantages, believing that "an orbed and balanced life would revolve between the Old and the New Worlds as opposite, but not antagonistic poles, the true equator lying somewhere between them." In spite of his anger at Britain's conduct during the Civil War and his pique at foreign condescension to things American, he kept separate in his mind literary and political England and numbered among his closest friends Englishmen like Thomas Hughes. Claiming for his countrymen complete independence of mind from foreign pressure, he yet spent twenty years teaching European literature to Harvard students and writing critiques of dwellers on England's Parnassus. The strength and weakness of the American literary health, and its possible improvement by foreign transfusions, were much in his mind.

He admitted freely what seemed to him just charges against

American letters. "New England," he remarked, "was all meeting-house when I was growing up"; and he campaigned vigorously against literary preaching. He conceded that Leslie Stephen was correct in explaining Jonathan Edwards's work as weakened by his literary isolation, and added that our authors still "lack the stimulus whether of rivalry or sympathy." He warned young William Dean Howells that abundance of talent could not compensate for care-lessness or want of scholarly refinement. "As a race," he mourned, "we care nothing about Art." Good artists must serve a long appren-ticeship; and in America, with little hereditary or accumulated cul-ture, this novitiate would probably last longer than in Europe.

To this unpromising situation, he felt that American criticism was an inadequate corrective. Complaining in 1858 of "the general laxity of criticism," he declared: "With few exceptions our criti-cisms are venal . . . or partisan. An invitation to dinner may make a Milton out of the sorriest Flecknoe, a difference in politics turn a creditable poet into a dunce." At times he felt that the "ideal dawn" which had broken in Hellas and spread to Albion's isle would find the Atlantic an impassable barrier.

The barriers did not, however, seem to him insurmountable. The first stage of the cure was to remember what earlier magazine writ-ers had known, that America was as much the heir to Britain's past literary greatness as was Britain herself. Next, authors should realize that universality, and not mere nationality, was the test of literature. "Literature that loses its meaning, or the best part of it, when it gets beyond sight of the parish steeple, is not what I understand by liter-ature. . . . Any verse that makes you and me foreigners is not only not great poetry, but no poetry at all."

Accepting Goethe's concept of world literature, he could not look with favor upon the claim of the New York enthusiasts that democracy, "the spirit of the age," would be the source of a new, essentially American literature. Democracy is too abstract a principle to serve as the "necessary Lucina of some new poetic birth." He remarked years later that many so-called spirits of the age, had proved so many will-o'-the-wisps to lead their devotees into the mire. Nationalism, he declared, makes its devotees vary between the extremes of overpraise and depreciation; it prevents our assessing any work at its true value whether we judge it absolutely by aesthetic values or relatively with regard to its milieu.

Another reason for Lowell's confidence in a coming American literature was that poetically endowed men may reasonably be expected to be born in America, that the proper study of mankind is man, and that human nature appears here as plentifully and in as varied manifestations as in Europe. Using the accumulations of the Old World and the materials of the New, he will be able to show man in all his complexity, not as a consequence of democracy, which rather tends to level man, but rather in spite of it.

But, Lowell had early insisted, "before we can have an American literature, we must have an American criticism. . . . with a few rare exceptions, America is still to seek a profound, original, and aesthetic criticism." He was asking for more than he himself, who was only half a genius, could ever provide, perhaps for more than can be provided; it is doubtful whether a truly original criticism can be valid. At the time, Lowell was censuring the criticaster in "the cast garments of some pigmy Gifford," who was the curse of the periodicals. He desired critical writing that, like creative writing, would combine the best of the New and Old Worlds into a product adapted to the New.

Lowell's judgment of individual authors varies considerably in quality. In general, he agreed with received opinions of greatly renowned or famous authors, though he arrived at his decision through his own study. In the case of his contemporaries, too, he made fewer mistakes than critics generally realize. Whitman he failed to appreciate, partly because he got his first impression of *Leaves of Grass* at second hand, partly because it seemed to him to belong to the "aphrodisiac or cantharides style of literature," which like the old inn signs offered "entertainment for man—and beast," but mainly, it seems probable, because Whitman belonged to the ultra-nationalist group of writers whose position he kept attacking as deleterious to the development of American literature. The case of Thoreau is somewhat more complex. First of all, the extrovert Lowell could hardly sympathize with the introvert Thoreau. Thoreau, too, without denying the value of European letters, expressed himself at times in an "isolationist" vein that was repugnant to Lowell. His hasty remarks on Bryant in "A Fable for Critics" he soon retracted.

On the other hand, he made a good many accurate assessments. In spite of his dislike of Margaret Fuller, he was not unfair in his picture of her. He was an early admirer of Hawthorne, and defended Cooper at a time when it was fashionable to defame him. He dealt fairly with Poe. He wrote a balanced review of Longfellow's translation of the *Divina Commedia*. He encouraged Henry James and William Dean Howells to follow their genius though their realism was not to his taste. And he estimated his own qualities accurately.

To many, Lowell's judgments have come to seem dated and superficial, an attitude which I cannot share. His shortcomings are obvious: his ignorance of America south of Philadelphia and west of the Alleghenies narrowed considerably his capacity to speak for and of the whole country; his aristocratic point of view, which he had inherited, made him unable to *feel* the nobility of toil; his inability to adapt himself to the age of science restricted his understanding of later writers; and he was too much Man Reading. In his earlier years, however, he fought vigorously against the nationalist heresy; and his later essays on the ageless masters of literature presented specimens of literary greatness to American readers and writers during the doldrums of the post-Civil War years.

EDWIN PERCY WHIPPLE

Among the Bostonian literary critics of the 1840's and 1850's, Edwin Percy Whipple, a critic now almost forgotten, held an important place. Poe ranked him, with the possible exception of William A. Jones, at the head of American critics. A popular lyceum lecturer, his articles appeared in the *North American Review* and other influential magazines. His 1859 Lowell Institute lectures, published as *Literature of the Age of Elizabeth*, were widely read. At the time of his death in 1886, however, his obituary notices read like reminders of past importance. Nevertheless, a man who for twenty years occupied a prominent position in the critical world deserves more than mere mention.

Bliss Perry has noted a close parallel between Whipple's career and Walter Bagehot's. Both, denied formal academic education, engaged in banking. Both read avidly and shrewdly evaluated what they read; and both were adept at transmitting to others their gusto for good books. Both wrote in a spirited, conversational style free from the precious affectation of academics like Edmund Clarence Stedman. Like Macaulay also, Whipple started his critical career early, curiously enough with an essay on Macaulay for the *North American Review*. Thus launched, he was for the next two decades one of Boston's most important literary lions. Whittier described him as "with the possible exception of Lowell and Matthew Arnold, the ablest critical essayist of our time."

Whipple made up for his educational lack by intensive reading. Though not acquainted with ancient languages, he knew Aristotle's criticism; and he subdivided poets into the same two classes into which, until the recent correction by Alfred Gudeman, Aristotle was believed to have classified them: the plastic and the enthusiastic. English poets are comprehensive or intense; the former combine according to objective laws, the latter by subjective laws. The comprehensive poet sees things after their own laws and relations, with no wish to mold the world to his own heart's desire. Possessing strong feeling, he is never possessed by it; he never fails to see both particular and universal as they really are. He is the highest sort of poet soon to be described by John Ruskin in his famous discussion of the "pathetic fallacy." The intense poet's individuality overmasters his mind and causes him to color what he sees with his own emotions and prejudices. With unusually keen insight into some realities, he is singularly blind to others and so lacks the universal view; but the intensity of his vision makes him fanatically sure that his views are true for all mankind. Recent English poets, Whipple declared, display many of the faults of the intense poet, Scott alone being free of the "impassioned declamation on man and nature" which in their poems substitutes for true representation. If Wordsworth, Shelley, and Byron had only possessed the saving grace of humor, it "would have given them sufficient tolerance of practical life to have represented it without exaggeration." Lacking its perspective power, "they too often flew into a passion with the world, and narrowed the range of their vision by dwelling too much on particular subjects."

Bryant showed similar narrowness. Creative power of high quality includes, Whipple insisted, the broader scope which the romantic writers lacked; its chief exponent was Shakespeare: "all that Shakespeare created he individually included."

In order to discern clearly the universal in the particular, Whipple required the artist to be a well-educated man. His own deficient preparation no doubt sharpening his emphasis, he detected in Charles Dickens the ill effects of a similar lack. If Dickens had been early made acquainted with general principles in history, government, political economy, and philosophy, "such knowledge would have checked and corrected the fallacies into which he was sometimes whirled by the intensity of his perception of unrelated facts, and the unwithholding warmth with which he threw himself into the delineation of exceptional individuals." Scott possessed the comprehensive view bestowed by broad knowledge. Whipple reported with awed respect and for once with uncritical receptiveness Goethe's detection of esoteric meanings in *The Fair Maid of Perth:* "Goethe judges Scott as it is fashionable among us to judge German authors.... We see one of the greatest and most comprehensive minds in modern times, one, too, particularly gifted with a clear perception of objective qualities, discovering in Scott such pre-eminent intellectual excellences."

Moral awareness, too, was essential in Whipple's artist. Whether a poet was personally upright did not concern his aesthetic nature— a doctrine in which Whipple found few American sympathizers. The writer must, however, possess at least an intellectual perception of the essential difference between good and evil in order to show that truth to the nature of things which is the test of poetry. In Whipple's day, fiction had finally broken away from ultra-respectable characters; but it had gone so far beyond Fielding's practice of representing blackguards and villains sympathetically that Whipple doubted whether its authors knew who should be in jail and who out. Accurate representation of life unfortunately shows rascality to play an important part in life; and the author can justify himself for making most of his characters more or less wicked. "But there is a great difference between exhibiting criminals as they are in themselves, and exhibiting criminals as proper objects of extreme and moral approbation. . . . Provided a writer respects the natural relations of things, there is no danger in his delineations of criminality." Whipple here struck a weightier blow than Poe's against the heresy of the didactic. He went beyond Howells' realism in admitting that the face of American society is not always smiling and in mentioning the seamy side of life.

Coleridge, Whipple's most admired critic, supplied his realism with a concept of the imagination. It is the shaping power, always in earnest, whereas the careless play of fancy contents the reader only momentarily. Taste must select the materials of the poem, but imagination fuses them into the new creation. Any limitation of the imagination by defining it, he steadfastly opposed. In response to Talfourd's restriction of it to the discerning, suggesting, and combining of analogies, Whipple protested: "Is this the whole of its province? Are not the creation of individual characters, and the invention of incident, among its legitimate efforts?" G. P. R. James was "emphatically a literary mechanic," putting characteristics and episodes together with nuts and bolts. Poetry "is not necessarily opposed to prose, but to what is prosaic. . . . The soul of poetry, indeed, is impassioned imagination, using words."

The epithet "literary mechanic" indicates another of Whipple's debts to Coleridge. In 1846, in an essay "Coleridge as a Philosophical Critic," he discussed favorably Coleridge's doctrine of organic form. Although he had doubtless read Emerson's organic theory in "The Poet," which was published in 1844, he relied here upon Coleridge. "Coleridge had a clear notion of the difference lying at the base of all poetic criticism, between *mechanical regularity* and *organic form;* and in the disregard of this distinction by critics, he saw the numberless fallacies and falsities which vitiated their judgments." Poets had been tried by arbitrary tests which their writings had never been intended to meet. Analysis by any set of critical rules will expose the weakness of a mere collection of loosely strung parts; but "the process by which imposture may be exposed is not necessarily that by which truth can be evolved. A life spent in examining quackeries and deceptions produces little fruit." Jeffrey, though doing yeoman's service in condemning false poetry, had been quite unequipped to recognize the genuine when it happened not to fit his formulas. The just critic is tolerant of another's mind and alert to its idiosyncrasies. In fact, the critic's point of view determines in large part his estimate of the artist. "The mind, untrammelled by forms and rules which bigotry has put into it, has a sense for the beauty of all new objects, and sees them in relation to their own laws." Such a mind does not ignore rules and principles which are founded in nature, for it is from nature that its canons are deduced.

The tests applied in such a critical attitude are fully as rigorous as those embodied in the old rules, but less rigidly molded because they are based on the fact that each work has its own organic life. Once the nature of that life has been determined, any deviation from its proper nature merits severe censure. Though this criticism is sympathetic, it requires absolute fidelity to the nature of the organism.

Contemporary criticism Whipple scored as being in most cases "merely the grating of one individual mind against another." The critics of the day, ignorant of almost everything except themselves, substituted their individual peculiarities for considerations of taste and beauty, or sneered in their reviews because the work under attention did not conform to established practice. As criteria for the good critic, Whipple asked: "Was his taste catholic? Did he perceive and elucidate excellence as well as detect and punish pretension? Did he see the dawn on the mountain tops, as well as the will-o'-the-wisps in the bogs beneath? Did he have any principles on which to ground his judgements, apart from the impertinence of his personality?"

More than a decade before Arnold made it notorious, Whipple had exposed the biased criticism of his time. He charged British critics with political distortion, violating the plainest principles of taste, morality, and benevolence, and preventing, by their misrepresentations, good authors' works from exercising the benefit they otherwise would have contributed to their times. Carlyle's criticism of Scott attempted "to sacrifice one man's genius to another man's prejudice"; his tone was a "low, melodious growl." Macaulay let his political bias edge the cutting sarcasm with which he assailed Croker's edition of Boswell. Macaulay exemplified also the current vice of undue severity: "his critical severity almost actualizes the ideal of critical damnation. There is no show of mercy in him." Talfourd displayed the opposite extreme of undue lenity; Whipple in a startlingly mixed metaphor declared that "he festoons the scalpel of the critic with roses." The golden mean was approximated by Sir James Mackintosh: "it was natural for him to look at things with an impartial desire to arrive at truth, and to view both sides of every question. His mind was ever open to new truth. As far as his perceptions extended, he ever did full and complete justice to all systems of philosophy or legislation which came under his notice." He was Alexander Pope's ideal critic with a freedom of range that Pope could not have envisioned.

Several minor critical matters in Whipple's position are important. First, the minutiae of revising and correction to which Poe devoted so much attention, though necessary and significant parts of literary work, should not be dignified with the term criticism. Secondly, Whipple accepted no promissory notes from the author and advanced him no literary credit, but operated on a strictly cash basis —a chafing hindrance to some ultra-nationalist critics, but a salutary rebuke to their exuberance. Thirdly, the critic must link literary history with history as a whole, and view literature in the light of political, social, and cultural matters—a lesson many scholars still need to learn.

On two matters Whipple showed himself to be modern beyond the point of his usual openmindedness. He conceded that poetry need not be metrical when most New England theorists, except the Transcendentalists, still disagreed with him. Though poetry doubtless finds its happiest expression in the verse of the greatest poets, "sometimes verse is a clog, and its management a mechanical exercise." None can doubt the poetic quality of Milton's prose, or of the prose translation of the Psalms of David. Imagination directed by poetic sentiments and passion to poetic ends make the poet. Whipple's well-known witticism that Whitman's *Leaves of Grass* contained every leaf but the fig leaf was in no way an objection to the form of Whitman's work.

The second matter, which the New Critics ever since T. E. Hulme have been pressing, concerns the poet's capacity to bend or twist or warp words to serve his purpose. This idea, implied earlier by William Ellery Channing, is a natural development of the plastic artist's problem of the ductility of his material. Whipple mentioned this faculty in discussing the economy with which great writers and orators compel common words to bear a burden of thought or feeling which mere rhetoricians can never load upon them. Though Whipple uses the metaphor of imprinting instead of bending the word, he furnishes another instance of the awareness of earlier critics that the artist finds words malleable to his pressure.

Whipple has been credited with more encouragement to American writers than any other critic of his day. His habit of looking at the facts and the common sense that had made him a competent banker, counteracted in him the tendency of many formally uneducated Americans to assume that their literature had already arrived at greatness. "We have no desire to exalt American poetry above its merits. We are sensible of its deficiencies, as compared with the great creations of English genius." These outstanding creations were not, however, in the current British literary product. He could not understand why British authors of the nineteenth century, "whose literature is stained with so many metrical productions offensive to good taste and good morals, . . . whose miscellaneous and magazine verse is, at the present time, inferior to our own," should sneer at the work of American poets. Though not sharing Lowell's early Anglophobia, he was irritated by our subservience to British comment on American books. And why did Americans pay attention to the childish tattling of these pert coxcombs? Partly because we still lacked a real literature of our own.

Whipple admitted that we lacked a literature partly because the imaginative energy of many Americans was being diverted into non-literary channels. It was not our authors who most clearly reflected the spirit of our institutions. Yet only literature could worthily express the American spirit, that "voice more majestic than the roar of party, and more potent than the whine of sects." Nor is the true vitality of a nation seen in "the triumphs of its industry, the extent of its conquests, or the reach of its empire; but in its intellectual dominion. . . . A nation lives only through its literature, and its mental life is immortal." He would probably have laughed at our effort to preserve our record in time-capsules.

Like Bryant, Whipple declared that the materials for an American poetry were available here in profusion. They must be presented in a tone essentially American, not a "feeble or sonorous echo of Germany or England." The higher life, the ideals of America must be shown in the midst of her turbulent and often degraded phenomena. It is a poetry that shall speak in loud, clear tones to the people and make them more in love with their native land, not by pandering to their lower feelings but by using our materials as images of lofty thought. "It shall disentangle freedom and cant and senseless hyperbole, and render it a thing of such loveliness and grandeur as to justify all self-sacrifice." It shall break down the thin partitions of conventionalism and expediency in order to vindicate the majesty of reason, strengthen the voice of conscience, give new power to the affections, and "speak out in the high language of men to a nation of men." In these words Whipple combined the desires of the chauvinists with the more reasonable principles of the better informed. Our hindsight shows his eclipse to have been a severe loss to our literary guidance at the very time when his sanity was greatly needed.

Lowell's Epigoni

Although not the founder of a school, Lowell profoundly influenced a number of younger thinkers. Of these, Edmund Clarence Stedman and George Edward Woodberry were so close to his ideas that treatment of them immediately justifies a slight violence to chronology.

Edmund Clarence Stedman

Born of a mother with considerable literary talent, Stedman was briefly a student at Yale, then a Civil War correspondent, and for many years a member of the New York Stock Exchange. He was a meticulous student of contemporary verse. His *Victorian Poetry* (1875) still repays study; his *Poets of America* (1885) by far the ablest study of its subject then made, deserves more attention than it now receives. *The Nature and Elements of Poetry* (1892), though unduly florid in style, stated clearly his tolerantly conservative poetic creed. Though not a pioneer in critical theory, Stedman summed up and evaluated the many tendencies of his day. He belonged to that front of literary criticism which abuts upon literary history, and his combination of faculties made him an extremely significant figure. His pronouncements were accepted during the eighties and nineties as those of a literary arbiter.

Stedman was well read in the critics from Aristotle's day to his own and drew freely upon his store. Of all critics, he held Coleridge in most reverence; he devoted a good deal of attention to the nature and function of the imagination. Of this faculty he recognized two levels: a lower, which appears in some intensely passionate and re-vealing phrase—Lowell's flash of lightning—and a higher, the shaping and unifying faculty. Its twin is emotion. It is only from the union of imagination with passionate emotion that poetry comes into being. The imagination, after the poet has carefully considered the objects which he plans to use, conceives new, yet natural, and more exciting combinations of them; then the heated emotion an-neals the elements—like most other poet-critics, Stedman hunts up a new metaphor to describe the process—so as to produce a new, unified creation.

Closely allied to the imaginative process, Stedman believed, is that unconscious process of the soul which we denote as intuition, insight, genius, or inspiration. This, too, must be present before poetry can be made. Of these three powers the imagination is sovereign; a poet's ability is co-ordinate with the clarity and staying power of his imagination. Vigorous intellect, though perhaps not on a parity with the other three, is always present with strong imagi-nation. "*Other things being equal*, the poet who 'mixes brains' with his measures steadily draws ahead and keeps ahead of the mere tunester and artificer." Intellect prevents the poet from trying to create something contrary to nature; "beauty of the fantastic or grotesque is not the highest beauty." Poe suffered in Stedman's eyes for his failure to realize that beauty dwells in the world of Raphael, not in that of Doré.

Mastery of technique, though not a substitute for imagination or thought, is also essential to poetry. The poet's technique comes partly through intuition—Stedman did not wholly discard Emerson's doctrine of organic form but declined its full implications. It comes pretty much as Addison had said that taste is acquired: through environment, reading, and experience. When the poem is well made, it accordingly combines soul, matter, and expression annealed into a whole. Its beauty, as Aristotle had said, includes shape, arrangement, and proportion; the excessive or unnecessary, especially ornamentation, is removed, so that the poem is an organic unit containing nothing alien to its aesthetic purpose. A carefully wrought product requires the skill of a master craftsman; he distrusted the poetic amateur.

Based upon this concept of the poem, Stedman ventured a definition: "Poetry is rhythmical, imaginative language, expressing the invention, taste, thought, passion, and insight of the human soul." He drew from Aristotle the idea that poetry is a structure built by imitation through imagery, whose end is delight. From Horace came the declaration that the poet must feel strongly what he writes. He is devoted to universal truth expressed in particulars. On the other hand, "the romantic—the word being Latin, the quality German—is all depth and tenderness." Classic and romantic, he believed, are not mutually exclusive terms; the romantic revolt provided "a fresh originality that is not radically opposed to principles already established." In all the greatest work classic and romantic qualities unite.

Like Lowell and Legaré, Stedman strongly advocated classical training. He used to say: "The Latin Grammar I knew by heart, the English Grammar by inference." Classical prosody had been so thoroughly drilled into him that he never felt a need for exhaustive study of the principles of English verse. His most valuable discipline had been his absorption for two years in the Greek Idyllic Poets. Desiring to translate their work, he had found it first necessary to form his own Greek text before he could proceed. Though the translation was never published, the scholarly discipline repaid his efforts. "After it I wrote with twice the ease, certainty, and—I think—

clearness of vision. In short, it braced and rendered flexible whatever faculties I had." Such classical discipline, which he noted in Landor and Arnold, he would have available to all artists.

Instead of studying handbooks on poetic technique, he urged young poets to study the masters of verse: "study Tennyson, being careful, however, not to become Tennysonian." Study the poet's technique, even his punctuation. Even more important, however, is the way they thought. Like Edward Young, Stedman advised younger writers to observe the mind and art of great writers from all ages, but to emulate only the best. The poet should learn from the master how to solve his own problems in art.

Though less fanatically than Poe, Stedman objected strenuously to pure didacticism in poetry. Formulas of truth "preach . . . the gospel of half-truths," uttered by those who have not the insight to perceive the soul of truth, the expression of which is always beauty. Anticipating John Crowe Ransom's differentiation between the poetic and scientific inspection of an object, Stedman declared that the preacher directs our attention not to the ultimate truth conveyed by the object, but to some application of it, some partial incomplete statement. The true poet "is your only truth-teller, because he gives the truth complete in beauty or not at all." Keats's enigmatic equation of beauty to truth was much in Stedman's mind. His admiration for Longfellow did not prevent him from noting that "he tacked a didactic moral, like a corollary of Euclid, on many a lovely poem"; and he admitted that his master Lowell, "when called upon, as he supposed, to make a choice between Taste and his conception of Duty," sometimes let Taste go to the wall.

Lack of a suitable theme, Stedman blamed as the principal reason for the deficiencies of nineteenth-century poetry. Not only must the theme be within the powers of the poet—and few poets realized as clearly as Longfellow where their limitations lay—it must also be great enough to give room for full exercise of such powers as they possess. There is something amiss in a writer who has to grope for his theme. Lack of a great subject cannot be atoned for by abundance of "images, quaint words, conceits, and dainty rhymes and alliteration," or by laborious search after "themes to constitute the groundwork over which these allurements can be displayed."

Such verse after pleasing briefly passes into oblivion. Perhaps Stedman's own constitutional inability to attempt great tasks—a defect of which his letters show him fully aware—emphasized for him the vital need of a great theme. Certainly he was correct in calling it a major lack of his fellows.

Stedman disagreed with Milton and with many of our contemporary poets in believing that poetry should be written for the people, not for the fit though few; in this he was at one with earlier New York critics. The rude ballad is more genuine than the poem designed for a restricted audience. The latter seldom possesses enduring quality. "That a poet's verse should require a commentary in its own day is not, all things considered, the best omen for its hold upon the future." He would have held out little likelihood of longevity for Eliot's *The Waste Land*. He would probably have been doubtful of our current metaphysical boom in poetry for much the same reason that he suspected the attempted revival of old French verse forms by Austin Dobson and Edwin Arlington Robinson, "the quest for values so long unwonted that they seem new." New types of genius will no doubt "add new species to the world's *flora symbolica* of art and song," but he would have been skeptical of the attempt to revive a form both old and difficult to understand. "Though it be true that thought may be so analytic that its expression must be novel and difficult . . . , as a rule the better the poet the more intelligible."

The manner in which art represents life also occupied Stedman's mind. A good Aristotelian, he naturally saw poetry as opposed not to prose but to fact; in his day science occupied literary men's minds pretty much as history had occupied Aristotle's. One can paraphrase the *Poetics* for Stedman and say that poetry differs from science in being more philosophical and serious; it represents the true image of nature, from seeing which historian and scientist are alike barred by interposed facts. Fiction must not give mere photographs of everyday life; "rising above mere introspection and analysis, poetry (*i.e.*, imaginative literature) must be not so much a criticism as the objective portrayal and illumination of life itself." Writing which attempts to criticize life, like didactic literature, works from preconceived ideas, sees what it looks for, and is little concerned to show life as in itself it really is. Poets vary, he admitted, in the scope of their view of life. Most can draw only the types under their direct observation. Greater truth to life, however, comes not so much from the realist's portrayal as from the enlarged sympathies of the poet. Resorting to German terminology, he differentiated poets according to the "Me" and the "Not-Me," the former possessing self-consciousness only, the latter able to represent life and thought apart from their own personality. True poetry approaches universality in emotion and thought, and embodies this universality in real personages and situations.

Whether the poet be subjective or objective, major or minor, "some kind of faith, with its resulting purpose, has engendered all poetry that is noteworthy for beauty or power." These convictions have commonly been religious, but they may be "certain convictions as to their art, themselves, and 'the use of it all.' " But the artist must have something to pin his faith to. "If I were asked to name the most grievous thing in modern art, I should say it is the lack of some kind of faith." In this belief, which Stedman shared with Lowell, he again anticipated a conclusion of many of our contemporary critics who declare that the only possible future continuance of our art must be based upon some belief.

As a critic, Stedman, like Horace, was committed to the tenets of no school; he favored "a generous eclecticism, or universalism, in Art." Like Lowell he combined judicial criticism with almost impressionistic appreciation. The judicial side, however, predominated: "The canons are not subject to change; he [the future critic], in turn, will deduce the same elements appertaining to the chief of arts, and test his poets and their bequests by the same unswerving laws." His eclecticism showed in his perception of the basic likeness of both classical and romantic systems, and its liberality in his welcoming radical new poets like Whitman into the poetic fold. "The catholic reviewer," he wrote, "will not shut his eyes to the value of new modes"; he was more receptive of Whitman's innovations than of Austin Dobson's revival of old forms. He saw "that conventional criticism, which holds to accepted canons, has its use as a counterpoise to license and bewilderment." Even the neoclassical narrowness, which did not suit his temperament, seemed to him to have its uses.

[152]

Stedman's definition of criticism was at once judicial and impressionistic. "Criticism is the art and practice of declaring in what degree any work, character, or action conforms to the Right. Conversely, and implied in this definition, the office of criticism is to see and declare what is wrong—*i.e.*, in what degree a work fails to conform to the Right." The critic's primary qualifications are accuracy, taste, and honesty. His task is "to distinguish between what is temporary or modish, and what is enduring, in any phase, type, or product of human work." Less judicial qualities present in this definition appear in the emphasis upon taste, which was no longer formed by a single pattern as in Addison's day, and in his eclecticism, which forbade him to follow slavishly any established canons. Without going to the extreme of impressionism, Stedman here shows a freedom from arbitrary judgment in which the impressionist may take comfort. The arrogance so objectionable in many judicial critics is also conspicuously absent in Stedman's critic; in performing his duties he will be actuated by humility. This humility will be caused partly by realization of critical frailty, but more by his awareness of past instances in which readers, whether instinctively or capriciously, have reverted to literary forms and ideas which critics had presumed to be extinct. He will also be on his guard against letting the characteristics of his age distort his judgment of values, as Poe sometimes did; he must try to judge *sub specie aeternitatis.*

Several suggestions for the practicing critic are to be found in Stedman's works. First, since the poet's true quality appears in his best work, evaluate him by that work. Indicate where he has fallen short, but only as warning to his readers or as possible guidance for him or other writers. And do not let romantic occurrences in the poet's life sway your judgment of his work. Poe's much romanticized life had given his work a glamor which Lowell's relatively unromantic life and assured social position could not contribute to his books; readers should not let such extraneous matters color their judgment.

A second suggestion warned that the poet has the right to make his own rules. He studies in his own atelier. "He is not made, his poetry is not made, by *a priori* rules, any more than a language is made by the grammarians and philologists, whose true function is simply to report it." The old may verify the value of the new, but tradition is merely monitory, not lawmaking. Further, if the poet may make his own rules, he may also demand to be judged according to them—a principle which earlier Americans had learned from Goethe. Presumably, the author believes that truth to nature requires what is novel in his work. He may be correct, or there may be a better way to do what he has attempted; but Stedman conceded to him as did Henry James the right to try his own way. If he has succeeded in doing well what he sought to do, the critic must not condemn him for snatching a grace beyond the preconceived reach of art. "An author is grateful to any critic who will take note of his major premise, rather than of matters that are minor and auxiliary."

A third suggestion directs the reader-critic to judge a work according to the principles governing its literary genre. Longfellow undertook to write according to the principles of German romantic poetry; the work thus produced should be judged according to the principles of that kind of poetry. Though Stedman was disturbed by post–Civil War tendencies in our architecture—as who has not been? —even there he remarked: "The critical question, I take it, is not what fashion should be outlawed, but whether the thing done is good of its kind." The true critic does not pronounce the rose superior to all other flowers, but asks, "How is this rose as a rose? How does this lily compare with other lilies?"

Averse though he was to destructive criticism, he had to admit that it had its place in the literary scheme. In editing Poe's criticism, he admitted that Poe had contributed only a few significant canons, none of them really new; and he conceded Poe's frequent dishonesty, vulgarity, and prejudice. The literary edifice of his day, however, needed housecleaning, and Poe's hatchet-swinging had made room for a new growth in American criticism. A body of criticism like Poe's in another era might well be not worth preserving. But his work was important if only for what it did to sweep obstruction from the path of our literature when it was just beginning to take form. His extended apology for including in his edition of Poe several volumes of his criticism seems laughable today, but his knowledge of American literary history in this case went far toward establishing Poe as one of our important critics.

Stedman's criticism is a constructive and evolving art. It promotes higher standards in its own sphere. Each great critic adds "a step to the stairway from which it takes a more penetrative and enlarged view." Such insight into the nature of criticism could belong only to the man who possessed a more systematic knowledge of Anglo-American literary and critical history than any American up to his time.

Stedman's *Poets of America* not only indicates the breadth and depth of his knowledge of American poetry; it makes equally clear his wide acquaintance with American prose, except perhaps with the less-known writers of fiction. This historical survey made him aware of a quality in American literature which had escaped Lowell. In the preface to this volume, he berated Americans for their failure to appreciate their authors' accomplishment. Our instinctive deference as a younger nation to the older members of the family, and their frequent snubs, have made us too willing to accept their depreciation of our writers. Actually, "the literature—even the poetic literature—of no country, during the last half-century, is of greater interest to the philosophical student, than that of the United States." Without chauvinist braggadocio, he quietly maintained for our literature an interest and value that its very possessors had been underrating. In poetry, he added, "we have already had the first period of what may be called, for want of a better term, a true American school." Though it had been regional rather than nationwide, it would father a literature of the entire nation. It was not "democratic literature," that will-o'-the-wisp of the pre–Civil War days, that he had in mind; but he believed that art, "under the free system of a democracy," would at least equal the product supported by government patronage.

American criticism, Stedman regretfully admitted, had not kept abreast of authorship. Within his own memory, critics had repeatedly veered from adulation to utter condemnation of American writers; they seemed unable to find a median position. The most sincere critics seemed to be at a loss as to the nature of art, and approached specimens from metaphysical or doctrinaire points of view. Americans were only beginning to see the efficacy in a criticism "which is penetrative and dexterous, but probes only to cure; which enters into the soul and purpose of a work, and considers every factor that makes it what it is;—the criticism which, above all, esteems it a cardinal sin to suffer a verdict to be tainted by private dislike, or by partisanship and the instinct of battle with an opposing clique or school." Though the critics who were practicing this sort of criticism were still occupied almost exclusively with "foreign or recondite subjects"—an implied criticism of Lowell's subjects surely appears here—the beginnings which he could descry would grow steadily until sound critical methods should be applied to American products and pressing literary problems. Such a hope was already being realized in the monthly pronouncements of William Dean Howells in *Harper's*; Howells was among the first to review with intelligent appreciation Stedman's *Poets of America*.

Though Stedman was not an originating critic, he was the first well-equipped man of letters to turn his attention systematically to American literature and the first to examine it on both historical and aesthetic principles. George E. Woodberry's statement that in 1885 Stedman was the only man who could be said to practice criticism in America was very slight exaggeration.

GEORGE EDWARD WOODBERRY

George Edward Woodberry entered Harvard when Lowell was finishing his career as a professor. Lowell became interested in the impecunious undergraduate who aided in cataloguing his library, and in 1891, shortly before he died, recommended the young scholar for the new chair of comparative literature at Columbia University. There for fourteen years Woodberry taught. He established the new department upon the firm basis which has ever since been its characteristic, and inspired in his students, among whom were Joel E. Spingarn and John Erskine, the same love of letters which had been developed in him by Lowell.

Woodberry was a curious combination of characteristics. A Yankee by birth, he learned at Harvard to love the Mediterranean lands and literatures. Spingarn described him as intellectually a frustrated effort to combine the individualism of the transcendentalist, which had inherited a Calvinistic substratum, with the European Platonic and Roman Catholic tradition. In spite of his assertion that Athens was the finest achievement of man and her defeat at Syracuse the great tragedy of history, he was more Hellenistic than Hellenic. In him the classical spirit was overlayed and to some degree alloyed by the demands of scholarship and by the feeling that he was singing the classical song in a strange land. He was excessively attached to tradition. John Macy called him the last of the Lowells instead of the first of the Woodberrys, a man so deeply concerned to transmit the traditional torch that he made no addition to its light. The charge, though not baseless, is somewhat too severe. His strange combination of motive forces, which he denoted his "agnostic, pagan, and Puritan instincts," inevitably produced a novel outlook upon life. In preaching the idealistic gospel of Lowell, he contributed to its several new tenets.

Two characteristic attitudes contributed heavily to his work. His nieces and nephews once decided that his most characteristic expression was the question "Why?" Persistently for all his shyness, he tried to satisfy his curiosity as to the "whys" of life. The second habit was his repeated recognition of likenesses. North Africa reminded him of the plains of Nebraska; a gravelly brook near Taormina took his mind back to the Berkshires. Both New England and North Africa were "marabout-breeding" countries, producing revivals, transcendentalists, and new lights in religion. A curious, imaginative man alert to note resemblances is well equipped to appreciate and criticize what he observes.

The critical problems of interest to Woodberry were those which naturally concern the idealist, particularly the relation between genius and training. Whittier was Nature's demonstration that the die she casts may be better than the diploma of the schools. Had he read Theocritus, he could never have written "Snow-Bound." Genius makes a very little art go a long way. As a rule, however, the greatest poets have been the greatest scholars in the living knowledge of their age. They have firmly grasped literary tradition and the great ideas that concern mankind as well as the great forms in which these ideas have been cast. They have not been professional scholars. Woodberry bewailed the modern shift of scholarship to a near-scientific pursuit, more like law or medicine than an item of civilized culture. The concurrent disappearance of classical studies as the *sine qua non* of scholarship was the greatest single loss to modern culture that Woodberry could envision. The methods of classical study—which he still thought of in Renaissance rather than German terms—might communicate little to the modern man; but he should at least be well read in Greek and Latin literature.

Woodberry declined then to accept the popular American belief in genius without benefit of culture. Once the materials of culture have become part of the artist so that he uses them instinctively, they function as a part of that power which we call genius. The creative faculty uses the entire personality of the artist; in creating literature the mind acts, employing all its powers just as men in other callings perform their functions.

Following Aristotle, Woodberry saw art as a new creation, as "nature regenerate, made perfect, suffering the new birth into what ought to be; an ordered and complete world. . . . The reality that remains in it out of the world that was, is only a residuum; the characteristic part, the vital and illuminating part, is what the artist has brought new-born in his own soul—that which never was before." Art remolds the world like clay to the form the artist's soul desires. Art is therefore freedom, while nature is necessity; art is soul, nature is body; art is spirituality, nature is materialism.

Reasoning in this Platonic-Aristotelian vein and reinforced by Sidney, Wordsworth, and Shelley, Woodberry followed the traditional differentiation between poetry and history in his distinction between scientific and imaginative truth. "Science and philosophy formulate truth and end in the formula; literature, as the saying is, clothes truth in a tale," by the aid of the imagination. He approved with Aristotle the use of historical plots in drama and narrative as wise economy; with well-known characters, much is done for the audience before the story begins. Distance also lends an unreal air to what is gross; the story of Oedipus is relieved by its unreality from much of that crudeness which would make a similar current event too crude for artistic treatment.

On one classical principle, however, Woodberry disagreed with tradition; he denied that impersonality is the mark of the classical artist. Not self-effacement, but universality, produces the so-called classical objectivity. In dealing with universal truth, the author omits his own idiosyncrasies and hobbies, but not his basic personality. Aeschylus no more effaced his personality from his plays than did Shakespeare; both authors are present in all their works with their human characteristics effective rather than their peculiarities. To speak of classical impersonality as opposed to romantic subjectivity seemed to him absurd. The classical tradition as much as the romantic requires that the poet sincerely feel what he writes; how then can he be objective?

Upon another matter of importance to classical theory, Woodberry felt that a change of emphasis had come with the development of the reading public. He insisted upon proper arrangement of parts —"the theory of art is most fixed in the doctrine of order"—and demanded that the work possess organic unity. Upon the relative importance of plot and character, however, he deviated sharply from the accepted interpretation of Aristotle's principle. Interest in action is the interest of the boy or the practical man whose meditative life is barely begun. Once man has begun to meditate, he ceases to be satisfied with action in itself and finds his true interest in what action reveals of the character of the agent. Character in the Greek tragedies was simple, being set forth by its ruling passion; agents were more nearly types than those created later, as in Shakespeare's plays. The more mature mind, he insisted, finds special interest in character because it is more profound than plot. Scott was one of the first to show how character should be presented: being and doing should be fused; Scott "achieves expression in its highest form—the expression of a soul using its human powers in earthly life." He agreed with Aristotle that action, emotion, and thought constitute experience and are the major concerns of the writer. His different emphasis from Aristotle's upon plot and character may be more apparent than real, for it is quite possible that tradition has set a greater gap between the importance of the two in his scheme than he actually intended; and Woodberry realized that Aristotle was writing of characteristics of earlier Greek tragedy and epic, not legislating for all literature.

Artistic purpose and moral precept, Woodberry declared, have always been the two aims of poetry. Somewhat like Yvor Winters, he equated morals with mores, the principles by which men live; and "one can no more imagine life truly without ethics than he can imagine mass without cohesion." Somewhat like Poe, he felt that the moral effect derived from the work is not the major intent of the poet, but derivative from his portrayal of life. Like Poe again, he believed that poetry should gratify those who "take pleasure in loveliness. . . . The direct aim of all art is to please, and to please immediately." The value of the work is in fact not what the author intended but what the reader receives. "It is common enough for the reader to find meanings in a book that the writer did not consciously put there; . . . and moreover, the reader may respond to the work with greater sensitiveness than belonged to the creator and in new ways."

Woodberry's specific critical practice is best observed in his lives of Emerson and Poe, and his editions of Poe and Shelley. He showed himself to be a sympathetic interpreter, appreciative of the author's efforts, and an equitable judge of his attainment. Perhaps his most detailed statement of his critical position occurs in *Two Phases of Criticism, Historical and Aesthetic,* published in 1914 as a response to the recent upsurge of aesthetic criticism under the leadership of his former pupil Joel E. Spingarn. It was a contest of highly qualified scholars on both sides. Woodberry defended that historical approach which Spingarn, though trained in it, had discarded.

Limitation of poetic criticism to the world of aesthetics, Woodberry declared, becomes invalid as soon as the poem is written down. It then becomes a part of the actual world, and therefore subject to judgment and evaluation. Even reputed success of a poem is not final; "it is still pertinent for criticism to inquire into the quality of the success, its value; and I am conservative enough to add that the critic may even ask whether it was right." While aesthetic freedom is a variety of free speech, such freedom does not liberate the poet from judgment of the wisdom or value of what he has said; the freedom implies the probability that he will incur such judgment. In a world that needed so desperately the guidance of reason Woodberry looked to criticism to "declare the judgment of reason on the intellectual and moral values of art."

After his attempt to establish the duty of criticism to judge,

Woodberry proceeded to validate historical criticism. Even if one should accept the aesthetic concept of criticism, that it attempts to re-create the work of art as it was in the mind of the creative artist, this very act places the so-called criticism in the field of history, the past. The only hope of successfully studying the past lies in study of the period and the personality of the author himself; that is, in biographical and historical study. The universal element in all art must be appreciated in the garb it has put on before one can truly enjoy it. The aesthetic critics wanted to reach the dessert before eating the meat and potatoes. The would-be critic, if he is to practice with any scope, must be a scholar versed in the ways of people of all ages who have produced poetry or have contributed to its production. Of course one would like to penetrate the author's mind; but this is extremely difficult to do even with contemporaries. The offerings of the psychological critics he brushed aside as too much concerned with possible pathological states of the author and too little interested in the universal. And if the process is difficult with men of our own time, how can we hope to enter the mind of the Anglo-Saxon Wanderer, the troubadour, or Omar? Whether the critic likes it or not, he must be an historical critic.

He was aware of the danger that historical criticism cease to be the tool and usurp the place of the product; this very dereliction had turned men like Spingarn away from it. But the correction for overemphasis upon historical background is surely not to resort to other ancillary studies like medicine, pathology, sociology, or the subconscious. Woodberry would have the appreciative reader approach the poem adequately prepared to understand its content, evaluate it, and enjoy it. If he remembers that the poem's the thing, he may use to advantage any knowledge that will throw light upon it.

Woodberry showed only occasional interest in the progress of American literature. He was attracted to Hawthorne's and Emerson's work, and he admired Lowell. Poe interested him chiefly as a literary symptom of his time. The great literary tradition occupied his mind almost wholly; his shyness and lack of social connections probably contributed to his unconcern about the literature of his native land. Stedman and Lowell felt deep interest in the growing American literature, a concern which one might expect Woodberry to have shared. John Erskine has noted, it is true, that he tried constantly to open the eyes of his Columbia students to see literature as belonging to the entire world. He kept directing their attention to the possible future America, which would not be regional, nor of any one racial stock, but would amalgamate the energies of all lands and races. It is regrettable that he failed to incorporate his ideal into an intelligent concern with current literary problems as they aided or hindered the realization of his ideal.

His lack of interest in American literature led him at times to superficial judgments. The flowering of New England he attributed to local conditions and to the classical instruction given at Harvard. He failed to note the low grade of classical instruction at Harvard to which the early nineteenth-century graduates had attested; and even more strangely, he ignored the significant awareness of the Bostonians of literary and cultural happenings in Europe. He dismissed the contents of the *Southern Literary Messenger* while Poe was its editor as "exceedingly tame and dreary" except for Poe's own contributions—a statement which examination of those numbers does not support. As for American writers, "all authors have a sponsor": Joaquin Miller found his in Byron, Bret Harte in Dickens, Cooper in Scott. Such a belief indicates that he accepted without much examination charges advanced by bilious Anglophiles of the earlier years. Spingarn has noted that he brushed aside as unimportant the racier writers like Walt Whitman, Thoreau, Mark Twain, and Herman Melville. He declared openly that genius had fled from a barbarous, materialistic America, which because of its lack of idealism could give birth to no poets.

With Woodberry, the school of Lowell came to an inglorious halt, until it had a rebirth in the New Humanists. His indifference to the immediate American literary scene save to condemn it made him unable to contribute greatly to American readers, though he did serve as a reminder to the few who appreciated him that idealism was a tenable literary position.

Chapter 8

The Realists

AFTER THE CIVIL WAR the realism which had been sporadically appearing in America took on new life. Under William Dean Howells and Henry James, characteristics in literature which had appeared in Sylvester Judd's *Margaret* and a few other works made a renewed bid for attention. Lowell and other romantic critics had written in high praise of *Margaret;* but when younger novelists began to make realism the basis of their writing, Lowell could not bring himself to approve of their principle. The movement had to struggle before it found acceptance in America, and it never succeeded in displacing the romance among general readers. It did, however, after some decades of striving, win a commanding position among readers of literary tastes.

WILLIAM DEAN HOWELLS

The credit for the success of realism in America belongs largely to Howells. From 1860 until his death in 1920—perhaps the longest career of any American writer—he published regularly, and before his death he was credited with greater influence upon the American novel than any other person. Largely self-educated, possessing only a smattering of the ancient languages, he remedied this deficiency by careful study of Italian literature and of Greek and Latin authors in German or English translations. He was widely read in the English classics and American authors, and as editor of "The Editor's Study" and "The Editor's Easy Chair" of *Harper's*, he for twenty-five years examined and commented upon a large fraction of the total publication during those years. Though a Midwesterner by birth, he was accepted by the Boston and Cambridge Brahmins. His genuine love and respect for them did not, however, blind him. to their ignorance of changing American mores; as a man of the people he knew his fellow-Americans far more intimately than most of the writers on the staff of the *Atlantic Monthly*. He had no desire to relive the romantic past, and if at times he dreamed of a Utopian future, he kept his eyes optimistically fixed upon the contemporary scene.

Howells' well-known definition of realism as the "truthful treatment of material," by leading one to ask Pilate's question, requires the clarification that can be drawn from his frequent discussions of it. From this material he made one noteworthy excision: though it must be nothing but the truth, it is only that part which his somewhat prudish standards conceded to be fit to print. The reason for this limitation of material was the predominantly feminine audience of the literary periodicals, but it was undoubtedly his own preference as well. Maupassant's literary skill seemed to him inadequate excuse for his indecency; there were many writers whom he would like to take out and step on. He considered the horrible equally unsuitable for these readers.

In his early days as critic for the house of Harper, Howells labored to establish realism as the legitimate successor to the romantic novel. Both had been designed to break down the barriers against aesthetic freedom and to liberate literature from its bondage to tradition. Romanticism had exhausted its powers, and realism must now assert that fidelity to everyday experience and probability of motive that he believed to be essential to a great American literature. In him the preference for the American theme over the foreign did not, as in earlier theorists, outlaw the use of foreign materials too; but the American material needed presentation, and only an American could do it. Howells' realism was in fact a graft upon the earlier romantic novel, differing little in organization and possessing similar universality; it insisted upon naturalness and greater probability of events. Whenever realism simply heaps up facts, "maps life instead of picturing it," it will in its turn perish. If it follows the line marked out for it by Hawthorne, it can be developed indefinitely. Far from being antagonistic to poetry or genuine romance, realism may well in its highest form show the presence of both poetry and romance where readers have never dreamed of their existence. That false romance which left Hawthorne's course, he labelled "romanticistic" and unsparingly attacked.

In attacking false romance, he remarked that while some of us like to see life in literature as it really is, the majority prefer it decked out in spangled tights like the young man on the flying trapeze. "There is a chromo appetite in human nature," he conceded, "which legitimately demands satisfaction. . . . The true criticism will not regard it with contempt but will endeavor to convert it to a taste for higher things." He demanded that this higher fiction cease to lie about life, but portray real men and women, not puppets: "Realism alone has the courage to look life squarely in the face and try to report the expression of its divinely imagined lineaments." He professed inability to see much difference between literature and real life; writing which failed to display true life he suspected of being misnamed literature.

Restrictive tradition chafed him. In an often mentioned apologue in the 1887 "Editor's Study," Howells pictured the traditionalist peeping and entomologizing over a grasshopper. This pseudo-scientist, he remarked, resents as uncultured the attempt to describe it as in itself it really is. He prefers to depict a typical grasshopper, "which has been evolved at considerable pains and expense out of the grasshopper in general," made out of wire and cardboard but conventionally painted and warranted indestructible. It may be artificial but it is that ideal which the artist has been told to cultivate. Books are full of its kind but show hardly a trace of the natural specimen. In such ironic belittling of tradition, most of the fallacies which Howells was fighting appeared: worship of tradition, the assumption that an artificial type is the only ideal, and the notion that the everyday person or event is vulgar and commonplace. Though yet far off, he predicted, the time will come when men everywhere will reject the burden of this pseudo-ideal grasshopper in favor of the real. To reply to such irony puts the defendant in the position of a man tilting at windmills; and the defenders of a dead tradition were at a loss for a reply.

Continuing his campaign, he desired in 1905 that "that luminous word normal" be set before the public immediately. He liked Charles Hanson Towne's courage in calling things by their actual names: why not speak in poetry of the Elevated Road or the Hotel System? Arnold Bennett in *The Old Wives' Tale* constructs admirably credible persons out of his heaped-up details of situation and character. Hamlin Garland's heroes are honest men, and his heroines not "women one would be the better for not having known," because he wisely puts his faith in the good he sees as well as in the evil. Lowell's *Biglow Papers* remain an American classic because they are a superb expression of Yankee character "with nothing false in nature or parlance." His demand for truthful treatment of material remained his prime test of literature his life long.

It was natural that Howells should look with disfavor upon the historical novel for its temptation to write in the false romantic style. Though he admitted that an author could produce the same effect by assimilating the facts of a remote time that he would produce by close observation of contemporary life, the historical setting seemed to him to give an air of superficiality to the representation. *Romola*, though true to human nature and moving naturally and livingly, "is a sufficiently dull and tedious book in some respects, as a historical romance must be." Reade's *The Cloister and the Hearth* is not only a mass of undigested facts but its characters are "capriciously, slightly, and theatrically portrayed." Walter Scott was utterly damned with all the sins of the literary decalogue. By falsifying historical perspective he confused youthful readers about the facts. He blindly worshipped mediaeval ideals; he was tiresomely descriptive and endlessly verbose; "he had no trust in his readers' intuitions but always spelled out everything emotionally for them." He must be presented to that young reader who is never far from Howells' mind with a warning how false and mistaken he often is.

With naturalism he had little sympathy; it merely mapped life instead of picturing it. He disagreed with Zola's theory of the novel as a controlled experiment patterned upon experimental medicine. Frank Norris' novels were selective and poetical. The novel is not a photograph, showing all details, but the naturalists are more concerned with the trees than with the forest as a whole. Moreover, the naturalists are preoccupied with the ugly; many of them seem to regard it as more worthy of representation than the beautiful; they concentrate upon the abnormal, the eccentric, the psychologically diseased, the exaggerated, the pathological. "Why shut the normal out altogether?"

Perhaps his strongest objection to naturalism stems from his prudishness. He frequently referred to "certain nudities which the Latin peoples seem to find edifying." Even when no great harm was done by them—and he thought this to be seldom—they showed the author's lapse in taste. Naturalism "has possessed itself of the good name of realism to befoul it." Howells seems to us nowadays excessively prudish as to what constitutes decency. He felt, however, that circumstances supported his position. American authors who habitually represent people of lax morals as American seemed to him to be untrue in their treatment of material. However the facts stood on the continent, immorality was not characteristic of life here. Even if it were, the nature of the American audience prevented the author's telling the whole truth. Such materials must not be presented to young women. Finally, even conceding that the representation of vice was true of American life and that it would not harm young women to read of it, editors of magazines would not print such portrayals for fear of public sentiment. Howells was a shrewd businessman; he knew that such novels would damage the subscription lists as irretrievably as the morals of the readers.

The aesthetic opposite to naturalism, art for art's sake, was a great though lesser peril to American letters. Howells attacked it in 1886 as a "make-believe Greek theory ... as if the Greekest of the Greek art were not for religion's sake, as the Greeks understood it." Two years later he noted with satisfaction that "the old heathenish axiom of art for art's sake is as dead as great Pan himself." Almost thirty years later, however, he nervously hoped that the vague seeking after beauty of poetry in 1917 did not betoken an abortive revival of the doctrine. Art for art's sake was dead never to return, and those

[167]

who tried to revive it were following after not only false gods but dead ones.

Equally mistaken were those artists who placed undue reliance upon learning and scholarship. Though far from being an obscurantist, he noted with approval in 1890 the American revolt against the notion that literary culture alone produces great literature. The author's excessive interest in such matters "is always tempting him to mistake the outward shape for the vital inward structure, and to prize what has been put in more than what has come out." Lowell had himself warned Howells of the danger in the poet's seeing from too far behind the eyes. Literary knowledge should supplement insight into actual life, not supplant it.

Howells' concept of literature inevitably clashed with the reverential attitude toward established classics. It was nothing new: "whatever is established is sacred with those who do not think." At least three-fifths of the so-called classics "no more lives than the poems and stories that perish monthly in our magazines." A superstitious piety preserves it; but except as reflection of past moods or revelation of the author's character, nobody finds enjoyment in it. Two-thirds of the British classics would be rejected today by a conscientious editor because "they were wanting in form, or wanting in truth, or wanting in art, or wanting in humanity, or wanting in common decency." Howells' obviously overstated attack upon accepted classics was no doubt envenomed by frequent failures to gain approval for realism; yet one can readily see that, like Emerson, he demanded that classical works convince him personally of their quality. He was so far from accepting Lowell's fulsome praise of Shakespeare that he rather conspicuously noted his faults while admiring his virtues. Unreasoning acceptance of Shakespeare would produce merely a horde of imperceptive zealots who admired indiscriminately and a few furious unbelievers who scoffed at his true greatness; not a critic in the field. Let the classics meet the same test that he applied to a new book: "Is it true?—true to the motives, the impulses, the principles that shape the life of actual men and women?" In any case, no classic could replace realism, the spirit of the age, as characteristic as its social, economic, and political circumstances.

Howells opposed also the traditional notion that the poet is "a sort of puissant and very admirable prodigy which God has created out of the common for the astonishment and confusion of the rest of us poor human beings." This attitude first appeared in 1886 in his discussion of statements defending the theory of genius and inspiration by Stedman, W. J. Courthope, and Edmund Gosse. Stedman retorted in his essay "Genius," after which the argument came to a brief lull. In *Criticism and Fiction* (1891), Howells returned to the fray. Belief in genius is a mere superstition, generally mischievous, seldom believed by the very writers who proclaim it. By genius, he suspected, writers meant simply that mastery achieved by any man according to his powers and diligence; poets and novelists excelled most where they worked hardest. Any honest author would admit that doing a work over made it twice as good. Though he once at least admitted that authors are sometimes aware of a mystical power which enabled them to achieve exquisite results, he was, like Castelvetro in the sixteenth century, the apostle of hard work rather than the hierophant of inspiration.

Aside from these literary heresies, Howells was in most respects fairly orthodox. Propriety of diction frequently found him its defender. His journalistic apprenticeship had made him aware of the temptation that newspaper parlance spreads before the author. Though aware of differing levels of proper diction, journalese seemed to him to have no place in literature. He quoted also the example of "the Greeks, who knew pretty well everything" in censuring the uncontrolled emotional outbursts prevalent in popular writing. And he accepted the classical theory of originality, that the new mind gives novelty by its refraction of the idea to the oldest concept. So long as this quality pleases and attracts readers, it matters little whether he breaks new ground or tills old. As Howells realized, such a concept of originality is almost obligatory to the realist.

On the nature and functions of the critic, Howells spoke from long experience with the *Atlantic Monthly* and with *Harper's* Magazine. Stedman had, it seemed to him, come close to being the ideal critic in his *Poets of America*. Such a critic is judicial and to the extent of his knowledge just. He tries peaceably to ascertain the place and qualities of the poet under consideration. His work shows his interest in background material, his quick sympathy, and his unerring pleasure in beauty. He is never harsh or arrogant, and if he censures he is always kindly and observant of the proprieties. Both in his own criticism and in his estimate of other critics, Howells always adhered substantially to the picture here drawn.

Additional details may be found in other pronouncements. He came out strongly for critical frankness, if necessary for candid severity. The editor will not capriciously demand changes, but will leave the contributor to himself so far as possible. He preferred that criticism which neither condemns a poet for his bad work nor acquits him for his good; it should simply point out the genuine poetry in the work along with the prose that has crept in. An author is generally, he said, the best judge of his own work, especially when he condemns it.

The critic must realize that literature is not static but progressive; not the imitation of masterpieces, but the representation of men living and acting. With changing social, political, religious, or economic conditions, the literature which represents men must undergo corresponding changes in order properly to portray them. More and more, criticism "must concern itself with ascertaining currents and tendencies, and not proposing to direct or stop them; more and more it must realize that it is not a censorship." It is scientific, not impressionistic, in its method; as soon as people realize this principle, he dryly remarked, many flourishing critics will be forced out of business because they know only what they like or dislike. The critic will do acceptable service to the public "by observing the traits of our growing literature, by recognizing and registering its facts, and by classifying books as they appear." Howells' practice for twenty-five years of literary comment in *Harper's* was an honest attempt to perform precisely such services for Americans.

In keeping with his concept of literature as a progressive art, Howells accepted the gradual changes in the poetic practice of successive centuries. He noted the advance from the mere metrical form as the criterion through the addition first of thought and feeling, then of elegance and beauty. Thence he traced the shift from the epic to the poetic novel and versified tale of Scott and Byron, and finally to the modern novel, which has supplanted all these in popularity. Each stage of advance, he declared, was justified in spite of its having been a departure from accepted canons, because each was suited to the needs of the age in which it was employed.

A noteworthy instance of his openmindedness was his frequent discussion of free verse—he preferred to call it shredded prose— from 1888 to 1917. He never got over his dislike of it. He did not, on that account rule it out as a poetic form, but gave it careful and, on the whole, fair treatment. Emerson's "beautiful lawlessness" he excused as the consequence of his impatience with smoothness and irregularity; he insisted, however, that a considerable conformity to standard verse forms was the rule with Emerson. In Emily Dickinson's poems he found evidence that "the author spared no pains in the perfect expression of her ideals"; her poems were a distinctive addition to the literature of the world.

It was Whitman and the later writers of free verse that Howells chiefly discussed. Somewhat surprisingly, Whitman's "gospel of nudity" shocked him little; "the judicious pen of the editor" could excise the few offensive lines if the author would permit, and leave the remainder blameless. When in 1889 he noted that the author had shown no readiness to disavow these lines, he merely expressed a mild hope that he soon would omit them. His attention was far more occupied with the form of Whitman's work. "He produced a new kind in literature, which we may or may not allow to be poetry, but which we cannot deny is something eloquent, suggestive, moving, with a lawless, formless beauty of its own." Howells was fairly trapped into this admission; Whitman was doing in his way what Howells was doing in the novel, refusing to do the thing that had repeatedly been done before. It would have been inconsistent in Howells to rule out a fellow-practitioner who held ideas similar to his own.

Within Whitman's work Howells found characteristics which he was free to oppose. American artists, he remarked ironically in 1891, had not arrived upon the literary scene until all the forms had been invented; consequently, nothing was left to their inventive genius except to "discover" formlessness. Since Whitman had exhausted the possibilities in formlessness, nothing but servile imitation was left for his followers. Lacking, then, any national form for our literature, our best refuge now is to be national in spirit and ideal. In this respect, both Whitman and Longfellow had been American and truly original. Each illustrates one of our prevalent national moods; their modes of expression have nothing to do with their nationalism. He admitted that meterless rhythm can express poetry superior to some metered verse—Macpherson's *Ossian,* for example, was superior to Samuel Johnson's verse. As a rule, however, meterless poetry seemed to him unnecessarily to sacrifice many legitimate poetic advantages, to be "cavalry fighting as infantry."

Later writers of free verse fared no better than Whitman. Amy Lowell best showed her poetic capacity when she employed rhyme and measure. The formlessness of Edgar Lee Masters contributed nothing to his expression. James Oppenheim and John Gould Fletcher apparently wanted not to sing their songs but to talk them. If free verse had come to stay, he admitted, no opposition could oust it; but though interesting as an experiment, it failed to convince him that it had permanent value. His courteous restraint in opposing what he actively disliked, and his eagerness to give it a fair trial, are a credit to his tolerance. But his delighted note in 1917 that the new verse had largely stopped "stumping along on the prose feet of free verse" indicated where his heart set him in the debate.

The critic, who must progress with the art he evaluates, combines historian and scientist. "His office is mainly to ascertain facts and traits of literature, not to invent or denounce them; to discover principles, not to establish them; to report, not to create. . . . Aesthetically or specifically we critics are of no use, and . . . we are only useful historically; . . . we may register laws, but not enact them." The critic is like the policeman who exercises his function upon the *corpus delicti:* the crime has already been committed. It is usually too late for him to save the author; in fact, criticism has not made for greater works of art: "the greatest books seem to have come first." Under this circumstance, criticism can only hope to edify the reader, though it may thus indirectly, by enlarging or diminishing his audience, sway the author in subsequent compositions. In all his comments, the critic will remember that an author must freely develop along his own lines; he cannot be rerouted into some course preferred by the critic, but can only be shown how better to follow his own bent.

Howells looked with a jaundiced eye upon current criticism. It was bad, falsely principled, and conditioned in evil. Critics in 1890 were almost without principle, and the anonymity of most reviewers gave these conscienceless men a free rein. For principle, many reviewers substituted so-called literary laws that would force literature to travel in a vicious circle, never going beyond the point of departure. By 1911, in swinging from barbarity, critics had arrived at its opposite evil of fulsome praise. Critics were learning their art at the feet of the advertisers; they dealt in superlatives. Reviewers, moreover, were by 1912 so restricted in space that they could present only one aspect of a book to the reader. They could hope only to interest the reader sufficiently to make him read the book for himself. Such conditions were the ruin of just judgment.

The *fin de siècle* American critic found Howells an unsparing castigator. Sometimes, acting under instructions from an editor, this reviewer "denounces because it is the tradition of his publication to do so." He passes quickly from censuring a work to censuring its author, and feels it his privilege to "assail with bitterness and obloquy those who differ with him in matters of taste and opinion." He has no principles, only an assortment of prejudices, which he intolerantly parades as final judgments. He unhesitatingly misstates the position of anyone with whom he disagrees, only to attack his opponent for what he had never actually said. Then, turning abruptly to the palliating circumstances that had produced this impotent critic, Howells ascribed his vitriolic nature more to ignorance, with the fear which it breeds, than to malevolence. A far better-informed reviewer, he adds, would be incapable of examining the number and variety of books which the American critic is required to pass in review; the only cause for surprise is that he is not even worse than he is. Glowing exceptions were Stedman, Lowell, and E. P. Whipple. Later, he ranked William Crary Brownell with the French and above the British critics.

This unusually passionate attack upon reviewers followed prolonged opposition to his realistic novels in the reviews. Three years later, when his irritation had evidently died down, he asserted that the American standard was as high as any in the world. As proof, he offered to compare an average review in the Sunday papers with the really capable criticism of the heyday of British reviewing. American literature and criticism were both advancing in the right direction. By 1912 he declared that our criticism was more intelligent and better mannered than it had been nine years earlier, while the public had kept abreast of it in intelligence and breadth of reading.

Upon the hardy perennial question of nationalism, Howells spoke significantly. We may as well admit, he wrote in 1891, that our literature is American-English, just as English literature is English-European. To expect 100 per cent American literature from a hyphenated source was preposterous. Furthermore, as Longfellow and other earlier writers had declared, "the great things in literature nowadays are not the national features, but the universal." To demand that our writers be anything but universal was to limit them to mediocrity by ruling out the greatest themes. By being as universal as they can in their outlook and at the same time writing naturally, they will write "as Americanly as possible."

That near relation of nationalism which had sprung up in the nineteenth century, the demand for the great American novel, found in Howells no encouragement. In 1891, he facetiously remarked that all America could only be expressed in a novel conceived in encyclopaedic proportions, "with a force of novelists apportioned on the basis of our Congressional representation, and working under one editorial direction." Twenty years later, he declared more seriously that the novel of the United States would never be written, and would be not worth reading if it could be written. It was less a possibility in the United States than in most other countries. Literature proceeds from the provincial through the national to the universal; and Americans, the most decentralized people in the world, had never yet achieved in culture any stage beyond the provincial. Our novelists are born in some locality to which they remain attached; and unless some genius can contrive to be born all over the nation, his regional outlook will fatally limit him from national scope. The humorous note is evidence that Howells did not intend to be taken too seriously. He considered the pother over the great American novel a waste of time, and reduced it to an absurdity in order to laugh it off the stage. He never actually doubted the future of American letters as a part of world culture.

It seems fitting to conclude the discussion of Howells' criticism on this mock-serious note. Much of his success in molding literary opinion came through his urbane humor. It frequently penetrated beneath the specious surface to open diseased spots; and if at times it touched a nerve, the obvious kindliness and good intent of the critic deadened the pain. He wrote to the people as one of them, not set apart by class or formal education from the average man. His intense patriotism and genuine love of everyday America enabled him not only to depict it but to prescribe for it in literary matters. He could sugar-coat the pill of adverse criticism with optimism for the future. Few men have exerted a wider, none a longer, influence upon American letters; from few men have we received more consistently beneficial advice.

Henry James

In Henry James, Howells had a fellow-laborer for realism. Though disagreeing with him in important details, James demonstrated by theory and by practice the values of realism over romance on the one hand and naturalism on the other. In addition to a notable body of critical essays, he late in life wrote for the novels in his definitive New York edition prefaces designed as a *vade mecum* for the novelist and the attentive reader. For this literary discussion he was well prepared. His environment as a boy and his years abroad gave him a cultured, international point of view which few American critics except Lowell possessed. Recent study shows, too, that James built these advantages upon a far stronger foundation of ancient classical literary theory and practice than had previously been supposed. With these unusually combined qualifications, he ably defended the ramparts of realism.

"The celebrated distinction between the novel and the romance," which had concerned Simms and Howells, seemed to James to have little basis in reality. There were simply two classes of novel: the good and the bad. As he explained in his preface to *The American*, strangeness and distance do not make romantic situations; they are the currently unknown, but not the unknowable. He defined as romantic things we can never directly know, which can reach us only through our thoughts and desires. The real is that which, whether presently known or not, is within the bounds of our first-hand knowledge. The varieties of the romance—the adventurous, the cloak-and-dagger, the historical—are all reducible to the principle that the protagonist should face the bright eyes of danger, successfully if possible, manfully in all cases. Now pursuit of danger is one phase of pursuit of life itself, which is the avowed purpose of realism. The only general attribute of romance is in dealing with experience liberated from the restraints of actual life. Inasmuch as readers have "a sense of the way things happen," this liberation is likely to rouse their objection unless they have been artfully drugged so as to make them accept the impossible as actual. James is not hospitable to Coleridge's request for the willing suspension of disbelief for a season. Since this kind of writing does not represent life on any actual level, James implied without actually asserting it, these so-called romances are simply bad novels. "There are two kinds of taste in the appreciation of imaginative literature: the taste for emotions of surprise and the taste for emotions of recognition." Life is recognizable, and the element of surprise in it is relatively small. The true novel will employ the unexpected, to be sure, but it will primarily cater to the emotions roused by recognition.

The novel, then, as James envisaged it, was "a picture of the actual, of the characteristic—a study of human types and passions, of the evolution of personal relations." It was not an "excision from life," but a representation of life as it logically may be expected to be. James strongly opposed the superstition shared by Victorian novelists that the sentimental key unlocked the door to all experience. Such an approach to life was "shamelessly 'dodgy,'" and could not be authentic; it was romantic in the worst sense. The material of the novel is the stuff that life is made of, though not the factual record of it. The novel's success may be measured by the amount of illusion of reality it produces; "that illusion makes it appear to us for the time that we have lived another life—that we have had a miraculous enlargement of experience." But it is experience on the level of actuality.

In the novel genuine life is deepened as well as enlarged. Mere ability to keep our curiosity alive is not enough. While it requires skill to picture "the multitudinous, adventurous experience of the senses" as Daudet and Maupassant have done, much greater and rarer is the power to depict "the deeper, stranger, subtler inward life, the wonderful adventures of the soul." This spiritual insight creates a work true to human nature and to life. Often recognizably like some actual event, it is still a new body and soul after Aristotle's conception of artistic imitation.

"The only reason for the existence of a novel," James wrote, "is that it does attempt to represent life." It resembles painting, an art which James had studied; and both novel and painting resemble history. The novelist differs from the epic poet, as Walter Scott should have seen, in that the novelist is not without obligation to historic truth. The novelist must convince his readers by an illusion of reality, without apologetic comment that his work is make-believe prearranged by the artist. He may of course—a common fault today—fall on the other side and be half-smothered by the historian in him. To escape both Scylla and Charybdis, he must steer a median course between them.

The realist treats his agents as he treats his facts: both are generalized though at the same time they remain clear and specific. To portray characters, he must understand character, possess "that extensive human sympathy, that easy understanding of character at large, that familiarity with man, from which a novelist draws his real inspiration, from which he borrows all his ideal lines and hues, to which he appeals for a blessing on his fictitious process, and to which he owes it that, firm locked in the tissue of the most rigid prose, he is still more or less of a poet." An author's paramount charge is the cure of souls. "Let him look to his characters; his *figures* will take care of themselves." They must be animate beings, however, not merely clothed dolls, if the reader is to show interest in them. James objected to Hawthorne's people in *The Scarlet Letter* in that they were all representations of the same state of mind, while those in *The House of the Seven Gables* "are all figures rather than characters—they are all pictures rather than persons." On the opposite extremes, Dickens' people are particularized but not generalized; "we do not feel their continuity with the rest of humanity." In short, James's characters, like those Aristotle noted in the drama, should be true to type yet at the same time individual.

"Art," James continued in the classical vein, "is essentially selection, but it is a selection whose main care is to be typical, to be inclusive." Balzac's descriptions depict objects only in so far as they bear upon the action; and incidents too should be selected for their contribution to the general effect. The most interesting problem facing the artist is to convey all the sense without all the substance. The result, as well as the method, is in the radical sense of the word exquisite. Life is inclusion and confusion; art is choice and selection in order to find and use what will convey the hidden value which alone is its concern. All else is excess.

With this concern for selectivity, James inevitably looked with distaste upon naturalism. After severely censuring many shortcomings of Trollope, he added unexpectedly that Trollope "tells us, on the whole, more about life than the 'naturalists' in our sister republic." These members of the new French school have visited many corners and touched upon many subjects which Trollope ignores; yet his perception of character is more exact and wide than theirs. James's objection to naturalism, as Morris Roberts has shown, is that it lacks what makes art attractive—significance, as well as insight, humanity, and a taste for the supersensible. The naturalistic predilection for the debased and ugly seemed to him not only one-sided but seriously disproportioned. If one looks steadfastly at the carnal side of man, it naturally seems the most characteristic. "The more you look at the other, the less the whole business to which French novelists have ever appeared to English readers to give a disproportionate place—the business, as I may say, of the senses—will strike you as the only typical one."

The naturalistic "slice of life" was, if anything, even more repellent to him. The slice, he remarked, tried to butter itself thick and spread on jam to attract and satisfy us; but the spread is manna from another heaven than that of invention. From a happy-go-lucky way of working, nothing artistic or trustworthy can proceed. As Morton Zabel has pointed out, the perils of the various sorts of naturalism had between 1880 and World War I entrapped many British and American novelists, and James was one of the earliest major prophets to proclaim the need for selective taste and literary form.

James's concept of art, Morris Roberts has also pointed out, accepts the traditional view that art is method. Roberts has assembled evidence of James's condemnation of Tolstoy, Dostoevski, Balzac, and Robert Louis Stevenson as in varying ways deficient in form and method. He might have added to the list Swinburne, whose *Chastelard* James complained had no backbone, and Arnold Bennett, whose novels seemed to him amorphous. "A dramatic work without design," he declared, "is a monstrosity"; and he applied this principle to other forms as well. Among realistic works, *Madame Bovary* was his instance of perfection in form. Though it deals with sordid, unrefined matters, "the work is a classic because the thing, such as it is, is ideally *done*, and because it shows that in such doing eternal beauty may dwell." James was so entranced by method and form that R. P. Blackmur has with some plausibility accused him of delighting in a complicated effect where simpler handling of the problem would have served as well.

Included in design is of course the plot or action. In an early review James echoed Aristotle, "The soul of a novel is its action." By their doing and suffering the agents best displayed the depths of their character. Mere complexities of plot may entertain "those jolly barbarians of taste who read novels only for what they call the 'story' "; but without ideas and depiction of character such a work is "a very bad book." The plot must grow naturally, with no indication of artifice, out of the agents and the situation; it must be closely knit in causal relationships; and it must come to a necessary or probable conclusion. Parts and whole must harmonize and work smoothly together, for the novel is an organism.

In line with Goethe's famous dictum, James insisted upon the right of the author to choose his story. More exactly, his story comes to him—perhaps out of his subconscious mind—as the germ of an idea. This he must work up after letting it lie fallow for a time; the function of a germ is to germinate. The subject chosen is of the highest significance; James wished authors to use only the richest. The first criterion in choosing it is, however, its value in the author's eyes; he must please himself with it, in the hope of pleasing many discriminating readers as well.

In handling his subject the author must be fully objective. He joined Howells in condemning Thackeray and Trollope for their asides to the reader in which they expounded their personal feelings as in the parabasis of the Old Greek Comedy, or gave their reasons for giving the story some turn of development. Objectionable as in many respects he found Zola's work, his detached attitude was highly commendable. Balzac offered him a more congenial model for objectivity. His story "stands complete before his mind's eye"; he sees "his figures clearly and fully as with the eye of sense" and therefore can present them to the reader in minute detail. Such clear, objective vision conveys that illusion of reality without which the novel is so much dross.

In demanding that the novel represent life, James had to face the age-old questions of decency and of the didactic uses of the novel. Early in life he declared that "intelligent realism, in art, carries with it its own morality." The measure of a novel's merit is its truth to something "however questionable that thing may be in point of morals or taste." Richardson, Fielding, and Smollett are "emphatically preachers and moralists"; only with *Waverley* do we begin to find novels that undertook to prove nothing but facts, however sentimentalized. This attempt to prove something through the novel is as harmful to the novel as it usually proves disastrous to the theory. The reader's illusion is rudely shattered by the sudden realization that "he is, after all, learning a moral lesson." Yet some natural sense of morality, even of a false morality, is vitally essential to the novelist. The negative morality of British novelists is better than the amorality of the French. To James, morality was not convention but a way of life. The novelist with no morality—one might almost say no mores—lacked all conception of the orderliness of life. "It is as difficult to describe an action without glancing at its moral history, as it is to describe a motive without glancing at its practical consequence."

As to conventional morality, James was far more liberal than

Howells or indeed most American writers of his age. To the charges that the plays of Dumas *fils* showed great moral impropriety, he replied that silence on such matters was hardly constructive: "Whereas we like to be good, the French like to be better. We like to be moral, they like to moralize." Our writers avoid reflection as "a practice of course essentially indelicate, as it speedily brings us face to face with scandal and even with evil." He conceded that British and American writers catered to a youthful audience for whom some restraints in subject were advisable. He admitted the right of society to set up certain taboos that vary with the society which established them. Within such limits as society permitted the artist to range, he felt, questions of morality will not greatly concern the artist. Their settlement lies outside his bailiwick as an artist. He reminded his readers, however, that moral quality does not determine the greatness of the work. No superficial mind will ever produce a great work; and the mind that can learn the causes of things will go far deeper than any sphere where morals reign.

Where convention had not clearly marked the limits, morality seemed to him to consist in the avoidance of grossness. Though he abhorred prudishness, his strong sense of decency barred the obscene. Propriety was a mean somewhere between these two extremes. If the author's tale requires mention of immorality, "he will speak without intellectual prudery and without bravado." He will not hesitate to call a spade a spade, but will treat it objectively as an element of life which a true picture cannot delete. Such statements are in no way pornographic or objectionable to the thinking man in any society.

James saw indecency in literature as a danger to literary art no less than to public morals. When complete licence is granted to the writer, indecency tends to swallow up all else; truth is first sacrificed, then beauty, to sensationalism; James wondered whether the partial misrepresentation of life in the English novel by prudish omissions were not more truthful than the out-of-balance picture in the "novels of passion." To the claim that such novels in portraying "the absolute ravage of Venus" present a moral lesson, he responded that he was concerned with the fable, not the moral. For English audiences at least, love presented under such trappings bore no resemblance to the emotion recognized in English life—a position like that of Howells with the prudery extracted. He doubted moreover whether it was the emotion generally so called on the Continent. Such novels, instead of showing the innermost meaning of life, expose us to a new kind of literary vulgarity of which life already gives us enough specimens. As untrue representations of what life really is, they are bad novels.

Most of what has been reported of James's literary theory belongs equally to his critical principles. So far as possible, the critic should enjoy the freedom of the creative artist. He is, however, restricted by the book which he has undertaken to examine. He is reviewing that book, not writing a dissertation upon the subject, as was formerly the case. In analyzing and evaluating the book, however, he is not bound by any principle, doctrine, dogma, or party allegiance.

James recognized two levels of criticism, the great, represented by Goethe, which verges upon philosophy, and the small, practiced notably by Sainte-Beuve, which deals with specific matters. If a dash of the philosophical view be added to the lower-level criticism, the acme of criticism is reached. James was fully appreciative of historical criticism like Sainte-Beuve's, provided that in the term noun and adjective rigidly keep their respective values. When they are reversed, as in Taine, we find not a critic but a historian. Instead of discriminating minute shades of difference, he focuses his vision upon generalizations, and is too eager to prove his theory to preserve the vital objectivity. The critic best uses his ability to see minute differences when he retraces the course of the man of letters. He must "repair the inevitable small injustices committed by other writers," and restore "the perverted balance of truth." It is hardly surprising that James considered the true critic a very rare specimen.

Having presented the author's work with such adjustments as are needed to show it in true perspective, the critic must also evaluate it. Sainte-Beuve having consistently avoided judgments of value, the precedence must be given to M. Scherer, in whose works one sees active the capacity to distinguish beauty from ugliness, aesthetic right from wrong, and moral good from moral evil. Sainte-Beuve and Scherer, taken together, compose that "compromise between the philosopher and the historian" which forms the true critic.

James's most comprehensive statement of the critic's nature oc-curs in his essay "Criticism." In terms that go far beyond Walter Pater's impressionism, he would have the critic project himself, feel until he understands, and understand so well that he can say. His perception remains objective even "at the pitch of passion," and he is "infinitely curious and incorrigibly patient, and yet plastic and in-flammable and determinable, stooping to conquer and serving to direct." When one adds to this capacity to receive and disengage impressions the ability to evaluate them, it becomes clear that James has incorporated the best of impressionism with sound judicial qualities.

In such a practitioner, the prime office of criticism is not what Turgenev imagined it, not the mere "amusement, the exercise, the subsistence of the critic." Nor is it what its lower manifestations some-times make it seem, "an unprecedented invention for darkening coun-sel." Its effect is rather "to make our absorption and our enjoyment of the things that feed the mind as aware of itself as possible." This awareness stirs the mind, which as its interests ramify wanders farther and farther for pasture; the process is steadily educative. As the process continues, the demand for refinement and for those matters which can be refined more than most becomes for us of the greatest importance. "Then we cease to be only instinctive and at the mercy of chance, feeling that we can ourselves take a hand in our satisfaction and provide for it, making ourselves safe against dearth, and through the door of that perception criticism enters, if we but give it time, as a flood, the great flood of awareness." For James, criticism is first of all a process of self-culture; one becomes more humane, more tastefully perceptive, before he feels prepared to disseminate his gains among his fellows.

The method of James's criticism is comparison: "it may be said that the study of connections is the recognized function of intelligent criticism." Examination of a book by itself can demonstrate some-thing of the talent and character of its author in kind, but only in its relations to other books can its degree of quality be discovered. Comparison opens up also other qualities of the book, for the view widens to include not merely the specimen but its genre, other related genres, other related arts, the culture of the nation, possibly the culture of the world. The imprint of Diotima's discourse in Plato's *Symposium* is as deeply stamped here as is that of Aristotle in other aspects of James's thinking.

Such intense application, it need hardly be added, is merited only by books with content to validate the labor. With the American and British scramble to notice every book published, James had little patience. They manage these things better in France, where they "publish hundreds of books which are never noticed at all." When the French reviewer deigns to criticize a book, he "handles the subject with finer finger-tips." Our critics blunder in a rough-and-ready way into their task, so that it is remarkable that a work of art survives their clumsy touch at all. The French by noticing only the best have materially raised the level of the novel; in England, where all works receive notice, the flood of novels has overwhelmed the incompetent critics with its bubbling and noisy waves. At best, the English reviewer points to the matters of interest in his subject, but has no conception what is the nature of that interest; he cannot disengage it and make it known. "Is this all?" James asked. If so, it is not enough. Mere response to stimuli is not a testing or evaluating of literature.

James, then, tried to impress upon English and American writers and readers the artistic nature of the novel as a means to picture the depths of life, not merely the surface. Into this conception he tried to fit the various problems faced by artist and critic in order to present a rounded, harmonious theory of the novel as an instrument in the widening of man's humane experience. It was unfortunate that he paid so little attention to American letters; yet he contributed greatly to future readers and authors by his appreciation and evaluation of the life and letters of the Continent. Americans needed just such a mediator as James to present to them the French gospel of art in a form applicable to the Anglo-Saxon world.

MINOR REALISTS

Howells and James were supported in their campaign for realism by many lesser writers. *Harper's* Magazine and the *Atlantic Monthly* both exerted their considerable influence in its favor. Both periodicals fostered the belief that character is more interesting in a novel than action, and from this position they naturally were led to support the truthful treatment of material about men. The 1859 *Atlantic* declared: "We cannot know too much about men. No man's life is so uneventful as to be incapable of amusing and instructing. The same event is never the same to more than one person; no two see it from the same point of view. And as we want to know men more than incidents, every one's record of trifles is useful." Another reviewer of a realistic novel that ended in a stereotyped romanticism wrote that it began in the spirit of Jane Austen but ended in that of Jane Porter. A third reviewer praised J. T. Trowbridge's *Neighbor Jackwood* because parts of it "were as full of honest human nature as those of the conventional modern novel are empty of it." Realistic writers, he added, should avoid Dickens' error of inserting unessential detail: "to be graphic is to tell most with fewest penstrokes, and to be poetical is to suggest the particular in the universal." Already the coming plethora of detail characteristic of later naturalistic novels was under fire.

The *Atlantic* gave space also to the opponents of realism. In 1860 a writer declared it "all bosh" to assert that Nature in New England is the same as nature anywhere. Lacking the centuries of habitation in lands where "the whole atmosphere of thought is hazy with the Indian summer of tradition," New England gave an infertile soil for writing. The Puritans had in breaking the ties with the Old World disinherited their descendants of that past which is essential to literature. "Not a single stage-property of poetry did they bring with them but the good old Devil, with his graminivorous attributes, and even he could not stand the climate. Neither horn nor hoof nor tail of him has been seen for half a century. He is as dead as the goat-footed Pan, whom he succeeded, and we tenderly regret him." How could the truthful treatment of such unliterary material produce literature?

James Eliot Cabot presented more serious arguments against the realistic desire to copy nature. He complained of their "pious tenderness towards barns and rail-fences and stone walls and the confused monotony of the forest, not as having any special fitness, but because they exist." "This slippery word, Nature" can be all things to all men. To the realist with photographic tendencies, the scene appears as if its components were fixed quantities. He forgets that the same forest will be to one man merely firewood, to another an arboretum, to a third a workshop, to a fourth a poem. The artistic genius is not measured—as Hawthorne had also argued in *The Marble Faun*— by his fidelity in reproducing objects, but by the depth to which he has penetrated them. "The test of 'truth,' therefore, in the sense of fact, is insufficient. The question is, Truth for whom? Not for a child or a savage. . . . We demand to be raised above our habitual point of view, and be made aware of a deeper interest than we know of."

Cabot's well-thought-out argument should be construed not as hostile to realism, but as corrective of its superficiality. As a reviewer of Longfellow's translation of the *Divine Comedy* remarked in 1867, "there is a wide difference between genuine realism and that literalism which is sometimes mistaken for it,—as wide as the difference between truth and fact, between the spirit and the letter." Between true realism and the standards of a romanticist like Lowell, the difference lies chiefly in the material to be presented, very little in the method of presentation.

As the century drew nearer to its close, writers on realism became increasingly aware of that naturalism which maps life instead of artistically imitating it. *The Nation* in 1880, admitting that the well-organized plot shows a more orderly progress from cause to effect than is seen in nature, declared that a report of events as they occurred in life would differ in no way from the columns of a newspaper. The conservative O. B. Frothingham insisted that though art will accept truth in the form of beauty, its quest is for beauty instead of truth. Like Diotima in Plato's *Symposium*, he declared that beauty rises in successive levels of manifestation from the sensual to the sensuous, the intellectual, and the imaginative, until the highest poetic attainment is reached. The average realist, he feared, would be lucky to attain the second level.

Charles Dudley Warner asserted in 1883 that since art differs from nature in selecting and arranging its data, "one of the worst characteristics of modern fiction is its so-called truth to nature."

Although current psychology might warrant some sacrifice of plot for greater intellectual entertainment, portrayal of character is a means to develop the story, not an end. "The highest fiction . . . embodies both; that is, the story in which action is the result of mental and spiritual forces at play." If the pessimism of current novelists showed mental and spiritual forces as they were, he concluded sadly, America was "in an irredeemably bad way."

John Burroughs, a popular commentator, tried to resolve the quarrel between realists and idealists by declaring that, provided the result be literature, it matters little whence the author draws his materials. They are "only a means to an end, . . . not the literal truth, but the ideal truth. . . . The artist must give us a true picture, but he must give us more than that; he must give us himself." Hamilton Wright Mabie added in 1892 that the work of art should "discover its connection with an ultimate order to which every real expression of man's soul bears witness." H. H. Boyesen asserted that the romantic spirit had never been indigenous to America; if Americans had not left it to chronicle their own social conditions, they would never have developed a literature worthy of serious consideration. So ran the demands for an idealized realism.

A dissenting vote to this chorus was sounded in 1894 by Hamlin Garland in his theory of "veritism." Veritism is the result of a passion for truth and individual expression caused by observation of "the verities," not derived from any theory. Its writer needs a powerful, sincere, emotional concept of life and the power to convey his concept to others. Putting aside all models, the veritist stands on his own feet, except of course for subconscious influences over which he has no control. "The past is dead, and the future can be trusted to look after itself"; the present is his sole theme. Unlike the idealizing writer, he looks for the specific and peculiar, not the characteristic or universal: "difference, not similarity, is the vitalizing quality, there is no sorrow at change." His little book *Crumbling Idols* survives, like his theory, only as a literary curiosity. Veritism may, however, be considered a small weight added to the cause of the coming naturalism.

The attempt of many realists to heap up needless details, another foreshadowing of naturalism, was attacked from slightly different angles by Hiram Corson and Paul Shorey. Writing from the scholar's point of view, Corson warned readers that details must be responsive to the informing life of the work in which they appear. The author who begins by contemplating details usually assumes that they may be studied per se, and therefore is incompetent to gauge accurately their relation to the work as a whole. In 1896, the classicist Paul Shorey described the "new spirit" in literature as a foredoomed attempt to write a democratic literature—this catchword of the 'forties cast a long shadow indeed—that would not "idealize or schematize life" but "paint it with relentless fidelity and analyze it with scientific precision." The common man, he added dryly, will continue to read the newspapers; "little as he may care for Wordsworth or Milton, the veritist novel of the day leaves him still more indifferent." Literature for the common man, if read at all, will not find him reading it.

At the turn of the century there appeared a strong champion of realism in Frank Norris. In phrases foreshadowing the nervous journalese of Mencken, he defended the realistic novel as the true expression of modern life. It alone conveys the true picture and quality of the times. No veritist, he wrote for realism with the crusading zeal of a missionary. "The people have a right to the Truth as they have a right to life, liberty, and the pursuit of happiness. It is *not* right that they be exploited and deceived with false views of life, false characters, false sentiment, false morality, false history, false philosophy, false emotions, false heroism, false notions of self-sacrifice, false views of religion, of duty, of conduct and of manners." He did not seek "the Realism of mere externals (the copyists have that), but the Realism of motives and emotions." His storyteller should tell not what life factually is but what it looks like to an interested, intelligent, impressionable man. What reasonably might have happened is, for literary purposes, true; even the historical novel, written on these principles is acceptable realism. What is desired is to get at the life—an immensely difficult task, because the artist is not only close to the canvas but is himself in the picture.

Prosser Frye in 1908 expressed the median position occupied by many of the critics. The best training for the novelist is not a system but experience. The give-and-take of life lets the hard facts batter their way to recognition. Trained by this life, the novelist's ideas come from the world itself already embedded in individual examples. The rearrangement and classification of his knowledge is his own, not made by some set formula. But, however satisfying and flattering it was to an age not conspicuous for imagination or sensibility to assume these qualities to be frivolous, something more than a documentary report on the details of life is needed—the conception of a moral principle active in the affairs of men. The determinism that was creeping into realistic literature allowed only for representation of the hard facts; it gave no scope for insight into their significance. The determinists were, however, too well established to yield to any such compromise; and realism as a force passed over into naturalism. Such a movement was, under the circumstances, almost inevitable: an age that had abandoned orthodox Christianity and supernaturalism for a mechanistic view of the universe, which its pessimism rendered palatable as well as seemingly scientifically supported, would hardly be satisfied with the realism of a Howells or a James.

The uniformly hostile reception of naturalism in the United States was based almost entirely upon its subject matter first, and only subsequently upon its form. The reviews of Swinburne's *Laus Veneris* in 1866 forecast by their horror at its immorality the reception Zola was to receive a few years later. Zola in the minds of most Americans stood for naturalism and his work was everywhere excoriated. Sidney Lanier declared that Zola was "defiling the whole earth and slandering all humanity under the sacred names of 'naturalism,' of 'science,' of 'physiology.' " Lanier's attack was directed particularly against Zola's celebrated treatise, *Le roman experimental,* in which the French writer attempted to apply the methods of experimental medicine to the novel. Lanier denied that Zola's realistic bits of observation in hospitals constituted the use of controlled experiment; even if such an "experimental" novel could be written, it would be no more a work of art than Huxley's treatise on the crayfish.

Others joined the onslaught on Zola. The 1881 *Atlantic* remarked that Zola had merely succeeded in knocking out the legs from under the romantic school. Thomas Sergeant Perry declared: "There is hardly an expression of his own opinion in the whole book [*Nana*]. . . . He simply takes down the side of the house,—a disorderly house,—and lets the reader see and hear what is going on under its roof." The workmanship, indeed, was skilfully done; but DeFoe and Swift had invented the form before Zola and had used it to give a rounded picture of life. Zola had omitted all the honorable data from his account. O. B. Frothingham classed Zola's stories with the tales of Boccaccio or Marguerite de Navarre: historically interesting accounts of a decadent, alien period, but not representative of what could happen here. Like unwholesome insects they were confined to certain climates and localities, but would quickly perish when transplanted.

One can see that on account of its emphasis upon the gross and depraved and its lack of an artistic conception of life, naturalism before the twentieth century found little but opposition in the American magazines. Its objectivity, though in part commended, was too factual and lacking in ideal insight to please American thinkers. Its reduction of life to a deterministic level repelled a nation proud of its initiative and free enterprise. And since it was regarded as a debased form of realism, the cause of realism suffered from its alleged shortcomings in spite of efforts by Howells and others to dissociate themselves from it. During the 1890's indeed, the adherents of romanticism were convinced that realism was doomed. William Roscoe Thayer in 1894 declared that the success of Hall Caine, Arthur Conan Doyle, S. R. Crockett, and Rudyard Kipling sounded the knell not only of realism but of "Zola's plausible fallacy" too.

By 1900, in spite of all opposition, realism was well established as the form expressive of the later nineteenth century. The idealists were still holding their own in a sort of literary compromise with the factual writers. Among the general public, romantic novels on all sorts of levels were still preferred reading.

Chapter 9

Other Late-Century Movements

WHILE THE BATTLE OF REALISM was raging, another school of literary theory and a significant literary development provided skirmishes for theorists and writers. The impressionistic approach to literature and the regional treatment of the American scene both had their adherents. Both were of considerable importance in their own day, and both were to reappear vigorously in the twentieth century.

IMPRESSIONISM

Walter Pater's studies in the Renaissance touched off a considerable discussion upon its appearance in 1873. After the book's glamor has dissipated, the *Nation* declared, the reader will give up his first impression that Pater deserves a place among the best critics. "*Diletto* rather than *cognosco* is the root of his thinking." He can contribute mere assumptions without a sound basis of artistic thought. "It is the unreasoning and generally unreasonable expression of individual preferences and tastes, which may to-day be adopted as the standard from the personal prestige of the holder and to-morrow be rejected because another has supplanted him." Art is not whatever one chooses; it can be reduced to laws and defined. Pater has correctly noted that at the instant of enjoying the artistic experience only the most highly trained and specially fitted minds can simultaneously analyze this experience; but he has assumed this response to be all of criticism, that rules have no possible place in it.

A writer in the 1879 *Nation* deplored the attitude of the contemporary self-made critic in considering art purely a matter of individual taste; he felt the need of critics who know "as much of the subject as at least a clumsy surgeon knows of the anatomy of a limb he must operate on." Evidently some untrained reviewers, forgetful of Pater's restriction of the valid intuitive response to specially fitted minds, were using his impressionism as a shelter for their ignorance. Agnes Repplier in 1887 found also that the incompetent American critics were young men who presumed to judge with no knowledge of the classics or the continuity of literature.

Among the defenders of impressionism William Peterfield Trent and John Burroughs were conspicuous. Trent in 1899 divided critics into teachers, concerned to preserve the power of authority, and reporters, attracted to individualistic, impressionistic criticism because it possessed novelty and was therefore news. The latter usually possessed the broader culture, were more up-to-date in their interests, and were better able than the traditionalists to discuss the so-called "unclosed genres" like the novel and new writers. They were also superior in applying to past literature the novel approaches to it which new generations bring to its interpretation. His attitude reminds one strongly of that soon to be expounded by his younger colleague at Columbia, Joel E. Spingarn.

John Burroughs declared in 1902 that the critic deceives himself in thinking he judges according to the standard set by the best that is known and thought in the world. He judges by his own conception of that standard, by his own individual taste and judgment. Impressionism is at the bottom of all criticism; the critic can give us merely the impact of the work of art upon himself. Positive judgments in literature, art, or any matter involving taste, are dangerous because they tend to block progress in literary or other appreciation.

The usual compromise in debates of this sort was offered in 1900 by Lewis E. Gates. Criticism, he declared, has since Addison's day shown an increasing tendency in the critic to value his response to the artistic stimulus, to prize the passing instant of enjoyment, until latterly some modern critics have put all their reliance upon their instantaneous responses. The response of a man mentally and emotionally alert may be very close to correct. It cannot, however, take into account the value of the work as it appeared to the artist and to his age; and it ignores the pleasure which the work has given to successive generations since it was composed. Juvenal's ancient question, *Quis custodiet ipsos custodes?* must also be answered: "Can *criticism* properly confine itself to the record of a momentary shiver across a single set of possibly degenerate nerves?" To achieve all these ends of criticism, objective standards are necessary as well as subjective impressions.

Gates would not demolish impressionism utterly. The combination of instinctive reaction with a realization of the perspective through which literature must be considered is needed to produce "vital appreciation, which is indeed criticism in its purest and most suggestive form." Such a critic will approach literature through its history; but he will use historical method to catch the precise quality of the human spirit that speaks through the literary work. He will worm his way into the personality of the author until he feels the moods and driving forces which, perhaps centuries ago, activated the writer. His mood will add to the author's "a complexity and richness of suggestion and *motifs* that correspond to all the gains the human spirit has made since the earlier age." And, being in full sympathy with his own time, he will express his creative criticism in a form adapted to men of his own period.

In this attitude Gates was soon to find aid among the aesthetic critics, who owed much to him and to Henry James. A minor offshoot from impressionism which was closely intertwined also with realism was the doctrine of art for art's sake. The 1878 *Nation* published a review of Swinburne's *Poems and Ballads* in which this theory received rough handling. To the reviewer the doctrine presented itself as a denial of any relation between poetry, or any art, and morality; and the assertion that what or why the author wrote was of little significance beside how he did it. Literature is purely a question of form. "Poets who write with a purpose are merely clergymen in disguise. The content of a poem must never be examined; the only question is whether it is well expressed." Such a doctrine could not have found wide acceptance at the turn of the century in America.

Among those who attacked the notion in addition to William Dean Howells, Grant Allen in 1896 countered its claims with the assertion that the higher fiction has from the beginning increasingly shown a deeper purpose beyond mere expression; and he predicted that the coming century would demand more and more purpose of its writers. Lewis Gates also contributed to the onslaught by contrasting Hawthorne's depiction of sin, disease, and death with that of the modern decadent writer. Hawthorne dealt with these matters sincerely as components of normal life and human consciousness; the decadent writer juggles out of these evils some fantastically new effect without the least care for their ethical significance.

For the defense, John Burroughs in 1902 advanced the hoary charge that the American view of life, tainted with Calvinism, needs doctors of the soul who had no function in "the more healthful and joyous pagan world." In essaying his function, the poet is neither doctor nor priest. Art for art's sake, Burroughs insisted, meant simply that art, with no "partial or secondary ends," should disinterestedly hold the mirror up to nature. "Thou shalt not preach or teach; thou shalt portray and create, and have ends as universal as has nature." Such a defense, which unfortunately for it tried to convince American readers that nature is unmoral, was quite unable to aid the progress of the movement, which soon died of inanition. Like impressionism proper, however, it found some revival in that aesthetic criticism which, under the aegis of Croce, was soon to find a considerable following. The attitude of Henry Timrod in 1859, that "a complete poem is an ethical poem; . . . it acts upon the world to make for positive good," continued substantially to rule the century. Those who were unwilling to accept this strong ethical demand would generally accept Norman Hapgood's remark in 1899 of the theatre: "We need a message; but we do not want a moralizer." As Frank Norris was soon to add, the novel with a purpose may perhaps be considered a preaching novel, but it preaches "by telling things and showing things," not by precept. The author is obliged to seek a keynote in moral principle, but like the musician he is more concerned with the sonata he is composing. Beyond such demand that the author teach by example, not by precept, or at least that he write in accord with moral law, the American critic seldom cared to go.

REGIONALISM AND NATIONALISM

The second half-century saw the rise of a strong literary regional spirit. Local sentiment was nothing new; it was coeval with the settlement and founding of the country; but it had been primarily political, and literature had followed its path. In the post–Civil War era, regionalism was in part at least a conscious attempt to develop a literature devoted to local color and restricted to depicting the life and scenes of a limited geographical area. As such it was naturally opposed by the nationalists who were still looking for the great American epic or novel that should be as broad as these states.

The origins of regionalism are clear enough. In the South, local pride and nostalgia for the good old days were stirred by the evil days of reconstruction. In New England, where as Walter Prichard Eaton has noted the stock of the Puritans had been pretty well watered by foreign immigration and by the draining of the more adventurous men to the West, a like nostalgia led to the attempt to recapture the prewar, undiluted New England spirit. In other areas, where settlement was new, local pride on a level somewhat above civic-club boosting fostered local writers. The magnitude of the country dampened the ardor of many who had entertained the notion of an American novel or poem that should encompass the entire nation. Thus local pride and affection were strengthened by the greatness and infinite variety of the national alternative.

The seeds of local writing had been sown before the Civil War. *Russell's Magazine*, a brilliantly edited Charleston periodical, declared: "In our great country, though one, we are many. There will naturally arise, through its immense extent, shades and varieties of thought and sentiment honestly entertained, each requiring a separate exponent." In 1872, a reviewer praised J. W. DeForest's *Overland* as "strongly sectional, in geography of plot and in tone of coloring," but "none the less genuinely American for all that." To him there were many Americas, but each region was the whole of

America in microcosm. The 1875 *Nation* strengthened the region-alists by declaring that the monotonous lack of contrasts in our civili-zation made it the more necessary to use whatever minute detail might give it distinction. At the same time, reviewers began sharply to challenge the American attention to the differences between Americans and Europeans, urging that we "concentrate our wits on our affairs for a time," and forget how we look to England. Regional writers were ready to take advantage of all attempts to divert atten-tion from Europe. By 1882, George E. Waring, Jr., writing of George W. Cable's novels, focused attention upon the American southwest, particularly New Orleans, as ideal for literary treatment. It was "a community in which English influence has found no place, and which has hitherto been subjected to only a distant and purely external study." Cable's sympathetic portrayal of Creole life laid open this life which, though American, is "warm with a touch of the Southern sun, and throbbing with a life that is new to our colder zone. If we had no characteristic literature before, we surely have one now." New England quickly countered with local color in Sarah Orne Jewett and Mary Wilkins Freeman.

The situation of writers in the deep South is of special interest. Their difficulties have been amply attested by Paul Hayne and Sid-ney Lanier: the scorn of postwar Southern communities for the author; the lack of interest in literature; the poverty and loneliness of the writer. Many of them felt that Northern magazines would not publish their work. In despair they turned to romantic reveries of the departed South. To this attitude Joel Chandler Harris in his Atlanta *Constitution* vigorously applied a corrective. The only reason why Southern writers failed to market their wares was that these were defective. In 1879 he urged Southern writers to make full use of the unique, undeveloped materials at their disposal. They must, however, avoid sectionalism, which is literary weakness, and the local animus which accompanies it. "Whatever is truly Southern is likewise truly American." Localism, under such circumstances, is strength. Several months later, he admonished them to accept criti-cism as a spur to improvement, not as an insult to Southern honor. They should write as artists mining the rich deposits of literary ma-terial in the present Southern life, not indulge in romantic dreaming. Harris was evidently unable to move the writers from what he knew to be their faults, for in 1902, John Spencer Bassett noted that the Southern writer's problems were little ameliorated since the days of Lanier.

The characteristics of the regional writing which appeared in the late seventies and eighties have been carefully studied. According to E. W. Parks, most of the writers were women who, though endowed with ample ability, had been inadequately prepared by their sheltered lives to portray their locality as it actually was. Mrs. Murfree, for instance, brilliantly portrayed the Great Smoky Mountains, but her mountaineers were not clearly drawn. Such writers tend to cover their deficient observation by writing purple patches expressive of local pride. Carey McWilliams has noted also the pressure upon writers to omit new and often crude actualities that might offend readers. Moreover, once the local colorist had depicted the local scene and people, his materials were exhausted; he could then either repeat himself if he abode by his form or, if he left it, write realism or the historical romance. The movement bore in itself the seeds of its own death, which had occurred by 1907.

James Lane Allen, perhaps the leading theorist of Southern local color, in the 1886 *Critic* laid down rules for the local-color short story. It should focus attention upon atmosphere, sites, and monuments, instead of upon plot, character, and motive. Descriptions of scenery, being means to this end, should not take the center of the stage. The writer should have the observant eye of the scientist. He must be a stylist, willing to omit dialect speech and analysis of personality in the interests of higher literary effects. Such advice, which seems today extremely ill-chosen, may have contributed to the demise of local color.

Regionalism in literature, a more inclusive class than local color alone, enjoyed greater longevity. By 1892, H. H. Boyesen declared, hardly a dozen conspicuous states in the Union did not have each its local novelist bent upon recording the widely divergent phases of American culture. A year later, Hamlin Garland started the interest in the middle border by claiming that the West would have the honor of producing the real American author. The locality counts in literature, according to Garland, to an extent that Wordsworth would never have dreamed. The vast outlook of the prairies gives strength of general conceptions; the winds give power, penetration, and alertness; the woods add breadth and generosity of intellect. The West is already producing "a literature not of books but of life," that draws its inspiration from men and nature; and the future development of the West, once it shall have overcome its timidity, will be limitless. With Garland, excitement over regional writing temporarily died down among the theorists. Regional literature has continued to be produced, following Harris' dictum that what is truly regional is also truly American.

Meanwhile, the discussion over nationalism was proceeding. Richard Grant White led off in 1878 with the assertion that one cannot make a genuine distinction between English and American literature. For both nations standard usage and life was supplied by the aristocracy and upper middle class of England. Americans, though an English people, are not *the* English people, and should not hope to produce an independent literature. In 1884 the *Nation* asserted that the main current of American literature flowed through Lowell, Hawthorne, Holmes, and Whittier, not through Emerson and the transcendentalists—a clear choice of the European-American culture. Though disagreeing in beliefs, both these writers were opposed to the earlier nationalistic view of American literature.

Such statements were becoming increasingly rare. Horace E. Scudder in 1887 demanded that American children be nurtured primarily on American classics. "I believe heartily in the advantage of enlarging one's horizon by taking in other climes and other ages, but let us first make sure of the great expansive power which lies close at hand." Sydney G. Fisher in 1894 seriously discussed the question "Has Immigration dried up our Literature?" Our great American authors, he noted, were nearly all born before 1820, the year that immigration began to assume imposing numbers. During their growth to maturity, the American population was more homogeneous than it has ever been since; and he refused to consider the increase of foreign population and the lack of contemporary writers as unrelated. In 1894, Massachusetts had a population more than 50 per cent foreign; "her homogeneousness and her literature are destroyed." This specimen of the *post hoc, ergo propter hoc* fallacy has sired a numerous progeny.

Similar worries beset Hamilton Wright Mabie as the century ended. We need, he said, "a literature adequate in its power and vision to the range of life on this continent"; manifest destiny felt the need of literary props. Emerson, Lowell, and Whittier had struck the note of nationality; but the new writers, for whom the time is fast ripening, must play the whole tune. The 1902 *Independent* declared, however, that it would be a long time before the nation becomes one; and Frank Norris agreed that the Great American Novel will almost certainly be sectional. Our country is a union but not a unit; and a novel must be unified. Meanwhile, until it can be a unit, readers should not look for the great American novelist, but for the great novelist who is also an American.

So long as a novel was expected to have unity of structure, Howells' remark that a novel could not include all of America was undoubtedly correct. It was not until the advent of more loosely organized work, like John Dos Passos' *USA*, that a novel-form became available whose organization admitted such diverse, slightly related materials as the expected novel would contain. And by that time the Great American Novel had retreated into the background of literary desiderata.

Chapter 10

The New Humanists and Their Opponents

THE TWENTIETH CENTURY, which several reviewers had prophesied would inaugurate a new literary age, at first proved something of a disappointment. Its early years produced little of note in literature; and the critics, who appeared content to await some new manifestation, were for some years fairly quiescent. In 1910, however, the quietly simmering literary pot came to a rolling boil. Fuel to raise its temperature was added by Joel E. Spingarn in an address at Columbia on "The New Criticism."

A pupil of George Edward Woodberry, Spingarn was perhaps the best informed American on the history of literary criticism. Wearied perhaps by his long pursuit of critical theories, which do not settle problems but keep them in agitation—his opponents believed that much learning had made him mad—he reviewed the standard approaches to literature, cast them out as outmoded machinery, and arrived at the Crocean principle that art is expression, with criticism the study of that expression. The critic should be satisfied with answering Goethe's two questions: what did the artist intend to do? and how well did he do it? Criticism holds the mirror up to literature as literature holds it up to nature.

Though Spingarn retained scholarship as necessary to the critic, he deposed judicial criticism as it had previously been practiced. By concentrating attention upon the work of art, he also drove out the impressionistic adventure of the soul among masterpieces. This iconoclastic address paved the way for our twentieth-century criticism.

Prior to Spingarn's manifesto, impressionist and judicial critics had been skirmishing under seasoned leaders. For the former, James Huneker was the most versatile champion; for the latter, William Crary Brownell and the New Humanists Irving Babbitt and Paul Elmer More.

Huneker had since the 1890's been preaching the impressionist gospel and introducing Americans to contemporary European culture. Brownell had also been educated in France after his undergraduate years at Amherst; and the New Humanists wrote chiefly of English and Continental letters. An important effect of this transatlantic attention was that both camps tended to think less of literature as an expression of a national culture and more of it as an art. Their influence caused literature to become more and more divorced from American life and its problems. They did indeed make frequent but unusually contemptuous reference to American culture; and their at best patronizing air toward America weakened the power of literary men to express or to sway the American public. The naturalists alone looked at and criticized American life from their somewhat oblique angle of vision. Such change of direction ushered in a greatly altered concept of the nature and function of literature from those concepts of the nineteenth century.

Huneker preached the impressionistic gospel with gusto. Self-educated through a forty-year course of reading, he knew well the values of earlier literature. In particular, he objected to the new emphasis upon the "damned psychology and soul-belly aching" in current drama and fiction. Philosophy was dangerous for the artist; let him throw metaphysics to the dogs and so escape suffocation in a "misty mid-region of metaphysics." Huneker's breadth of reading appears startlingly in his criticism: Aristotle, Horace, Nietzsche, Pater, Shaw, and Croce rub shoulders in his essays. H. L. Mencken, who knew him well, has written of his gusto and enormous fund of anecdote about men of art and letters.

Huneker's versatility in the arts was unique in America. Primarily a student of music, he had added the other six arts to his province; his theories blended music, the plastic arts, and literature. He insisted that the boundaries which Lessing had indicated as separating the seven arts were no longer barriers. Modern artists were successfully composing tone poems, painting with words, and narrating in music. There were no schools of art, only artists. Though he damned perverse modern artists, he defended the most revolutionary attempts, provided they were intelligently undertaken, to widen the scope of any art.

Especially disturbing to conservative critics was Huneker's sifting of traditional criticism. For Aristotle as a guide he had profound respect; he even accepted the neoclassic rules after he had watered them down to valuable hints of pitfalls in the path of the author. His free remodeling of tradition, coupled with his wide reading, made him a dangerous foe to the judicial critics. They failed to realize that he was using the critical tradition constructively in applying it with modifications to George Moore, Ibsen, and Bernard Shaw.

Huneker's complete lack of racial prejudice further irritated the guardians of the aristocratic literary tradition. He loudly declared his belief that talent in an artist indicated Hebrew blood. He was moreover a devout Roman Catholic, a nephew of Cardinal Gibbons, in an America that was culturally still anti-Catholic. His Continental, "Bohemian" manner of life seemed to be an affront to the conventional manner of American life, which he, like Mencken, assailed at every opportunity as Puritan. Such a man was a dangerous foe to established critics. He blasphemed their gods, turned their traditional artillery upon their positions, forced them to engage him in fields of art with which they were relatively unacquainted, and did all this in a breezy, captivating style which they could not hope to match. Impressionist criticism from Huneker was a mighty weapon indeed.

On the judicial side, William Crary Brownell came the nearest to matching Huneker's breadth of culture. His two early volumes, *French Traits* (1888) and *French Art* (1892), demonstrated his knowledge of the Continent and of the plastic arts; he did not, however, continue, as Huneker did, to publish on the arts other than literature. His *Victorian Prose Masters* (1901) and *American Prose Masters* (1909) shrewdly analyzed and evaluated outstanding authors. The reader who labors through their turgid, complex sentences is still well repaid for the labor.

[202]

Brownell was no hidebound conservative. He ignored categories, though more considerately than Huneker; he saw, for instance, that romanticism differed from classicism in its greater awareness of the background. The better romantic writers practice a truly classic restraint. He agreed with Henry James that all human types are interesting even if morally unimportant; that each author's technique is his own business; and that he must be judged not only by absolute standards but also by standards of the era he represents. He accepted the recent preference for character above plot. Art becomes truly artistic, he declared, by virtue of the artist's sense of form and feeling for perfection—a position which, though sanctioned by eighteenth-century ideas of taste, seemed like a concession to the impressionists. And he insisted that the critic know history, a principle ignored by many conservative critics. He insinuated that a nation usually got as good artistic expression as it desired; the law of supply and demand worked here as in economics. He joined the new attack upon the affixing of labels to literary movements: classicism, romanticism, and realism were phases of taste, not mutually exclusive terms. Art is simply a sound and reasonable way to do things. Such a critic would not follow tamely in any trodden path.

Brownell's tolerance did not extend to impressionism. Although one can no longer speak of critical laws, he wrote, one can follow Aristotle and speak of literary postulates which have varied little since the Stagirite wrote. It is fatuous in the impressionists to presume that they have improved upon them. Taste must be rationalized before it can furnish true criteria of criticism. Judged by these enduring principles, a work of art has a value which must be found by measuring its merits and defects; the pleasure it gives is of less significance. Arnold's statement in 1863 of the function of criticism appealed to him as the best statement of it in modern times.

Brownell remarked that American critics genially assign to us great writers on the least provocation. Transcendentalism had made Americans see all their geese as swans; talent, he dryly remarked, was too weak a quality to be noticed by those who had held commerce with the Over-Soul. The New England critics had all drunk of this fountain. As for Poe, his criticism rarely got beyond the merely

[203]

technical. Though technique produces many immediate literary effects, its resources are mere devices in contrast with the deeper values to be sought in poetry. A critic must possess reflective power to reduce a work of art to a general concept in order to judge it. Our reviews show scholarship without the air of finality in their pronouncements. We mistake knowledge of an art for the capacity to evaluate it. What we most need is a critic like Arnold, who will channel the irresponsible freedom and eclecticism of our writers and clarify the relation of reality to the ideal.

In short, as Stuart Sherman later approvingly pointed out, Brownell believed that critical progress is achieved neither by denying *in toto* the achievements of the past nor by following only where the ancients had pointed the way. The vital critic will follow his great predecessors and progress beyond them in the direction which seems the most promising of success.

Brownell all too regularly hid his brilliant critical light under Scribner's publishing bushel, seldom emerging above his editorial duties. A somewhat narrower yet more frequently flashing ray was cast upon criticism by Irving Babbitt. As lecturer at Harvard and contributor to learned and literary periodicals, and as author of several controversial books, his influence upon American literary theory was profound. Lacking Brownell's ironic rapier, he resorted to a bludgeon. By indiscriminately swinging it at whatever seemed to him unsound, he alienated many who if more tactfully approached might have become more kindly disposed to his humanism, and at the same time gave a handle to his opponents in his sometimes sweeping generalizations.

To the intuition and gusto of Spingarn and Huneker, Babbitt opposed an almost deistic reverence for reason. There is a higher law, he declared, which man can rationally discern, and to which, by subjecting his emotions and his animal nature under his reason, he can hope to conform. As Walter Jackson Bate has pointed out, man in Babbitt's eyes should thus achieve the eighteenth-century virtue of decorum, and by harmonizing his conduct with universal law become "human." Without considering literary rules as Nature methodiz'd—he was no admirer of Nature in any sense—he held strictly to tradition, not as a policeman but as a rarely errant guide.

Tradition on the whole is rational, and whatever opposes the conclusions of reason must be discarded. Romanticism with its later incarnations in realism and naturalism is dangerous yielding to emotion. Babbitt took for his theme the ills from which society and literature were suffering as the effect of their having abandoned right reason.

Like Huneker and Brownell, Babbitt was widely acquainted with Continental literature and criticism, with special professional interest, as professor of French at Harvard, in the expressions of the French mind. His basic theory, however, went back to the founding fathers of letters. In 1897, objecting to the Germanized classical instruction in American universities, he demanded that students be made acquainted with classical culture directly, on as high a level as they could receive. If Pindar were above them, let them read Horace; if Horace proved unattainable, they should appreciate it in Molière. Terence's *humanum nihil a me alienum puto* combined in his theory with Horace's *nil admirari* to produce the humanist, a term analogous in sense to that humanism of sixteenth-century Europe. The proper study of mankind is man, who is to be observed with a rational detachment devoid of that enthusiasm which obscures judgment. The neoclassicists, in spite of their obvious defects, were defenders of the rounded man against the one-sided specialist, and exponents of measure, judgment, and objectivity. Such uncompromising championship of what the twentieth century regarded as a defunct cause brought Babbitt plenty of opponents; and, being a fighter by preference, by the time of Spingarn's manifesto he had drawn the fire of many writers in response to his own heavy salvos.

Disorder in literary thinking irritated Babbitt; a notable weakness of his criticism lay in his inability to practice that very emotional detachment which he advocated. Impressionism had perverted the "honest liberty of taste" of the Latin *de gustibus non est disputandum* into licence to ignore its complement, *est modus in rebus.* Standards do exist by which to criticize literature, partly outside the individual, partly within him. The real problem is to find some median position between the legalistic Procrustes and the amorphous, impressionistic Proteus. Such a standard employs the universal part of the individual, that which he shares with all men, and a discipline based upon past practice without being purely traditional. By constant and clear thinking it adjusts the experience of the past to the changing needs of the present. Lacking any such standard, American critics are unable to distinguish the excellent from the inferior, a deficiency which according to Goethe is the earmark of barbarism. As in many later papers, Babbitt made the moderate thesis advanced in his paper unpalatable to his audience by his blunt denunciation of the men for whom it was delivered.

Equally disorderly seemed to him the literary movements which he lumped together as essentially romantic. In *The New Laokoön* (1910) he examined as Lessing had done the misinterpretations of Horace's *ut pictura poesis* which had led literary artists to seek after the effects normally produced by music and painting. Disagreeing with Huneker, he insisted that the demarcations drawn to indicate the areas of the several arts must not be summarily removed. Though the neoclassicist had erred in binding poetry with the strait jacket of prescription, the romanticists and their successors, in seeking to arouse wonder, had extinguished common sense. The true humanist attempts to satisfy both the imagination and the understanding. He imitates, as Aristotle advises, human actions with a definite plan and purpose, not realistically as they are but as they ought to be, having removed the local and the accidental, the abnormal and eccentric in order to afford full play to the universal.

As a New England teacher impressed by Emerson, Babbitt agreed that the critic's judgment is partly intuitive: one must believe in the existence of something beyond the grasp of the intellect. He made a jest of the absurd lengths to which judicial criticism had been carried. Beyond these admissions, he refused to budge. Criticism remained for him to his latest years the application of a correct scale of values. Important as technique undoubtedly is for art, it remains, he insisted, only a means; and the study of means, like the study of origins, is less important than the study of ends—a point to be labored by later critics.

For his attacks upon realistic and naturalistic developments from romanticism, Babbitt added Longinus to Aristotle as authorities. Longinus had insisted that literary excellence is the echo of a great soul, which is attained first of all by greatness of ideas. Americans,

Babbitt declared in 1912, lack ideas; instead of reflecting the American scene, writers and critics alike echo European pronouncements of from five to forty years earlier. We trail as far behind Europe in art as we precede her in sanitary plumbing. Dreiser throws back to Zola, Dos Passos to the Goncourts, our free-verse writers to the French symbolists. "In general," he declared in 1928, echoing Emerson's words of ninety years earlier, "it is not fitting that a great nation at the very height of its power should go on indefinitely trailing after Europe. It is time for us to initiate something of our own." He hastened to add that a truly American literature will not immediately inbreed its own originality; it will, however, question that spurious originality which for a century and a half has literally tried to express only its temperamental self; and it will be sufficiently informed to refuse the title of original to those writers who attempt to palm off as new the castoff literary habits of Europe. What we need is such standards as an American culture alone can supply, and our higher education makes no effort to supply them. Mencken, whom he cordially detested, proved his own charges against our education: if we had grown culturally as we should have done, Mencken himself would have been impossible.

Babbitt's running mate in the cause of humanism was Paul Elmer More. The two had begun a lifelong friendship in the 1890's as graduate students at Harvard. More had soon abandoned the academic for the journalistic life; by 1910 he had won a prominent place among American literary thinkers, whom he further influenced as editor of *The Nation*. His humanism differs from Babbitt's chiefly in his closer adherence to Christianity, and his consequently greater emphasis upon the moral purpose of literature. Though both men were condemned as Puritans by opponents, More's ethical discussions were much more detailed. As Morton Zabel remarks, More found Arnold and his contemporaries lacking not in moral earnestness but in a positive principle capable of effectively uniting their moral with their aesthetic sense. Through the gap left by this disunity had entered all the movements which lacked the rounded view of life demanded by the humanist: impressionism, naturalism, subjectivity, and moral anarchy. The unreadiness of Protestant sects to close the breach against these enemies probably contributed to More's temporary desertion of Christianity. Humanism alone could defend culture until Protestantism began to take thought of eternal life as including a rounded existence upon earth preliminary to a higher existence after death.

Against both romanticism and naturalism, More fought desperately. Romanticism is adrift, without a planned existence. The romantic critic joins to the sensibility and fluidity of the revolutionary temperament the historical critic's attempt to enter into and become the types he studies. Such a critic hardly differs from Anatole France's impressionist; being part and parcel of his object, he cannot judge objectively. The true critic, like Ruskin's parallel class of greatest poets, enjoys with gusto what he is considering, but at the same time conceives clearly the values of the object he enjoys. Poet and critic differ slightly in the location of this restraining principle; in poets it works unconsciously from without; in critics it proceeds consciously and from within. More spoke of this principle as the will to refrain, the inner check, which curbs the opposed will to act; proper interaction of the two produces art from the artist and insight into art from the critic.

In one respect, More infuriated his opponents even more deeply than Babbitt had done. If Elizabeth's court, he speculated, had sheltered a critic of Boileau's character, Shakespeare might have been taught to lop off his redundancies, clarify his language, and get rid of his barbarous denouements; other dramatists might have learned to create simpler, better plots and more conceivable characters; the sonneteers might have learned common sense; Spenser might even have learned to tell a story. Lack of such a controlling influence at England's great expansive moment was a loss for which no other gain can ever fully compensate. Again, after defining the critical temperament as consisting primarily in the linking together of literature and life, he qualified this generally acceptable statement by adding that it included the leveling application of common sense, an ingredient violently repugnant to the proponents of the *furor poeticus* and critical intuition. Whether designed to needle his opponents or not, these blasphemies against the current literary theology goaded them to fury.

More had no desire to preach a prescriptive literary theory. An ·

art, he wrote, is something to be perceived and felt, whereas a science is capable of demonstration and supports argument. He objected to Brunetière's raising the banner of pure authority: we need instead of written codes to know those unwritten codes resident in man himself, of which the old rules were an imperfect embodiment. If we do not find unity of taste and morals on the higher plane of our common humanity, the impressionist will persuade us to discover it on a lower level. The true critical spirit as More saw it boasted a genealogy from Cicero through Erasmus, Boileau, Shaftesbury, Sainte-Beuve, and Arnold. These discriminate the false from the true, the deformed from the normal, and spread the gospel of harmony, proportion, order, and taste. To benefit the present, which occupies their interest, they try to salvage the living power of the past. Like Arnold, their motto is *semper aliquid certi proponendum est,* and they labor to make that certainty known.

Like Babbitt, More found little to praise in the current American scene. The few who had overcome their lack of background had succeeded by retreating into unreal worlds. But a canon of taste was even more needed than a literary background. America had lagged behind the England of Tennyson and Arnold by supposing that the artist should abandon himself to his genius without exercising his will to refrain upon his vagrant imagination. Whitman, in whom More unexpectedly shows deep interest as an artist, most clearly showed the effects of these two deficiencies. Both More and Babbitt were wholly unsympathetic to that desire for a democratic literature which had never died out among American theorists. As they saw the situation, literature should be written by the fit few on a level to which the worthy should be aided to attain: instead of reaching down to the masses, the writer should attempt to elevate their taste to his higher level. This writing should not be esoteric—More vigorously condemned that excessive emphasis upon metaphor and that complex meaning which were becoming the hallmark of twentieth-century poetry. In some respects the New Humanists seem like Federalists born a century too late.

More wrote forcefully about individual critics. Pater was to blame for the moral breakdown in letters with his emphasis upon the fleeting impression. Bergson's theory of consciousness as an uninterrupted stream of activity which selects and focuses critically upon one aspect or another of an object, More felt to be rich with applications for the theorist about cultural development; the rest of Bergson's significant work he left unmentioned. Croce, being the basis for Spingarn's theory of literature as expression of impressions, fared badly at More's hands. He objected vigorously to Croce's assertions of the artist's moral irresponsibility for his works and of the complete divorcement of art from pleasure and philosophy as well as from morals. Such a writer, said More caustically, can be not only immoral but a liar as well; he is dangerous, even deadly. Man is a moral, responsible being, whatever Croce, I. A. Richards, or James Joyce may affirm to the contrary.

For T. S. Eliot, though he professed himself unable to discover the meaning of some of his statements, More expressed respect. As the pupil of Irving Babbitt, he had at least the right to be heard for the good that was in him. Eliot's theory of dissociation of sensibility in the postmetaphysical English poets seemed to him to have some validity. The statement that while literary standards determine whether a work is literature, nonliterary standards must decide its greatness as literature, More accepted as "a complete truth perfectly formulated." Eliot was one of the few contemporaries not wholeheartedly humanistic whom More approved.

Perhaps the most violent New Humanist was Stuart Sherman, whose late academic training developed in him some of the traits which amused Theophrastus in the late learner. His first enthusiasm seemed to burn itself out, for in the early twenties he deserted the ranks. He was notable for the vigor with which he preached the gospel according to Arnold and for his fierce onslaughts upon H. L. Mencken and Ludwig Lewisohn in defense of the American cultural tradition. These alien-minded critics, he declared, in discarding the American past were condemning their followers to sterility: the present must always grow out of the past. The American writer grows dull when severed from his heritage, not from contact with it.

Gorham Munson, another New Humanist, declared that Babbitt and More alone had clarified the literary situation by defining the terms of the debate and bringing a significant order to the confused world of letters. He divided American critics of the twentieth

century into three generations: the elder, headed by Babbitt and
More; the middle, led by Van Wyck Brooks and H. L. Mencken;
and the younger, among whom the better known were Kenneth
Burke, Yvor Winters, and Allen Tate. The elders were classical;
the middle group represented the romantic revolt against the ethical and intellectual checks of their predecessors; and the younger
group, though still not wholly formed, were showing mingled romantic, neoclassic, and religious strains, with intense interest in writing techniques and aesthetics. The elder group, he felt, could hardly
expect to hold the influence they had attained, the younger was still
unformed, and consequently the field would for some time be left
to the middle group. This estimate of the literary situation, made in
1928, was remarkably accurate, except that the younger group,
among whom were leaders of the new criticism, came to power
sooner than he had prophesied.

G. R. Elliott also defended the New Humanists. Like T. E.
Hulme in England, he saw the romantic movement as having
almost expended its force and a classical revival as imminent. Unlike
Hulme, who defended the newer movements in poetry, Elliott saw
them as tangential to the poetic cycle; the imagists, he declared,
were moving steadily away from its course. Longfellow indicated
the correct course for American poetry. Using material wherever he
found it, at home or abroad, he shaped his works from the life; he
did not think that poetry should be crammed with real life, but
produced from it. Poetry is neither hard, angular facts as the imagists
thought, nor is it vaguely generalized; it is universalized out of
life. American poetry, in particular, must proceed in its traditional
line of descent, shaping its works from the entire American scene
though not restricted to it. Of this scene, Longfellow and Whitman
are complementary parts.

Elliott went even beyond More in denying the naturalistic
assumption that adequate religious truth or genuine beauty can be
found outside Christianity. The Christian course is the direction in
which criticism must move if it is again to become vitally effective.
Christian art can take the materials of naturalism and shape from
them a thing of beauty. This art, he felt, would not support More's
intense concentration upon ethical principles; yet of the two hu-

manistic leaders, More had a sounder conception of its nature than did Babbitt, who had departed from the Christian tradition.

IMAGISM

The immediate beginning of the imagist movement came from the English poet and critic T. E. Hulme. In America the movement was given publicity by Ezra Pound, and was supported by the purse and prowess of Amy Lowell. Hulme's essay "Romanticism and Classicism" (1914), unpublished for a decade but privately circulated, though it provided ammunition for the imagists, stated principles reaching far beyond them. He attacked romantic poets for their vaguely imaged pictures and their boundless self-confidence. The new poetry, he declared, now shows a precision that fancy with its hard, dry outlines furnishes better than does the imagination. Man, a much more closely limited agent than he generally supposes, cannot properly employ his imagination. A new classicism derived from the fancy is at hand, to be expressed by poets aware of the mechanistic forces that direct the universe. Hulme's theory tied poetry to twentieth-century philosophy and science, a connection which later theorists were to find somewhat embarrassing. Our immediate concern, however, is the violent tempest stirred by imagist doctrine.

In defense of imagist practice, O. W. Firkins in the 1915 *Nation* described it in impressionist terms as the immediate and complete response of the momentary expression to the momentary thought. Such poetry could be achieved only with complete freedom in meter. A more detailed statement of the imagist creed appeared the same year in *Some Imagist Poets*. Briefly stated, imagism professed to use the exact word, not the proximate or decorative word; to create new rhythms, whether metrical or in free verse; to allow the poet absolute freedom in choice of subject; to present an image in exact detail, without vague generalities; and in consequence to produce poetry that is hard and clear. The imagist poets honestly labored to write according to this creed.

Opponents, however, immediately charged them with failure.

Conrad Aiken characterized their verse as "unmixedly decorative," with no organic movement behind its hard, clear images. They were trying to make poetry of that sensory world which had been the poetic background for the masters from Chaucer and Shakespeare to Coleridge and Keats. Imagist verse is therefore a setting without a play. It never stirs the reader's emotions; the adjectives one instinctively applies to the best of it are "interesting," "delightful," "charming," but never "moving." In 1916 Lewis Worthington Smith, describing the trend toward imagism and vers libre as a revolt from prevailing literary forms to a more elementary level, asserted that this reversion carried with it a corresponding elementary substance. These minor poets, overwhelmed by the variety of human experience, have unwittingly taken a position which forces them to treat experiences one at a time. They respond to and represent impressions singly, omitting the correlation and expression of their impressions in a connected organism. Max Eastman in 1918 branded them as trying to express incommunicable special values.

For the defense the ablest spokesman was the redoubtable Amy Lowell, whose influence soon so dominated the movement that disgruntled writers nicknamed the movement "Amygism." In the 1917 *North American Review* and in her *Tendencies in Modern American Poetry,* she delivered telling blows in support of her school. All poetry, she declared, contains two ingredients: vision, from its lower form as Fancy to its higher levels Imagination and Inspiration (she here departed from Hulme's elevation of the Fancy); and words. Older and modern poetry differ in the idiom employed. Modern poetry works by suggestion, invoking an image instead of describing it, but using the word that exactly renders the suggestion. A fine scholar herself, Miss Lowell did not claim that older schools were wrong and hers alone right. Poets have always written of what they saw, but the new poet sees a different world in a different way. Taking issue with the humanists, she declared that a literary work has interest only on account of its aesthetic significance; conceding that its beauty had to grow out of a soil capable of producing it, she nevertheless denied that the forces which incited the poet possessed any interest or significance for poetry. Modern poets, she added, being concerned with truth instead of dogma, see the universe in

Emerson's terms as a huge symbol, which so thoroughly absorbs their attention that they feel no need to dwell constantly upon the meaning of this symbol. This idea was later to figure largely in John Crowe Ransom's theories.

Miss Lowell admitted that imagist poets had at first produced poems unduly simple and deficient in organic movement. The name imagism, she insisted, belongs to the product; it is wrongly attached by critics to the poet's object. The imagist should not merely present images but a clear picture of whatever he wishes to convey. His scope is all-inclusive. Her definition of the poet makes him "a man of extraordinarily sensitive and active subconscious personality, fed by, and feeding, a non-resistant consciousness."

Within a few years, internal dissension among imagist poets brought an end to the movement. Its importance lies chiefly in those ideas in its creed which were to gain wider acceptance. Its emphasis upon symbol and image was taken over by adherents to the fringe of the movement, by the transplanted T. S. Eliot, and by theorists in America, into the new poetry and criticism which have drawn the lion's share of attention during the last two decades.

OTHER OPPONENTS OF TRADITION

The imagist attack upon tradition was almost eclipsed in the public estimation by the vigorous onslaught upon the American cultural scene launched by Henry Louis Mencken in the decade following World War I. Mencken, a sworn foe to American literary tradition as embodied in the works of the New England writers, spoke for many young liberals and radicals of the time. Upon Puritanism and what he assumed to be its offshoots, he blamed most American ills; his concept of Puritanism included the "Comstockery" of New York and Pennsylvania and the inhibitions of the Southern "Bible belt" with his hostility to New England.

Mencken described the Anglo-Saxon mind, which he declared had been vitiated ever since the British Reform Bill of 1832, to be culturally middle class, superficial, smug, essentially moral in its estimate of values, and incapable of that skepticism, "save as a passing coryza of the spirit," which is the mother of true wit. In consequence, Anglo-Saxons are constantly victimized by quacks. In art, their habitual reference to an ethical scale of values makes them incapable of aesthetic appreciation. The moral obsession of America has deified New England authors and relegated to neglect her greatest literary figures, Melville, Whitman, and Mark Twain. Conceding a modicum of merit to Emerson and Hawthorne, he denied it utterly to Longfellow and Whittier; the two former, though tainted by the pervasive moralism of their time, were at least strong individualists. All the other accepted American writers, and Emerson and Hawthorne too, lacked gusto—he evidently knew little of Holmes and Lowell—and without gusto there can be no art. Puritanism in its decline had bequeathed its opposition to earthly beauty and joy to its successor Philistinism.

Professing such a dim view of American letters, Mencken inevitably rejected American criticism. It was "too academic, too objective, too formal, too remote from life." Brownell, "the Amherst Aristotle," irritated him beyond endurance by what seemed to him his ironic superciliousness; the man with the bludgeon cannot engage the man with the rapier. The French have shown, Mencken stated, that literature is a live, exciting pursuit worthy of the best efforts of men in love with life, not something to receive the flabby notice of feminine specimens of either sex. In its academicism the American body of critics refuses to exercise its prerogative upon vigorous contemporary writers, who are surely as much its material as are the dead. It allows the Philistine American public to dim all its conclusions under the shade of ethics. Except Poe and Sidney Lanier—Mencken showed Southern preferences where Southern Puritanism was not concerned—American critics have all been incompetent.

Mencken's artist feels the wonder of life without the romantic confidence in man's limitless possibilities. Man is a mere sensitive organism, which the artist should try to record and, as Dreiser has attempted, to translate and understand. Though he rejected Zola's work as "empty, meticulous nastiness," he believed character in decay to be the subject most suited to fiction. To this naturalistic view he added for poetry—not for prose—some notions of the Greek tragic hero evidently borrowed from Schiller and Nietzsche. The novel is concerned with faithfully representing man in his actual state.

[215]

Mencken pictured his critic as actuated by artistic, not peda-gogical motives; criticism is an art, not a science. It is no science because it cannot make permanently valid judgments—the remark betrays a surprising misconception of modern science. The critic so interprets literature as to provoke reaction between reader and work of art. It proceeds empirically, using with a gusto like Huneker's whatever it finds available. Gusto is the parent of all true critical talents. Honesty, originality, beauty, and life are the only desiderata of literature. The critic should show the reader that the enjoyment of literature is a magnificent adventure, pursued regardless of criti-cal canons of professors and enjoyed regardless of its ethical effect.

Mencken approved of Spingarn's declaration that criticism is an intuitive creation of beauty. He felt, however, that this ideal lays a heavy burden upon the critic; it also ruled out nine-tenths of the "grown-up sophomores" who then constituted the corps of Ameri-can critics. Such decimation of the critics caused him no regret. Spingarn's error lay in his ignoring the interpretive function of criti-cism, which requires more than intuition and renders pure recreation of the work of art impossible. One cannot see beauty *in vacuo;* it appears alloyed with social, political, and moral implications. Spin-garn had, however, cleared the critical air by expelling from it many noxious vapors. The truth of the matter lay, he concluded, some-where between the professors and Spingarn, but nearer to Spingarn.

Spingarn, unlike the New Humanists, gained in critical urbanity in later essays. When setting forth in 1922 his conception of the American critic and his needs, without abandoning his basic position he withdrew some of his earlier assertions. American criticism con-tained abundance of brilliant utterances, which were isolated flashes rather than sparks struck out from any coherent theory. America lacks that philosophic insight and precision which come only from a tradition of aesthetic thought. An aesthetic theory the critic must have, a conception of what literature attempts backed by a philosophy of life; for criticism concentrates upon the artistic forms into which morals and life are transmuted. At its highest development, it is an expression of taste which, guided by knowledge, is transformed into thought. Lacking the critical ladder to attain this height, the American critic can hardly hope to arrive at even that level where he can imaginatively experience the artist's vision.

Three principal forces, Spingarn continued, pervert the American concept of literature: the concept of literature as a moral force; the concept of literature as propaganda for new ways of life; and the concept of literature as wholly external to man which in the later nineteenth century had produced the mechanical, sterile notion of art for art's sake. The artist's convictions about morals and social organization do not provide the entire content of his work. He seeks to compose, not treatises in economics, ethics, or sociology, but poetry, which by transcending them becomes something new and greater, a work of art. The critic must seek an aesthetic in the artist; all else is secondary. He must be a foe to anarchic impressionism, which, though a natural reaction against earlier mechanical criticism, leads the artist nowhere.

For criticism, Spingarn continued, sound scholarship is equally important with an aesthetic theory. In America, scholarship must discipline the critic to a wider international outlook and a deeper national insight. Cosmopolitan outlook is the surest remedy for our timid colonialism; it will teach the right valuation of native talent, avoiding the rampant chauvinism of the nationalist and the depreciation of the ignorant lover of things foreign. It should be a humane scholarship based upon the critic's search for his larger self and upon a tradition that is both part of the past and a state of the soul. It makes the critic more deeply sensible of art, for it is training in taste.

Attacks upon dogmatic criticism rapidly spread. As early as 1922, Henry Seidel Canby mildly complained at the rough handling of our literature by dogmatic critics so concerned with classifying a book or its author that they failed of specific judgment. The New Humanists served as the principal target. By 1930, opposition to them had crystallized into a symposium, *The Critique of Humanism*, which in attacking them delivered blows upon several dogmatic positions. Hartley Grattan charged them with thinking of literature as a source of moral precepts or pseudoreligious disciplines, not as a phase of human experience. With Malcolm Cowley he denied their right to the label humanistic: their emphasis upon the inner check stemmed from cloistered, censored academic life, not from humane concerns. Hardly a contributor to their symposium, *Humanism and America* (1924), had been a creative artist or could have sympathized with one. To them, literature was only what conforms to highest critical standards that leave no room for less rarefied pleasures or for revision of those standards. Henry Hazlitt added that some young writers had found humanism attractive because it had speciously offered escape from the unintelligible, incoherent barbarism of recent literature. The humanists were, however, academic, not humanistic, with no antidote for the crudity which these writers had disliked.

By the mid-thirties, humanism, with the various groups opposing it, had ceased to function as distinct movements. Dogmatism was to appear in other guises. Humanistic ideas recurred in the New Criticism while some of their opponents' ideas affected the actively practicing critics of the late thirties and after. As in other cases, the values in each group that were worthy of survival and usable to subsequent writers survived.

THE SEARCH FOR A USABLE AMERICAN PAST

Although John Macy had in 1913 broached the matter, the best-known spokesman for the seekers after a usable American past was Van Wyck Brooks. Writing in 1915 on "America's Coming of Age," he faced squarely what he considered the deficiency in nineteenth-century American literary men. Waiving the question of their talent, he noted that Whitman alone of them can personally move the modern reader. Emerson, Thoreau, Poe, and Hawthorne, though possessions to him forever, were powerless to sway his conduct, nor had they moved their readers in their own day, if their abortive attacks upon American materialism give any criterion. They were equally unable to adapt themselves to novel situations; consequently, they left no successors to speak for subsequent generations. The maelstrom of World War I and powerful new immigrant cultures found America without leadership to steer her thinking and its literary expression.

Brooks adduced as one cause of our earlier writers' incapacity to move later generations their absorption in creating a culture for their own, a problem which has appeared as paramount to the writers of nearly every previous period. This concern was probably a cause of their didactic moralism; they were intent upon teaching their countrymen what they were convinced the United States needed. They felt impelled to point the moral whether or not they successfully adorned the tale. When to this seriousness of purpose was added the reliance upon intuition taught by German transcendentalism, their sense of responsibility for their country's welfare reached its height and simultaneously its greatest success. Emerson still lives as a force in American culture. Writers lacking his source of power have lost their significance for their descendants. Lowell, with natural endowment and training surely second to none of the New England authors, in spite of his vivid, attractive personality has dwindled to little more than a lay figure in our culture, because he lacked substantial ideas or pressures like those which forced his transatlantic peers to bring their inchoate ideas to form. His strong social consciousness seldom found a cause adequate to call it into action: in verse it produced his fine *Biglow Papers*, in prose several excellent but dated essays. Though he did not bury his talent, New England buried it for him.

Brooks saw in the excessive refinement of these writers another American defect. They sublimated the American character until most of its daring and vigor had been pared away. To keep oneself unspotted from the world is good, but to preserve one's purity by withdrawing from the hurlyburly of life atrophies one's powers. Spiritual atrophy is the major defect in the genteel tradition.

Brooks's search for a usable American past ended in Whitman, who, challenging the abnormal dignity and aloofness of American letters, presented unpurified, unsublimated American life. Through the rude force of everyday folk Whitman saw shining an ideal America. Probably without realizing it, he pointed to the median course which to Brooks offered the only way of retrieving for our culture that combination of earthiness with idealism which was its natural possession. Whitman's thinking, Brooks admitted, did not measure up to his intuitions; yet among nineteenth-century American authors he stood alone in pointing to men the path between reality and their own souls.

[219]

In "Letters and Leadership" (1918), Brooks renewed his attack. Its burden was the American critics' failure to envision America as in itself it really is. The secluded, academic humanists refuse to look at the present save to condemn it. Younger critics, though aware of the immediate American scene, fail to realize what it actually contains. Neither can offer cultural guidance; so Americans are emotionally disturbed, timid, dissatisfied with the present but unsure what they want or need. They consequently substitute unsatisfactory monetary values, which they can understand, for the higher things which they vaguely feel they need. The critic, as cultural leader, must offer them an organized higher life, must present a coherent scheme for its attainment.

Brooks's violent onslaught did not go unnoticed. Waldo Frank pointed out the dangers in the "American jungle." Henry Seidel Canby, reviving a popular nineteenth-century argument, declared that the English tradition is as truly our inheritance as that of the British. The hostility of Mencken and his followers to this tradition is ill advised, inspired by Anglophobia rather than by love of things American. As Mencken has dimly seen, the faults in our tradition arise from our narrow loyalty to the Puritan-Victorian tradition; we forget the rest of our English heritage. Here Canby sides with T. S. Eliot. Brooks and his group, who see the genuine tradition in Whitman, also avoid the main stream of American culture. To neglect Mark Twain and Whitman is to omit an important part of America; to neglect Longfellow and Poe is equally disastrous. The local interests of the local colorists prevent their becoming national. Canby found a common denominator for these varied approaches to America by reverting to the English fountain and following its course through all its American streams.

Norman Foerster also entered the fray. The world war, he wrote, demonstrated our cultural impotence as clearly as our political and economic power. Our old and young intellectuals alike understandably felt the need to strengthen our culture. Like Whitman, most of them were revolting against an only partially known past; they betrayed scant acquaintance with America prior to Whitman. Foerster was less insistent than Canby that we look to our British heritage; our culture had since the first American generation steadily drawn away from England until the principal bond between the two was our language. Our literary expression was molded by the frontier spirit, the Puritan tradition, romanticism, and realism. Of these four, the Puritan tradition alone was of English origin, two were international, and one American. A literature so variously derived and compounded could properly be termed only American.

Brooks and Foerster found support. John Farrar deplored the unreflecting comments of critics upon the American scene. The Puritan tradition was superficially known to both its friends and its opponents; neither knew its philosophical content. More careful study of the American tradition, Farrar believed, would show it to have fully as great intrinsic validity as any other; it is always dangerous to be intolerant of household gods. Percy Boynton in 1931 reiterated the need for serious attention to the old American traditions. Mary Colum in 1934, by defining criticism as a principle through which the world renews itself, pruning old ideas to harmonize with new needs and desires, also supported tradition truly understood. And in 1935 Canby reproached the modernist critics for their fear of traditional questions about life and literature. Those who still talk of art for art's sake or literature of the proletarian revolution should not drive critics from asking "Does this reading make a better or worse man?" Though partisan pressures of all sorts are to be avoided, literature must be judged by its effects: whether its readers become more alive, more self-expressive, more understanding and happier, as the result of their reading. The prevailing American view of literature has consistently held to Canby's position.

Psychoanalytical Critics

Attractive material for critics was furnished by the rapidly developing psychoanalytical studies begun by Sigmund Freud and developed by Carl Gustav Jung. In 1938, Edmund Wilson noted that Freud had applied his scientific knowledge to an approach to literature earlier used by Dr. Johnson and Sainte-Beuve. To a less widely read age, that almost blindly revered science, his method, however, seemed novel and wonderful. By 1919, Conrad Aiken declared that Freud's ideas were known to most critics, though Canby in 1922 felt that they deserved still more attention. Aiken believed that, however inadequate and erratic in detail, Freud's relating of poetry to the dream was an important step in scientific investigation of the sources of poetry. Psychoanalytical studies like Brooks's *Ordeal of Mark Twain* began to appear. Setting a pattern for such works, Brooks declared that Twain was an improvisator, a potential artist degraded into a journalist, largely because he suffered a psychic trauma in early adolescence, inflicted by his sternly Calvinistic mother. Except in creating Huck Finn, he never escaped the censor of his own will to let his rebellious, creative self find free expression. In 1922, Frederick C. Prescott set forth in *The Poetic Mind* a detailed Freudian account of the making of poetry.

Few voices were raised against the new approach to literature. In 1922, Maxwell Bodenheim termed psychoanalysis "the spoiled child of a realistic age," badly in need of a metaphysical spanking: critics and creators alike used it as an excuse for sensual writing. They had changed Freud's modest suggestions into a swollen phallicism. Most of the influential critics, however, were adding it to their apparatus. Canby, asserting the importance of the subconscious as the medium which carries tradition into literature, declared that only the man whose wide, rich experience has sunk into his subliminal self can truly express his own observation against the background of our culture. Waldo Frank, in *The Rediscovery of America* (1929), likened the cultural bases of a work of art to the psychology, physiology, and sociology that go into the making of a man: to know man or book requires knowledge of this background prior to consideration of its more important aesthetic aspects. Objections like that of Joseph Wood Krutch in 1937—why should a psychological pattern or historical setting which applies to a whole group be held to explain some extraordinary member of it?—were airily dismissed as emanating from unqualified practitioners.

As time passed, however, more dispassionate judgment began to evaluate the new critical tool. Bernard De Voto in 1939, admitting that the making of literature and the dream had common characteristics, warned readers that such tools when handled by inexpert enthusiasts usually produced disastrous results. In 1940, Lionel Trilling cooled the ardor of some cult members by showing psychoanalysis to be simply another culmination of nineteenth-century romanticism; that period also was deeply indebted to scientific studies and devoted to investigation of the self. Such an unexpected connecting of the new literary method with the scorned previous century struck a blow to the wind of the enthusiasts. And in 1941 Kenneth Burke weightily conceded to psychoanalysis literary usefulness in so far as the symbolic acts of poet and neurotic run parallel—a value not inconsiderable, yet severely limited. To these critics psychoanalysis was a useful tool, but not the philosopher's stone.

Frederick J. Hoffman, in his *Freudianism and the Literary Mind* (1945) and "Psychoanalysis and Literary Criticism" (1950), has surveyed and ably evaluated the movement. Starting with the statement that artists allow psychoanalysis to supplement but not supplant other bases for judgment, he traced the movement through the twenties, when writers who believed sex to be their problem saw in Freud's teachings a means to its study, into the thirties, when the movement received more intelligent study. He distinguished between the true Freudian practitioner and the writer who uses Freudian methods. Of the latter group, he singled out two critics: Edmund Wilson, who used them as aid to criticism without ignoring other criteria; and Kenneth Burke, who treated psychoanalysis as an important source of knowledge without permitting it to draw his attention away from literature itself.

In his second publication, Hoffman noted three places where psychoanalysis impinges upon criticism: in language and style; in biographical explanation of the author's talent; and in esoteric allusion and myth. He mentioned modern concern with verbal connotation, and demanded that the critic concentrate upon the language and logic of the unconscious. At whatever expense, the critic must reduce their obscurity through rational paraphrase. At the second contact, Hoffman cautiously warned critics against using the work to prove a preconceived notion about the artist's life, instead of restricting his attention to the artist's psychic state prior to his making the work. Such conditions concern the critic only in so far as they clarify the work of art. In treating the work itself, he will use psychoanalytic means to determine the quality of the referents; he

[223]

will seek to discover how and how far the author's neuroticism has affected his work. The third contact concerns the recurrent myth, a point on which Jung disagreed with the master. Here, Hoffman believed, the critic is less concerned with the existence of these myths and the manner of their recurrence than with the way in which the artist has employed them. The directions taken by psychoanalysis are not always advantageously followed by the critic. Since psychoanalysis treats the relations between artistic creation and psychological ills, and between the artist's wish and the psychological explanation of his life, it overlaps but a small part of the field which criticism must survey. The critic must not think of art in terms of neurosis. His concern is the work, not the means of its creation. Hoffman's studies, with which Lionel Trilling in general agrees, sum up adequately the achievements of Freudian criticism.

Marxist Criticism

The Marxist approach to literature had been some time in the making in America. Karl Marx was strongly impregnated with Rousseauist thinking and with nineteenth-century humanitarianism. With his Utopian thinking, Friedrich Engels' economic ideas became associated, and later Taine's famous theory of race, moment, and milieu, with special emphasis upon its third ingredient. As Edmund Wilson has pointed out, the writings of Marx and Engels lent themselves readily to exploitation by less idealistic men. They had shown appreciation of literary values. Uncultured men like Stalin did not share this attitude. When Marxism came to dominate Russia, inevitably literature, which under the Tsars had been used for political ends, was reduced to propaganda. Russian criticism likewise ran in double harness with politics.

American literary men watched the nascent Russian revolution with absorbed interest. Undeterred by the sorry denouement of the French Revolution, they welcomed in the downfall of Tsarist rule the emancipation of a large segment of the earth. The unlovely aftermath of our own Civil War, and the unscrupulous methods of some capitalists, had bred in their minds dissatisfaction with American democracy that made minds of little analytical power imagine that Russia was showing the way to something better. When the economic debacle of 1929 came, it seemed to many of these the inevitable folding up of capitalist society; and alert Communist propaganda lured many writers into sympathy and even into membership in the party. The thirties echoed with the party line in one or another dilution. Literary men, following the characteristic Russian-Communist pattern, conceived of literature in terms of propaganda. One finds as a result in America protagonists of a professedly atheistic movement crawling into the bed long reserved for Puritans and moralists. Some clergymen were dazzled by the movement. This sway of Communist literary and critical theory continued, though with gradually waning power, until Stalin's callous pact with Hitler in 1939 rudely snapped the Russian spell. Advocates of proletarian literature then, if they did not bolt the party, at least became temporarily less vocal. Our wartime alliance with Russia gave them some encouragement, but the literary popularity of Communism never recovered after 1939.

The Revolution had progressed for some time before anti-Communist writers realized its implications for the United States. Its doubters seem to have held a watching brief like Gamaliel. Among the first to be moved to opposition was Henry Seidel Canby. Americans, he wrote in 1918, should not look to foreign models, not even to English; they too are foreign to us and we need an American literature. Though our shaggy geniuses from the backwoods are indisputably American, their appeal derives from their strangeness rather than from any value; they cannot inspire us. We should look to the bourgeois literature which we have. Not of high quality, it nevertheless represents our society, and only by elevating this literature can we attain our literary hopes. America is not inert; beneath her monotonous surface boils an inner fire which requires only the cracking of that crust to let "the lava of new and true imaginings" pour through. Canby's use of the term "bourgeois literature" indicates that Marxist theorizing was in his mind if not on his pen.

Conrad Aiken's review (1919) of Louis Untermeyer's *The New Era in American Poetry* also foreshadowed war. Scrutinizing sharply Untermeyer's declaration that American art was once more expressing itself in democratic terms, he charged the author with excessive preoccupation with nationalistic and sociological approaches to literature to the neglect of its aesthetic side. Art is still art, even if it shows no contemporary social significance. American art need not display the "made in America" label to be national. Untermeyer wanted poetry with a message, Aiken charged, in support of his own politico-social views. Actually, social and political ideas are like fashions, local and temporary, superficialities merely and not elements of art. Aiken here indicated a latent danger to literature akin to that noted by Canby. Neither critic, however, represented the popular attitude. Americans like to see the American label on their wares, and instead of repairing or improving the old, they prefer to replace it with some new product.

The battle was soon to be joined, however. In the 1921 *Bookman*, Heywood Broun noted that during the past three years not a single book had been praised by both *The Liberator* and *The New York Times:* novelists were frequently judged, not on the time-honored basis of style, but on their attitude for or against Soviet Russia. The strife thus clearly marked could not be hidden.

Marxist critics found a vigorous proponent in V. F. Calverton. In the beginnings of proletarian literature, Calverton wrote, the proletarian was only the butt of humor or satire; at the best he was the frontiersman like Cooper's Natty Bumppo, useful chiefly to fight Indians. The advance of the proletariat, however, gradually forced authors to notice it. Even the unfriendly Lowell had to modify his bourgeois attitude to compose *The Biglow Papers*. After Whitman's elevation of the laborer above the bourgeois, the rise of labor organizations drew attention to that class consciousness which is a constant force in bringing proletarian ideas to the foreground. Environment originates every kind of literature, which reflects the dominant class, the class rising to power, or the declining class. The author's temperament is an immediate but not underlying cause of the work he produces.

Proletarian art, Calverton continued, represents the ascent of the proletarian and the concurrent decline of the bourgeois. Literary values obviously change as society changes; therefore, any criticism which tries to preserve the *status quo* viciously undermines social development. With the bourgeois society must go also its bourgeois virtues: honesty and chastity are verbal veneers to be ruthlessly stripped off to lay bare the elemental timber. American criticism has too long been quixotic, superficial, myopic, vague, uncorrelated, ineffectual. Americans need a new synthesis that will relate their art and criticism to life. Since criticism is a part of life, it can no longer be viewed as aesthetics, but must ally itself with the criticism of civilization which is implicit in the class contest. In Russia, where blind confusions do not exist, they have successfully solved the relation of art and criticism to life.

In the anthology *Proletarian Literature in the United States* (1935) a number of Marxist critics air their views. Michael Gold, an archangel of the movement, contrasted Eugène Sue with Walter Scott to Sue's advantage. Whereas Scott tried to revive a defunct feudal past, Sue, anticipating the future, traced the stages of proletarian martyrdom that stain the pages of history. He used the past properly, as a rich manure for the present. More recently Thornton Wilder in *The Bridge of San Luis Rey* had imitated Scott's attempt to revive the dead past in the proletarian present. What has this to do, Gold cried, with the true picture of America? Bernard Smith, who was soon to write his proletarian *Forces in American Criticism*, listed Huneker, Brooks, and Spingarn as the only significant American critics since the 1890's. Spingarn was now forgotten; Brooks was too narrow in his influence; Huneker, by giving Americans impressionism and Mencken, had been the great iconoclast of American bourgeois tradition. These three critics had paved the way for the current proletarian view of literature.

But the anthology also betrayed rifts within the proletarian lute. William Phillips and Philip Rahv, though they noted proletarian advances, were more concerned with recent difficulties. Writers, they remarked, had come to Stalinism from diverse areas, and inevitably bore the stamp of their source. A homogeneous proletarian literature must therefore reconcile opposites—a use of his phrase that would have startled Coleridge—and this reconciliation is the task of the Communist critic. By criticism, these writers explained, they meant the entire "organizational leadership of revolutionary literature." The proletarian critic, like the writer, could not treat of the class struggle without participating in it. Communist criticism cannot pursue a distinterested course.

Granville Hicks's *The Great Tradition* (1933, revised 1935) was perhaps the most generally read Communist critical work. Taking his cue from Calverton, Hicks conceded to Howells a measure of approval: his dim understanding of American life and its economic problems did not blind him to the existence of these problems. Other writers were overwhelmed by their bourgeois society. Fearing the post–Civil War industrial age, they for the most part escaped from it into a romanticized past or some Graustarkian or South American present. Stephen Crane's hatred of poverty and suffering was a more constructive attitude; the artist must hate rather than pity what he reports. Frank Norris, too, rightly identified realism with social purpose. Following these pioneers, American artists from 1912 to 1925 effected a renaissance in the novel, in poetry, in criticism, and in allied arts. Revolt was their keynote, not only against past standards and attitudes but also against any standardization that might destroy individuality. Since these writers did not yet see a remedy for the evils they condemned, they were uniformly pessimistic.

In this dolorous impasse a map-maker was desperately needed. Earlier literary cartographers had misled readers by their erroneous data. In particular, the restraint and discipline taught by the humanists contradicted the naturalistic view of man which science now taught. The crash of 1929 and the subsequent depression set the issue squarely before the revolutionists: either defend the *status quo* or attack it. The alternatives were hopeless pessimism or confidence in the emergent masses. Since Marx, Hicks concluded, offers the best hope for mankind, even in America, the portrayer of American life must ally himself with the proletariat or own himself defeated.

The weaknesses of Marxist criticism were ably shown by James T. Farrell in *A Note on Literary Criticism* (1936). Farrell, disclaiming the position of a professional Marxist, was not unfriendly to its doctrines. Literature is an instrument of social influence; it is also a branch of the fine arts. Human experience, he wrote, may be divided into aesthetic and functional categories. Since aesthetic experience is generally a by-product of the functional, the art of any society is likely to arise from its functioning. From Pater to Croce aesthetic critics have reversed this relation, concentrating upon the record of sensations instead of social values. To them content is either irrelevant or incidental to the emotional response generated by the work of art. Their critiques are not judgments but new works of art created in response to the object considered, in harmony with the dead theory of art for art's sake. The critic must be aware of life as it is lived.

There is, however, an aesthetic category of experience, and Farrell severely censured Marxist critics for neglecting it. Their one-sidedness is as culpable as that of the despised aesthetes. Completely severing the functional from the aesthetic aspects of art, they relate the functional side to sociology and economics, making these laws for man as thing laws for literature as well. The concept of literature as propaganda ignores the "persistence value" of works of art, which often outlasts their functional value. Marx's idea of society as constantly in motion requires that the effects of one set of relationships become causal factors of the next, producing a chain of tradition. One cannot therefore scrap all bourgeois literature; it contains progressive qualities which must be kept. "Leftism" too often ignores this carry-over value of literature.

Under such circumstances, Farrell continued, literature cannot be pigeonholed as purely bourgeois or proletarian. The Marxist who asserts the uniqueness of the proletarian novel fails to realize the true literary situation and attempts impossibilities. When Marxists legislate that the author must create characters out of concepts instead of life, they forget that a good novelist's people are both individual and typical; he uses specific human beings in some predicament to show general ideas.

Whenever literature attempts to propagandize, it ventures into prophecy and becomes banal. Instead, it should be treated as an instrument of social significance. Without necessarily judging life, it presents materials for the better understanding of life and judges these materials. Its readers become more aware of people's problems and predicaments, their thoughts and emotions, their times and milieu. It attains its effects by plausibly reproducing elements of life. The critic clarifies and evaluates the artist's picture. Until Marxist critics see literature as a development and expression of life, not as something to be composed according to absolute rules, there can be no truly proletarian novels. Farrell's censures in this and later volumes inflicted more telling blows than did the Marxists' avowed enemies.

Edmund Wilson, another former Marxist sympathizer, charged Marxism with grave injury to literature. In Soviet Russia, Communism has destroyed Russian literature by controlling its use as a tool for propaganda. Marxist jargon everywhere hides confusion of thought, insincerity, and deliberate fraud, which American converts have received as a new revelation. In trying to legislate for literature, Marxism goes outside the critic's bailiwick. Even if it stays within critical bounds, it can inform us only about the origin and social significance of a work; it cannot assess its value. The addition of Freudian analysis to Marxist materials merely enlarges the study of a work's origin. In liquidating Trotsky, who in spite of his shortcomings had some notion of the author's need for free expression, the Stalinists had driven literature from the Soviet Union.

With these not unfriendly critics severely attacking Marxist criticism, it is unnecessary to examine the work of its out-and-out enemies. The reader has already noted in proletarian literary theory a revival of the perennially recurring notion that literature must be didactic. American critics have lately been nearly unanimous in their condemnation of the Marxist literary position. Their rejection has been only in part a reaction against Stalin's aligning of the Soviet Union in 1939 with Hitler and against the callous conduct of Russian policy since World War II; the opposition has been, as we shall see, inherent in the principles of various critical schools.

Chapter 11

The New Criticism

BY FAR THE MOST NOTEWORTHY critical development of the past quarter-century has been the New Criticism. The name, as the New Critics themselves admit, has not been happily chosen. It came into general use after John Crowe Ransom published under the title *The New Criticism* (1941) studies of four leading contemporary critics, followed by a plea for an "ontological critic." It was not until quite recently that Ransom, perhaps the key figure of the movement, accepted the term as properly designating the movement. The student of literary criticism will readily appreciate his hesitation; the movement is more notable for new emphases in criticism than for novelty of ideas. If there had existed in seventeenth-century England a critical school parallel to the metaphysical school of poetry, one might with some propriety name them "The New Metaphysicals."

The origins of the movement are diverse. First no doubt was the wide dissatisfaction in America and England, at the beginning of the century, with the literary situation. The lack of fulfillment of the great expectations that writers had had for the new century may have contributed to this literary unrest. To many thinkers, literature and criticism appeared to be stagnant amid unparalleled scientific advances and equally significant social changes. Victorian literature, many believed, had been chiefly an attempt to salvage what could be saved for the arts in an age dominated by science; it seemed to be interested mainly in the moral, social, or religious uses of literature; and its romantic basis was now outmoded. Writers desired earnestly a positive approach to literary problems. Allied to this desire was the revolt, in nearly all critical camps, against academic overemphasis upon the background and environment of literature and concentration upon the author instead of the work. Spingarn's epoch-making address in 1910 was soon paralleled by Stuart Sherman's attack upon the training of English graduate students under George Lyman Kittredge.

Defenders of imagism also prepared the way of the New Criticism. Among them Ezra Pound was one of the earliest to indicate the direction of the new study of poetry. In a letter to Harriet Monroe in 1912 Pound insisted that American poets must look at poetry as an art whose techniques and media are constantly developing, and must study these aspects of poetry if they expected their craft to survive. T. E. Hulme's "Romanticism and Classicism" and the Imagist Manifesto gave added impetus to tendencies which the New Criticism was to exploit.

The movement also owed much to other preceding and concurrent movements. Its objection to the moralism of Victorian poetry no doubt gained new vigor from the Marxist attempt to use literature as propaganda. The ethical emphasis of the New Humanists contributed as much to the New Critics' opposition to didacticism as their insistence upon scholarship reinforced the demands for learning made by the new group. Spingarn's iconoclastic brushing aside of traditional literary conventions appealed to them, though their interest in what they considered the genuine thread of English literary progress prevented their full acceptance of his impatient proposals. Even Mencken's vituperative barbarism had elements which they found useful. None of these groups, however, fulfilled for them the prime need of literary study, which was, as R. W. Stallman expressed it, to "illuminate the center," the work itself.

One may add too the probability that the New Critics, by focusing their light upon the work itself, escaped from unlovely aspects of the times in which they were living. Some of their leaders had previously belonged to the Southern agrarian group, who had combated without success the urbanized, manufacturing life of the times.

Opposed as they were to escapist literature, they nevertheless unconsciously found relief in sailing with Yeats to Byzantium or speculating with Kant upon aesthetic knowledge. The student who is aware of the strength they derived from such investigations should not ignore their concurrent less desirable qualities.

Though the New Critics share certain basic attitudes, they are by no means unanimous in their beliefs; there exist sharp cleavages among them. For this reason, and because they are so close to us as to defy fully objective treatment, it has seemed best to discuss separately certain key figures in the movement.

THOMAS STEARNS ELIOT

Eliot is undoubtedly the most commanding figure of twentieth-century criticism in the English-speaking world. He stems from the New Humanist tradition presented by his Harvard professor, Irving Babbitt, and from the imagist school with its varied sources; but other ingredients flavor his thinking. The publication in 1917 of his "Tradition and the Individual Talent" has profoundly impressed both the New Critics and their opponents. This significant essay indicated where the new thought was to deviate from the New Humanists' concept of literary tradition. Eliot required that for the understanding of any living artist he be set for contrast and comparison among those dead artists who have preceded him. Since poetry is a living whole composed of all the poetry that has ever been written, the poetic tradition is not represented by any individual or group. Each new poet contributes to the stream of poetic tradition. All contributions, of course, are not equally valuable. Eliot himself preferred the metaphysical poets as indicative of the true course of English poetry which poets from Milton's time to the present have disastrously abandoned. He also took issue with the Wordsworthian definition of poetry. It is rather, he wrote, escape from emotion and personality. The poet's contribution is not that in which he differs from tradition, but that part of his work most in harmony with the dead poets who preceded him.

From these premises Eliot concluded that the poet's work must be judged by standards from the past. This is not the application of older canons of criticism; it means that his worth will be determined by the degree to which it fits into the tradition. Criticism is directed upon poetry, not upon the poet. The poet does not express his personality, but uses a medium which unites his impressions and experiences in special, unforeseen ways. These impressions and experiences are not those of most significance in his life, but may have been almost negligible. They are, however, significant with reference to the poetic tradition.

According to Eliot, the reader actively judges the poem as he reads it. If he is an instructed reader—and Eliot is not concerned with the ignoramus—he will react in terms of his acquaintance with the tradition and automatically fit it into its proper place in the tradition. The author, when he writes with awareness of the tradition, also exercises his critical faculty. Both reader and poet then must be the Biblical instructed scribes, able to bring out of their storehouses things new and old.

An excellent, concise statement of Eliot's critical position appears in Walter Jackson Bate's anthology, *Criticism: The Major Texts* (1952). Bate compares Eliot's view of tradition with Edward Young's statement about proper imitation of the ancients, that one imitates Homer, not Homer's *Iliad;* he could have added Longinus' emphasis upon emulation of Homer's spirit. As Mr. Bate puts the case, the significant artist may modify the direction in which the stream of tradition will flow; but he never abandons the stream, he simply produces it.

To the poet's objectivity, Mr. Bate continues, the critic offers a corresponding sense of fact. He does not use primarily any theory of criticism; he focuses his light upon the poem before him, responds to it, and evaluates it. Eliot deduces criteria from the practice of the metaphysical poets, who represent the farthest production of the tradition before poets abandoned the true course of the stream. (The reader may recall a similar belief expressed by a writer in the *Monthly Anthology* in the opening years of the nineteenth century, when Young was still read and honored. Like Eliot, the writer wished to transfer his homage to Dryden; his ideas were, however, engulfed in the romantic flood.) Eliot's resultant point of view Mr.

Bate describes as "an informed and unillusioned—as distinct from a disillusioned—sophistication," which presents itself in hard clarity of outline and strong feeling for structure. Such a combination of English tradition with a classical formalism, Mr. Bate concludes, is almost unique among modern critics.

Eliot's influence appears in phrases which have become standard critical terms. His term "objective correlative," though actually used earlier in America by Washington Allston, as M. F. Heiser has recently shown, has become the recognized term to signify the way of expressing emotion in the form of art. Eliot has expressed surprise that Eliseo Vivas and others have undertaken to clarify a term whose meaning seems to him self-evident. Another term, "dissociation of sensibility," Eliot used to indicate that inability to "devour any kind of experience" which in his eyes set Milton and even Dryden below the metaphysical poets and diverted English poetry from its proper channel. A third influence to be noted here was Eliot's contribution in 1929 to the revival of medievalism by his penetrating essay on Dante. His attention to Dante's famous letter to Can Grande della Scala about the interpretation of the *Divina Commedia* has added impetus to current interest in the hierarchical principle and allegorical modes of interpretation.

In opposition to Spingarn's belief that criticism may be creative, Eliot brought it abruptly back to a position ancillary to literature by declaring that it is not an autotelic art. Its end, he added, seems to be the interpretation of works of art and the correction of taste. Its work can be pursued only in collaboration with other studies, especially ethics and theology. Literary standards are adequate to determine whether a work is literature; its greatness as literature must be measured by other standards. Its function as corrector of taste, Eliot told a Paris audience in 1945, includes guardianship of the language. The good critic, whom every man should aspire to be, has keen and abiding sensibility coupled with wide and increasingly discriminating reading. Thus armed, he can submit himself to impressions by powerful personalities without fear that any will dominate him. Literary citicism is a means toward rounded, integrated life, not merely *ancilla theologiae*, but *ancilla vitae*.

As a pioneer in modern criticism, Eliot's significance is difficult to overestimate. Younger critics, it is true, often disagree with his pronouncements. His belief that English criticism should state beliefs rather than argue or persuade, has brought complaints that he has become prone to speak ex cathedra. Others have been alienated by his capping of literary criticism with theological judgment, which in his case means traditional, Anglo-Catholic Christianity. Still others, while agreeing that the critic needs a religious belief, have ludicrously tried to base a religion upon the law of supply and demand; and, not being conspicuously successful, have discounted Eliot's emphasis upon ethics and theology by asserting that he wanders too far from critical matters. In spite of these objections to his ideas, however, Eliot stands with Ivor Richards as master of those who know among the New Critics.

Ivor Richards, an English critic now resident in the United States, is credited by Ransom with beginning the New Criticism, and in the right way. His views have differed considerably from Eliot's; their icy courtesy toward each other indicates their lack of sympathy. Richards in the 1920's approached literature as a psychological, though not a Freudian, investigator. His analysis of the reader's poetic experience, which enters deeply into Ransom's thinking, suggested new insights into poetry which earlier investigators had been unable to discover. In several instances his conclusions have corroborated earlier statements from the time of Aristotle down to the present. His later interest in Coleridge's theory of the imagination, though interesting, has been severely handled by other critics. His analysis of poems in terms of language, imagery, and metaphor, has however been taken over by the New Critics and has become basic to their practice. Further discussion of him will appear in the account of subsequently treated New Critics.

KENNETH BURKE

Among the earliest of the New Critics to publish is Kenneth Burke, whose essays have been appearing since 1925. Though his philosophical approach to literature is deeply indebted to Eliot, he has consistently used both Freudian and non-Freudian psychology as well as his considerable acquaintance with modern scientific method. Others have been more vociferous and combative, but Burke has earned an established eminence both in and out of the ranks of the New Critics.

In 1925, a year after Richards' *Principles of Literary Criticism* had exemplified his use of scientific psychological methods in evaluating literature, Burke published "Psychology and Form." Taking *Hamlet* for his text, Burke advanced the proposition that "form" refers to the creating and satisfying of an appetite in the auditor's or reader's mind, so that proper form in a work is equivalent to the psychology of the audience. The Freudians, he charged, in focusing their research upon the artist's possible neuroses are investigating the wrong subject to furnish information about literature. In literature, form in our scientific age has been gradually supplanted by information; and we erroneously think of psychology as information rather than with respect to artistic effects. Science is interested in fact, not in aesthetic effect. It tends to lay emphasis upon information, analyzing the psychology of the hero rather than studying the effective arousal and satisfaction of the reader's desires. Form has in many cases become a mere literary adjunct, attracting little attention and that hardly favorable.

In art, on the other hand, information is merely matter used by form to attain its purpose; it is a means, not an end. Information once gained ceases to be interesting; information uses as its devices surprise and suspense; what has once become known possesses neither. Emotion, with which art deals, is universal and eternal. A true work of art can by eloquence and formal excellence arouse and satisfy emotion over and over again. One is reminded here of Horace's awarding the palm to the work that will give pleasure when ten times repeated. In art, excellence, form, and the psychology of the audience are practically synonymous: art converts emotion into eloquence, which coincides with form and so achieves that creation and satisfaction of desire which is the end of art. Such a theory reaches far back to Aristotle, Horace, and Longinus; it utilizes principles from classical rhetoric; and it evaluates the most recent hypotheses of psychology.

Later critical works by Burke apply his principle to various problems. In 1931 his essays, "The Status of Art" and the "Program" in his *Counterstatement* exposed the inconsistencies in the hypothetical "aesthetic sense" and the embarrassment of the artist forced to attempt to please conservatives and innovators. The artist's medium, he agreed with Eliot, is composed of survivals and his own few additions. The artist sees, too often to please the innovators, that their novelties simply revive the old and neglected or forgotten. Not usually concerned over contemporary problems, he is more interested in attitudes or emphases in which some political or economic policy may be implicit; but he may use the local and temporary to typify the universal. (It was on such terms that Burke discredited Marxist literary theory.) His work discusses and considerably clarifies the use and status of symbolism in literature.

Burke's few basic principles are far-reaching in their importance and give him a profound influence over recent criticism.

JOHN CROWE RANSOM

Of all the American New Critics, Ransom is the most significant figure. Like Kenneth Burke, he has distinguished and defended poetry from science; his work has been consistently polemic, though his attitude toward opponents has shown a uniform kindliness. He is well read in literature and philosophy, and displays an intelligent nonprofessional acquaintance with modern science. His importance for the New Criticism justifies the discussion of his work in detail.

God Without Thunder (1930) attacks modern social Christianity, which, Ransom charges, after getting rid of the stern, inscrutable Old Testament God, has evicted also the Christ of the New Testament with his concern for the individual sparrow. Instead, it has set up a deity who, like the modern scientist, thinks of genus Homo rather than individual man. Protestantism has progressively rationalized its doctrines; it has made occidental man see myths as lies or at best incorrect attempts to explain natural phenomena. The Oriental mind has always seen myth as symbolic representation of truth; the myth-maker never intended to be historical or scientific. Modern scientific man, however clear about general principles, has ignored those individual matters so vital to poetry; in viewing the forest he has overlooked the trees.

The World's Body (1938) differentiates further between the scientist's and myth-maker's world. Both see its actual body; Ransom has no use for romantic escapism. Poetry is to him a kind of knowledge—his idea is Kantian in origin—by which we learn to know objects as actual wholes, not merely in the scientific manner as specimens of a type; it attends to the differentia of things as well as to their genus and species. The poet contemplates the world's body, things as they essentially are. A good poet transcends his personality into perception of the universe and the things that compose it.

Poet and scientist approach an object free from prepossessions, stirred by curiosity about it as an independent object. But the scientist is the more easily satisfied. He examines it to obtain some physical satisfaction from it, to classify and control it; from his examination another may later put it to some practical use. The poet wishes to know the object for its own sake. He looks at the whole of it, unrestricted by any ulterior motive. He seeks, as Schopenhauer would have said, a knowledge without desire, to see the object as in itself it really is—though Arnold would perhaps have disapproved Ransom's interpretation of his famous phrase.

Ransom faces squarely the problem of poetic form, which has plagued modern poets ever since the imagists. Much vers libre, he explains, is unfinished because the poet is impatient with the carefully polished weakness of most conventional verse. In this the poet is mistaken; he should try to express himself formally in order to keep at the so-called aesthetic distance from his object, to contemplate the object and grasp its meaning, especially its symbolic meaning. Instinctive experience needs contemplation to transform it into aesthetic experience. The poets will sooner or later get over this affected roughness.

The imagination, Ransom says, approaching it from an angle unlike that taken by Coleridge and Richards, has a function parallel to that of sight except that its technique concerns images instead of objects. In both, the poet contemplates the particularity of nature, for he sincerely means these images also to be true to nature. By either course the poet arrives at more radical knowledge than does the scientist with his carefulness of the type that leads his attention away from the whole.

Aware of the shortcomings of scientific contemplation, modern poets consistently seek an aesthetic effect divorced from moral or useful ideas. As guides and teachers they have the French symbolists, who have shown them the need of wide knowledge; the imagists, who have shown the possibilities in poetry of things; and two poets, John Donne from the past and Ezra Pound in the present, who insist upon the removal from poetry of meretricious or adventitious ornament. Thus instructed, the poet now willingly focuses his attention upon a real or imagined object, leaving to one side verbal and metrical effects. His work in consequence shows the first unfinished motions towards poetic effect.

This modern poetry, Ransom continues, approximates pure poetry; it is poetry of things, not ideas. Victorian poets, supported by Plato from antiquity, preferred poetry of ideas; theirs was an age which suffered a dissociation of sensibility, as Eliot might have said, by which science became paramount. Ransom supports Hulme's charge that nineteenth-century poetry is vague. Man, he adds, is temperamentally more interested in things than in ideas; and though temporarily lured from things by science, he is reproached by his dreams and memory for his desertion of them for theories. Art, too, is always based on revived love—the pleasure of recognition—and as always man turns unsatisfied from generalizations of science to poetic contemplation of objects or images.

Poetry of things never occurs in a pure state. Genuine poetry may start as an idea and never fully depart from it. But the image, which comes to the poet as he considers the idea, quickly assumes control, until the idea may be ignored, almost forgotten. This image Ransom designates the texture of the poem, and the idea its structure. Though the structure may be almost forgotten, no poem can exist without both texture and structure.

Ransom discusses also the relation of the poetic statement to what is commonly called truth—in Aristotle's terms, history or matter of fact. In Ransom's picturesque phrase, scientific, surface-knowledge sees things thin and not thick, does not contemplate the inner essence. Though the poet's assertion may be mythical, it is nevertheless essential truth. He must present "this world's data" in their true, inner significance. The scientist has not truly examined the object because he has not looked straight at it or into it; his ulterior purposes in looking have distorted and partly clouded his vision. The man who feels no interest in individual objects should reclassify himself as a scientist.

In the present age, Ransom admits, some poets find everything so overrun by the prose of science that they take refuge in the past. Nowadays poetry has to become difficult and strange in order to remain poetry. Men are so thoroughly inoculated with the prose view that the poet must shock them out of it. Poetry reacts from the tyranny of factual prose toward the truth derived from intense contemplation; science is strong but prosy; and the reaction, to be effective, must surpass the force it opposes. Poetry must always amplify prose experience or observation into a total experience; but many prose matters are now so nearly insoluble in any poetic solvent that vigorous forces must be applied if the solution is to be made.

The critic who prefers Victorian verse cannot distinguish between things and ideas. With this statement Ransom disqualified as judges of the new poetry most of the older critics during the period of what Eliot had called the dissociation of sensibility. Ransom's opposition to this so-called Platonic criticism naturally inclined him toward Aristotle; and in *The World's Body* he discussed several Aristotelian principles as they seemed to him to relate to the twentieth century. Noteworthy among these principles are Aristotle's mimesis or artistic imitation and catharsis or the purgative effect of art upon the beholder. His treatment, though he obviously knows the scholarly discussions of them, hardly satisfies students of the *Poetics*. Ingeniously he uses Aristotelian terms to support his own theories, and considerably wrests Aristotle in the process.

Aristotle's influence is apparent in Ransom's insistence that criticism become more precise and systematic. The Stagirite would not, however, have agreed with Ransom that it must become the business of trained specialists; in his eyes, literature should be evaluated by the judicious amateur. Ransom finds the best place for its practice in the academic chairs of colleges and universities, by professors who already have the requisite knowledge if they will but apply it.

They must add to scholarship the competence of the artist and the philosopher. They must be objective critics who will report the nature of the poem they contemplate, not its effect upon them. This restriction rules out the followers of Croce and Spingarn. The New Humanists' rampant moralism makes them historians or moralists. Since they are not artists or philosophers, they are as incapable of objective judgments as are the impressionists.

In *The New Criticism* (1941) Ransom discussed younger New Critics and set forth his prospectus for the needed ontological critic. Criticism demands first consideration of structural properties, which is best exemplified in the criticism of Yvor Winters. The second requirement is appreciation and judgment of the texture or local peculiarity of meaning in the poem. The critic who can analyze structure alone is as much a critic of prose as of poetry. Winters' concern with morality classifies him as incompetent to judge the poetry of things, as a critic primarily of prose.

On the principle emerging from his judgment of Winters, Ransom in his critique of I. A. Richards differentiates prose from poetry. Though the work of art may commence from feelings and passions as well as ideas, it seeks appropriate objects, which speedily obtrude themselves. These push the emotions or ideas into less conspicuous positions or even lose sight of them. Constantly being added to the poetic texture are details which overflow or depart from its original configuration. A metaphor, for instance, does not become as a rule an integral part of the structure; Ransom does not consider the esemplastic function of the imagination which Coleridge and Richards maintain; the metaphor introduces a sort of second poem and so diffuses the reader's interest. Poetry thus often transcends its ostensible argument by adding an ambiguity or analogy, for analogy, however suspect by scientists, is valid for poetry. Since the textural quality of the poem so thoroughly overwhelms its structure, the critic should devote his most careful attention to texture, realizing that he is analyzing an ontology, an order of existence which cannot be treated by scientific modes of thought.

By this standard Ransom finds contemporary critics deficient. Eliot's scholarship, fastidious taste, and ability to prevent his own creative mode and religious convictions from limiting his critical judgment receive his unstinted approval. Eliot is a critical scholar after the order of Dryden or Dr. Johnson, the kind of critic Ransom wishes to find in professorial chairs. Less interested in startlingly new theories than Richards and Empson, he recaptures the old criticism for incorporation with the new. His lack of interest in literary theories and preference for comparison of passages make him perhaps more prophet than philosopher.

In classing Eliot with academic scholars, however, Ransom terms him "a Pharisee of the Pharisees"; Eliot seems to him essentially a historical critic, whose judgments place a poet in the tradition but fail to evaluate his work. His attention having been thus diverted from judgment, his sense of values becomes blunted. Since 1928, too, his traditionalism has increasingly shown in religion as well as in criticism. Consequently, Eliot faces backward instead of concentrating upon what lies ahead.

Ransom has also found it necessary to censure the younger generation in his own party. In 1947, his remarks upon Cleanth Brooks's *The Well Wrought Urn* indicated a rift among the New Critics. Reiterating his belief in study of the total connection of words, he deplored the confusion produced by this practice alone, and felt obliged to halt the analytical effort of the group. To many readers, excessive analysis had, he felt, made poetry seem so wholly without order as to make them doubt that a poem could ever be perceived as a whole. This centrifugal effect of analysis must be compensated by effort at synthesis. Brooks, in presenting paradox as a principle of poetry, had failed to establish a satisfactory unifying basis for the poem. Paradox is not rest, but a precarious state which the reader tries to escape by resolving it. Ransom recommends instead renewed attention to structure. The logical positivists, who are now in the saddle, can take poetry apart as they have analyzed theology; since they hold the initiative, the poetic challengers of their supremacy must let them choose the weapons of combat. The New Critics, strong in their mastery of language, are vulnerable in psychology, whereas their enemies have advantageously used psychology, especially by adapting Freudian knowledge and methods. The New Critic must also consider the use and motive of poetry. He must recognize that the poet uses the mode of feeling, not of logic, and that in poetry the syntax may so nearly vanish as to make the meaning nebulous. He must therefore now accept paraphrase, a device anathema to Brooks, as a legitimate critical tool.

Since the impure logical discourse that is poetry does contain a modicum of logic, the defender of poetry cannot ignore the pragmatic and naturalistic approaches to it. The New Critic's horror at such ways partakes of obscurantism; he cannot deny the validity of new knowledge, however unpalatable. He should accept the naturalistic concept of man as a defensible hypothesis if it can figure forth the whole man. Though Ransom believes that the naturalistic view cannot account for the poet and his world, he recognizes it as a position that must be faced, a challenge to be considered and met.

In 1948, Ransom widened further the scope of criticism. Literary judgment, he said, has two margins, the lower of which uses the tools of academic scholarship: study of the language, the period when the book was written, biography of the author—the data listed by August Boeckh as needed in literary hermeneutics. The upper margin is a speculative area, to enter which requires equipment for inquiry into final causes. On either margin there will always be room for investigation. Aristotle, besides his contributions on the lower level, in his ideas on mimesis and catharsis had led the way into the metaphysical realms of criticism. Following his course in either margin, we can reach knowledge beyond his attainment. Like the New Critics, Aristotle was more proficient in linguistic knowledge than in psychology; by combining with his attainments the modern psychologist's discoveries, they can advance farther into the literary empyrean.

Two articles in the 1950 *Kenyon Review* express later stages in Ransom's thought. "The Understanding of Fiction" ventures into a literary genre which the New Critics had for some time neglected. Ransom declares that fiction, like all literature, must possess style for its essential activity. Style he here defines as the sum of those characteristic turns of speech by which the author liberates himself from the bonds of logical prose expression. In fiction, logical interest must as in poetry yield to the concrete or substantial object. Naturalistic writers from Zola's day have lacked style in any developed form; when we progress beyond satisfaction by plot and character to interest in style, such writers cease to charm us. The linguistic analysis developed for poetry applies also to fiction.

Current critics, Ransom proceeds, attend inadequately to the emotional needs of readers. Passion for technique is not enough; the poet must also provide emotional gratification. The literary work takes us into a world of spontaneous and natural affections; Ransom here closely parallels Pope's declaration that it may bypass the judgment and directly touch the heart. The critic must be a psychologist; he suspects indeed that the literary analyst may arrive at sound psychological conclusions before the clinically trained psychologist arrives on the scene. The latter, being a scientist, has studied the affections only to classify them, whereas to the critic they are objects for contemplation in themselves. Much as Diotima taught Socrates the ladder of love, Ransom offers a "ladder of the affections" to guide the baffled literary man who is confounded by the present world.

The second paper, "William Wordsworth: Notes toward an Understanding of His Poetry," diverges still further from the Brooks-Richards reliance upon Coleridge. Coleridge's comments on Wordsworth's theory of poetic diction are misstatements based upon badly chosen critical principles. Wordsworth, whom Ransom now holds in honor, defends the diction that registers factually "a human passion for a concrete object." He realized that the animal, appetitive faculties, which science and business serve as instruments, deal in generalized abstractions, whereas the affections focus upon concretions. To support this new and startling application of Wordsworth's theories, Ransom introduced novel terms for three of the four devices which he noted in poetic language. These are first, Singular Terms or Spreaders, to illuminate the vivid concreteness of objects and events; secondly, Dystactical Terms or Rufflers, which deliberately cultivate logical confusion: inversions, ambiguities, ellipses, asyndeton, and the like; thirdly, Metaphorical Terms or Importers, which introduce foreign objects by analogy or association; and finally, meters. By using almost exclusively the first and fourth of these devices, by keeping his eye steadfastly fixed upon his subject, and by expressing in meter the fruits of his contemplation, Wordsworth composed poems whose purity of style has finally won Ransom's earnest admiration. He recognized here the similarity which was noticeable from the first between his and Wordsworth's approaches to poetry.

Ransom's criticism has held consistently to the superiority of poetry of things to poetry of ideas, and has regularly defended poetry against what seem to him the encroachments of science. He has also added to his earlier principles ideas from other camps as they seemed to him to justify themselves. Since he is the central figure of the New Criticism, he has been discussed in great detail; other figures in the movement will be considered for the most part as they impinge upon him.

ALLEN TATE

Allen Tate's prominence among the New Critics sets him in a position next to Ransom. Though a decade younger than Ransom, he emerged at about the same time as critic and poet; both were members of the Southern agrarian group; and in spite of significant differences in opinion they have enough in common to be treated together.

More than the other New Critics, Tate is concerned with the plight of twentieth-century man. Less theoretical than Ransom, he is afraid that the further criticism advances in system and method, the less aware it becomes of immediate occasions for its use. Tate evidently thinks the practice of criticism a clearer picture of it than any general statement. He shares the widespread apprehension that goes back at least to Huneker, that philosophy has invaded the field of letters and kidnapped criticism.

Tate has consistently opposed the theorists who have for decades been connecting literature with sociology or using it as propaganda. These friends of literature have been trying to justify it by showing it to be something else. The poet inquires how the work shall be done, not why, nor why it is what it is; and the critic likewise should find what poets actually have done or may reasonably be expected to have done in their time. What he thinks they should have done is not criticism. Poetry does not explain experience, it apprehends ex-

perience and concentrates it in limitations of form. Though in appre-
hending experience the poet does to some extent test it, he does not
express or confirm any theory—to do so would change poetry into
propaganda; the Victorian notion of the sugar-coated moral or social
pill derives from philosophical rather than poetic sources.

Tate has, however, been more receptive of ideas than Ransom.
Great philosophical poets, he says, treat a subject already fixed in
their readers' minds; they do not have to teach it. Mediaeval theology was for Dante a datum upon which his sensibility set to work.
By keeping his imagination focused upon this datum he concen-
trated his effort. Since the poem was not propaganda, Dante never
lost sight of its structure. A similar situation existed for Milton when
writing *Paradise Lost*. Idea and sensibility should together produce
a poem, not a didactic treatise. Without this central idea, the arts
have lost a common center of experience, feed upon each other, and
finally disappear into abstractions as much modern art has done.
Need of a common animating idea, which American critics since
Stedman have felt, appears in Tate's thinking as need for a religious
belief; the loss of this, which leaves artists with means but no ends,
he considers a fatal deficiency in American letters.

Tate finds himself accordingly in approximate agreement with
Eliot's emphasis upon tradition. The poet is no revolutionary; his
background is fundamental to his work. When he finds it no longer
intellectually or religiously adequate, he adapts it more closely to
the data provided by experience. He modifies tradition, does not
surrender it. Acting perhaps upon this principle, Tate has recently
gone beyond Eliot's Anglo-Romanism into the Roman Catholic
church. He believes that true poets such as Donne and Emily Dickinson are keenly aware of things as they are; their inherited culture
enables them to control the natural world for their purposes. In their
work a tension is set up between tradition and experience which
arrives at an equilibrium in which their poetic product rests.

This term "tension" has become associated with Tate's criticism.
In "Tension in Poetry" (1938) he developed a kinetic explanation
of the poem in contrast to Ransom's relatively static structure and
texture. The quality of a poem is determined, he writes, by its total
effect. To examine this whole, which results from its configuration

of meaning, is the critic's duty. The most common sort of poetry is generalized personal poetry, that usually results from sentimental, inaccurate observation and is used for propaganda. Its fashion was set by nineteenth-century poetry, conveying ideas and feelings which its writers privately felt could have been better presented by natural or social science. Its confused, frequently undignified imagery contrasts sharply with the coherent and at least apparently logical imagery of the metaphysical poets. These latter denoted in poetry objects undistorted by interposed ideas, and bent words to fit objects. Sentimental poetry treats objects irresponsibly. To indicate the denotative aspects of language, Tate uses the term extension; to denote its connotative aspects, intension. The equilibrium of these two forces in tension gives poetry its meaning. His metaphor conveys a more spirited notion of the vigor leashed in poems than does Ransom's.

Tate sees the proper critical position as somewhere between the historical and journalistic critic. The latter has but one criterion, intensity of feeling; the former, engrossed in irrelevant information, has no critical standards at all. Tate commends Irving Babbitt for recognizing the near impossibility of the young student of letters, as currently trained, ever becoming a critic. Babbitt, however, confusing the moral duty to judge with making a moral judgment, could not himself distinguish between literary and historical work. Historical criticism looks at literature as expressing life, not as possessing it. The critic makes not a moral judgment, which is partial, but, after regarding the work as a whole, delivers a total judgment.

Like Ransom, Tate believes that the attempt to order all experience scientifically omits too much human experience. Since the scientist must ignore in his work the spiritual realm, this realm seems to him to be mere irresponsible feeling; sociological and historical critics see in the arts no meanings beyond what their sciences lead them to expect. Forgetting the individual man, they tend with the professional educators—the worst enemies to sound culture—to look upon men as objects to be adjusted to society instead of individuals with intelligence to be developed. Facing these enemies of men, the critic must maintain and demonstrate the special, unique, and complete knowledge provided by the great forms of literature. Literature is a form of knowledge, not one of many varieties of social or political expression or, as Richards thinks, a kind of applied psychology.

The historical approach to literature, Tate continues, reflects monist philosophies of the nineteenth century. Under their sway scholars see literary works in the light of the currently popular science: under physics, they become forces or causes and effects; under biology, organic growths, developments, or evolutions; or materials for psychology, economics, or sociology. The critic must look at literary works as objects. He must first decide in what respect the work possesses objectivity, testing it not according to its subject matter, which does not share this objectivity, but by its formal qualities. He considers both the literary genre and the entire individuality of the work. He examines past authors' works in the light of the formal, objective expression of our time. Form in past works must be tested in comparison with our mastery of it today. Former authors, he agrees with Howells, should be reassessed every generation or two.

But criticism by formal qualities does not in Tate's view occupy the entire critical area. In the presence of great poetry, critics, being inadequate alone, must pool their effects. Together with examining formal qualities, other investigations contribute to overcome the difficulties in understanding great literature. By these combined efforts the reader-critic may approximate mastery of it, for much of our literature seems difficult only because readers expect to be passively pampered, not exercised by reading. The result of this effort, though not in accord with the scientist's view, will go deeper into life than attention to general qualities alone can penetrate.

All literature, Tate declares, has a social, moral, or religious purpose, which the great writer realizes along with his artistic representation. One must continually remind himself, however, that poetry cannot merely exhort man to perfection, or the purpose may override the poetry. Though he admits that the texture may extend beyond the structure—to use Ransom's terms—he nevertheless believes that the poem should be a complete organic unit. Here he gives structure more house room than Ransom allows it. Tate is, however, more concerned to estimate what poetry can accomplish by what it has achieved than to legislate standards for it.

Tate's more recent work has shown an almost Emersonian mysticism. "The Man of Letters in the Modern World" (1952) pleads for a man who, like Emerson's American scholar, will recreate the image of man for his age and distinguish facts amid appearances. For the present, he said, as Eliot had also told a Parisian audience in 1945, the responsibility of the man of letters is to preserve the vitality of language, distinguishing mere mass communication from the knowledge of man offered by literature. The arts exist for self-knowledge, the Socratic ideal, not for control of others. Those who are taught by literature do not merely communicate with others; they establish a literary communion of saints which wages a holy war against modern dehumanized society that has lost all sense of direction and without ends is engrossed in means. The dehumanizing powers strive to subject man to "drive," "stimulus," and "response," servile terms to which the liberal man opposes "ends," "choices," and "discrimination." This liberal man advances by discrimination, through choice, toward a worthwhile end. To successfully discriminate true from false, he protects the integrity of language in all its uses. His province is culture, and to the culture of language all other culture must yield. His language shows his genuine knowledge of human community, which, in the words of St. John, is communion through love. St. John's vision and the Christian way are in Tate's mind vital to America's survival; a society that has once been religious cannot sink to secularism without risk of spiritual death, of possessing means without ends. So far has Tate's love of language born him in mystical perception.

CLEANTH BROOKS

Of the younger New Critics the most widely known is Cleanth Brooks, who since 1935 has been publishing critical articles productive of spirited controversy. Though he does not profess to be the standard-bearer of the New Critics, his frequent publication, and perhaps his vulnerability, have led to his being singled out by opponents for special attack.

Brooks sounded his first note for metaphor as the prime characteristic of poetry in 1935. Modern conceits, he charged, are accurate, subtle, not sublimely vague like those used in the nineteenth century—one notes again the echo of T. E. Hulme—and they are intellectual, not merely rapturous. Though the poet may engage in an *altitudo*, he may not lose himself in it. Modern poets, in fact, are to the metaphysical poets what Wordsworth and Coleridge were to composers of the folk ballad, heirs of the estate who have developed the property.

Understanding Poetry (1938), by Brooks and Robert Penn Warren, is a landmark in modern poetic study. Though written for undergraduates, its clear, concise expression has stated for critics also the authors' view of the proper approach to poetry. The poem, they assert, must be grasped as a literary object before it can be otherwise considered. Though paraphrase, biographical study, and inspirational or didactic interpretation may be means to its understanding, they do not singly or together reach the whole poem. (Brooks was later to exclude paraphrase as remorselessly as a Covenanter elder would exclude it from worship.) Nor does the scientific view of objects explain poetry, for literature treats of materials different from those of science. It aims at precise statement of attitudes, feelings, and interpretations that ordinary viewing of objects at best vaguely suggests. A poem proves itself by its effect, and its effect arises not out of the things used but from the poet's use of them. Though prose fiction also seeks emotional response, it generally works by accumulation, whereas poetry employs sharp detail produced by careful arrangement of selected items. Verse controls words and entices the reader's imagination by its recurrent rhythms to the willing temporary suspension of disbelief. However much the authors' youthful singlemindedness may detract from its scope—and their opponents have not been slow to attack it—the book has stimulated more exact reading of poetry by a greatly increased number of readers.

Brooks reached more theoretical levels in his *Modern Poetry and the Tradition* (1939) and in *The Well Wrought Urn* (1947). The earlier book opens with Eliot's contention that each poet we read alters somewhat our total conception of poetry. Modern poets in particular have effected a radical modification of our conception. Dr. Johnson's view of metaphor as intended to ornament and ennoble the poem is, for example, invalid for modern poetry. It may now be the entire poetic statement. Moreover, the notion sponsored by Coleridge and Arnold, that play of intellect and wit is incompatible with the elevated, serious content of poetry, is incorrect. It rules out dramatic development of emotion and relegates to satire the use of ironic imagery. Arnold concentrates his effect by excision of all experience not an integral part of the poem; the modern poet, in this respect closer to Coleridge, almost fuses into a whole the conflicting elements of experience. Like the metaphysical poet, he gambles on the power of imagination to reconcile opposites. He retains the irony which in a fully unified work would disappear. Wit, whose penetrating quality would destroy the veil cast over so much romantic poetry, was excluded until the symbolists revived its use; modern poetry employs it freely. Metaphor, intellect, and ironic wit are major forces in Brooks's concept of poetry.

Brooks joins Ransom, Tate, and Richards in declaring that the scientist's question concerning factual truth does not arise in poetry. Neither do poetic symbols merely stand for ideas. The poem does not contain, but is, the communication; what it is, matters. Logic may be a powerful instrument of the poem, but no more. Science, to which logic belongs, was no problem for the metaphysical poet, but its assumption of control put an end to metaphysical poetry. After the founding of the Royal Academy, poetry and science were confused, and what Eliot called the dissociation of sensibility set in. The modern poet, in reverting to metaphysical practice, must face the problem raised by science concerning the nature of truth.

The New Critics' pronouncements against many aspects of academic scholarship brought against them the charge of hostility to such scholarship. In 1946, Brooks denied the charge. The New Criticism relies heavily upon the history of language and ideas and upon literary scholarship generally; it attacks only the academic failure to crystallize this knowledge into a critical attitude, the assumption that such studies of themselves constitute criticism. The New Critics, he added, are versed in rhetorical principles, one of which is to concentrate one's pressure upon the idea one wishes to promote, to the occasional exclusion of possibly related matter. Much of Brooks's writing employs this device; now adverse comment has made it necessary to round out the statement of his position. In *The Well Wrought Urn,* one finds more exposition and less rhetoric.

In the latter work, notwithstanding his friendlier tone toward the several literary disciplines, Brooks does not retreat from his earlier positions but rather strengthens them. He declares paradox to be the essence of poetic language. While science tries to stabilize terms, the poet tends continually to warp them in order to make them accurately fit his meaning. Connotations are as important as denotations: poets "by indirections find directions out." The subtle states of emotion which poets portray demand an accuracy of expression that can only be achieved by metaphor; and metaphor brings paradox. The effect is an extension, not a perversion, of language; the possible bad sense of the metaphor in "warping" does not enter here. To the reader willing to work out its meaning, even the ambiguity in ironic metaphor is not deceptive but enlightening.

In Brooks's eyes the basic critical ill is the tendency to confuse comment on the poem with its essential core. Critics are prone to restate the poem in a prose paraphrase as a step toward elucidating it. Such a procedure, he declares, presumes the paraphrasable part of the poem to be its essential part. But the act splits the poem, which is by nature a whole, into form and content; and the content differs hardly at all from a statement of science, philosophy, or theology. It totally ignores the poetic function of metaphor and meter. It substitutes for the imaginative coherence of the poem a logical coherence, and fails utterly to present the whole poem.

Brooks assures readers that the poem has ideas as well as attitudes; but its content cannot, so to speak, be poured out of its form as a prose statement. Form and content compose an indivisible unit. The ideas, moreover, though justified in the imaginative poem, may when stated in prose paraphrase appear nonsensical, even untrue. Poetic truth cannot double as scientific fact. The unity of the poem is, as Tate asserts, an equilibrium of tensions; extraction of any part leaves the remainder in imbalance. Words themselves are not the same in poetry as in prose; in poetry their relation warps them to fit the exigencies of the poem. The poet does not analyze actual experience like the historian; he synthesizes out of experience a simulacrum of reality that is in fact a new experience. For all these reasons, the heresy of paraphrase is as deadly a poetic error as Poe's heresy of the didactic.

A second critical ill consists in emphasizing differences between poems. Though these cannot be ignored, Brooks believes it more important to attend to their common qualities. By so doing we are led at once to levels of meaning, symbolizations, clashing connotations, paradoxes, and ironies, which bring us closer to the organic structural principle of poetry than any previously emphasized approaches. One may learn more about poetry by applying a single set of criteria to all poems than by looking at their differences.

His monistic position leads Brooks to disagree with Ransom, who seems to him to demand too systematic a construction in the poem, with all metaphors logically working out into a texture and structure as unified as warp and woof in a rug. Tate's kinetic metaphor of tensions in uneasy balance appeals to him as more descriptive of the conditions within a poem. Though Ransom's admiration for Donne's logical rigor is warranted, it does not justify his assuming one strategy to be the whole art. Poetic decorum—Brooks finds the term apt because Ransom's system reminds him of neoclassical regularity—is simply set by the poem itself. Whenever the devices used produce a coherent and powerful poem, it satisfies the proprieties.

Brooks's "Irony as a Principle" (1949) presented irony as closely allied to paradox, and metaphor as the matrix of both. Modern poetic technique consists in the rediscovery and full use of metaphor in poetry. The poet enters the universal through the particular, realizing the details in order to attain the general meaning. Metaphor prevents the tendency of direct statement to lead from particulars toward abstraction. In poetry, images or words or statements become so charged with significance from their context that images become symbols and statements dramatic utterances. The warping of statements by their context is irony, a phenomenon of practically all poetic statements. Only abstractions, which poetry avoids, escape such warping.

Brooks's concentration upon the pervasive function of paradox aroused outspoken opposition. Ransom's strictures have already been noted. A more vigorous and hostile reaction was Ronald S. Crane's review of *The Well Wrought Urn* in 1948, "Cleanth Brooks: or, the Bankruptcy of Critical Monism." Crane, a formidable opponent, begins disarmingly by approving the New Critics' insistence upon viewing poetry as poetry and not another thing, and their fight against the dictatorship of "factual science and relativism"; and he heartily endorses their careful textual study of poems. But, though he admits that paradox as Brooks uses the term is characteristic of all poems, Crane parts company with Brooks when he tries to set up this quality as their sole principle. A similar monistic fallacy, Crane declares, exists in Tate's reduction of poetry to tension, in Ransom's principle of texture, and in Richards' obsession with behavior of words. Crane is in fact only less concerned with the other New Critics than with Brooks.

Part of the New Critics' difficulty, Crane continues, stems from their attempt to reduce Coleridge's poetic theory in *Biographia Literaria* to a single principle. They diminish its greatness—it is far too big to be reduced to one source—by calling it a confused glimpse of the simple truth. Coleridge actually found that, though the imagination was more important for poetry than the other factors, in criticizing poetry one must take into account other qualities that enter into its composition. They also fail to note Coleridge's distinction between "poetry," or architectonic thought, and "poem," a composition in words of a special kind that differs from prose in their combination to meet the exigencies of "a different object being proposed" from that of prose. Poetry and poem refer respectively to an ideal concept and an actual object which have in common the idea of imitation. Brooks has combined part of Coleridge's definition of poetry with part of his definition of the poem in an endeavor to constitute poetry as homogeneous in structure throughout all its embodiments in poems by reason of one common characteristic, irony or paradox. He has ignored Coleridge's interest in the differences among poems. His attempted unification also fails to note distinctions between form and substance, the manner and matter, of poems. Furthermore, Coleridge found "poetry" in philosophical and scientific works, which were not "poems." His was a criterion of value, not a differentia of kind. Brooks's attempted simplification confounds confusion by mingling parts of two definitions and applying the compound as a definition of one of the two objects originally defined.

To Crane, Brooks is fundamentally a grammarian interested in the impact of words upon one another. His position has been the staple of rhetoric and poetic from the days of mediaeval literary study. Brooks has in fact reduced poetics to grammar. Since grammar is present in all poetry, Brooks's poetics cannot account for the special varieties of pleasure afforded us by such widely different poems as he discusses in *The Well Wrought Urn*. Criticism which ignores such differences is for Crane quite inadequate.

Crane suggests that Brooks and, by implication, the other New Critics, have taken hold of poetry at the wrong end. They have started not with poems of varying kinds as interrelated yet different wholes, but have instead commenced with their language, which is but one of their many components. He advises them to begin with the concrete poem, to argue a posteriori instead of a priori, to begin with immediately sensible effects—poems—and proceed to their proximate causes. His ironic turning of their own guns upon the New Critics has not, to my knowledge, been specifically answered except by restatement of their position and by their continuing conciliation of other approaches to poetry. Even with this concession, Brooks warns in the 1951 *Kenyon Review*, the New Critic should continue to focus his light upon the work itself, not permitting interest in author or reader to lure him into biography or psychology. Worthwhile as these pursuits are, they are not that "description and evaluation of its subject" which constitutes criticism.

R. P. BLACKMUR

Perhaps the least absorbed of the New Critics in their particular approach to literature is R. P. Blackmur, who since the early 1930's has been combining interest in language with attention to other aspects of poetry. His major concerns are the deficiencies of expressive form and the importance of adhering to the dictionary significance of words. E. E. Cummings and Carl Sandburg supplied his texts for attack upon writers who feel that their experience is real and final and that mere statement of their experience is poetry. Their notion he evidently considers to be a development through Whitman of Emerson's doctrine of organic form; he notes that Whitman mistakenly thinks the handiest word the best. The poet should exercise intellectual control over his materials, especially by selecting the most adequate words. Cummings' expression is either so conventionally obvious as to be flat or so unconventional as to be barely intelligible. At best, he provides notes for a poem, not the poem itself. Sandburg is a sensitive reporter with almost instinctive perception of the best way to report his observation. He needs, however, a controlling intelligence to recognize and order the confused irony of life. Reporting is ancillary and preliminary to the poem.

Intellectual control begins with use of words. Blackmur consistently minimizes the bending or warping of words emphasized by Ransom and Brooks. Good poets employ words faithfully to their definitions, and by so doing achieve the new and strange. Use of words, Blackmur admits, does slightly alter their dictionary appearance by selecting one from the several listed meanings and placing it in context with other words; there may even be some ambiguity of meaning. Further modification, however, nullifies the value of the word.

Important in Blackmur's eyes is the control of the poet's mind over his materials. Unlike Ransom and closer to Tate, he demands that the poem be as nearly as possible a unit; and its structure must be rationally conceived, its component parts arranged into a whole. It is not limited to the poet's self-expression, which is not poetry. If it were poetry, there would be no need for growth in intellect and taste and in the insight characteristic of the true poet. Unorganized personal expression is chaos, presenting materials without due regard for the niceties of language. It may even be irrational hysteria, which, though undeniably expression, must be analyzed to become intelligible. The great poet has always been, like Dante, profoundly rational even when most deeply moved; he is integrating and perfectly clear. Like Lionel Trilling, Blackmur refuses to see in neurosis or psychosis adequate expression of the poet's power, which is intellectual.

His account of poetic power opens the way to Blackmur's concept of the critic. One can, he says, judge only technical aspects of a poem, by showing how its parts bear upon each other and what tensions are produced among them. He can indicate how its words work together, sometimes elevating the commonplace to poetry, sometimes finding bare statement to be poetic. Such analysis can lead to the vision of that in the poem which transcends rational accounting. Like Aristotle, Blackmur stops as critic where analysis must stop.

The critical intellect must be supplemented by sympathy. In defining criticism as "the formal discourse of an amateur," Blackmur deliberately employs an ambiguity. The critic is, as Emerson said, the lover advised; not a professional practitioner of a science, he practices an art interdependent with the other arts concerned with life. As a lover of poetry, he seeks more intimate acquaintance with the beloved object, rearranging and identifying ceaselessly whatever it can impart in the hope of thereby knowing it better. He finds a complex approach rewarding. And he never lets his love blind him to the true nature of its object. Careful to avoid all preconceived notions of it, he tries to prevent personal bias from clouding his vision.

Without some ulterior purpose, Blackmur continues, criticism is unlikely to survive. It is a means, not an end; and the lover quite properly sees a use in the beloved object. This use, however, cannot displace the object in his affection. Failure to heed this latter warning invalidates Marxist literary theory, which keeps its eye, so to speak, on the dower instead of the espoused. Marxists, however, find their parallel in this respect in diverse groups: Christians and humanists, for example, are in this matter alike culpable.

As a preventive for criticizing by our personal perceptions, a set of objective standards outside of and antecedent to our own practice is needed. Here also is danger: these standards may develop into a system which blocks the activity of the individual imagination. Such a flaw Blackmur notes in I. A. Richards, whose legitimate scientific approach to poetic language mushroomed until it almost reduced criticism to linguistic science. His opposition to Brooks's critical monism probably grows from the same root.

These ideas were developed or adumbrated in *The Double Agent* (1935). A second collection of essays, *The Expense of Greatness* (1940), goes further into the content of poetry, not trying to analyze what Blackmur believes cannot be analyzed, but describing its problems. Paramount among requirements for content is a body of belief. In Dante and Milton, as Tate also points out, the poet's belief was already at hand when he began to write. Nowadays, the poet must create some personal belief like Yeats, revive some belief from the past, or seek some present but hidden system. In none of these attempts does Blackmur find poets to be wholly successful. Closely related is the need of a background of tradition, orthodoxy, or moral dependence to govern and provide atmosphere for literature. The writer's material is inevitably morals, mores as they are; he is steadily to see facts amid appearances. He will feel with it but at the same time judge it. In this function poet and critic merge. In the modern, secularized American world, morals and tradition have almost lost their sanctions; writer and critic alike act without a code to enforce. Either by revival of the old or by discovery, they must attain convincing values. In these essays Blackmur proposes no solution, being content to expose the perils of the situation and, it may be, feeling in 1940 not a little like Jeremiah.

In "The Enabling Act of Criticism" (1941), Blackmur proposed a tentative course for the critic in this near impasse. He must first admit that his peculiar approach to literature is not the full approach. Next, he must candidly apply certain tests to other approaches. He must consider whether these pretenders everywhere subordinate their claims to the interests of the work criticized or are instead subordinated to some extraliterary interest. If the latter, does that interest still illuminate the object? Like Eliot, he admits that nonliterary standards aid in determining the greatness of literature. Moral, social, political, and spiritual interests all must be examined in the way the writer uses them. Thus armed, the critic concentrates his full attention upon the analyzable techniques that interact in the work. He accepts whatever the words tell him until he can bring to bear extraliterary standards; having applied both sorts of tests, he will know whether it is literature and whether it is great. Blackmur's proposed procedure for the critic marks the limit to which a man skeptical of extensive critical theory probably cares to go.

In 1946, Blackmur developed further his concept of critical techniques. Still tentatively, he sets up four principal critical categories, allowing for subordinate techniques if needed. His first category includes meter and plot, which carry along the reader's attention and unite literature with its subject. The second, consisting of linguistic techniques, busies itself with images and tropes which give a certain validity to literature and indicate partially the richness of its materials. The integral, not ornamental, tropes combine the concrete image in the artist's view with something abstracted from another work or field of the mind. The third category penetrates more deeply into the activity of the imagination in attempting to show how the mind by images and idioms produces discourse as meaningful as the actual experience. For this the critic employs a variety of techniques: criticism of ideas, and deterministic, Freudian, or environmental theories, to name a few. These methods help to lay bare the truth about the object or idea contemplated. Interaction of theories with actual instances aids both creation and criticism; known conventions bypass needless explanations that would prevent one from ever arriving at actuality.

This imaginative activity having cleared the way to actuality, the artist is free to present it; and the critic's fourth category tests its presence and the degree of artistic attainment. Author and reader-critic alike must attain the closest possible rapport if this criticism is to be effective. The critic must give full assent to the writer while at the same time exercising analytical discrimination and, in the end, judgment.

In "A Burden for Critics" (1948), Blackmur commented upon the current situation of the critic. His task is to complete for the reader the form of the work of art. Joining the attack upon Brooks, Blackmur repeats that a monist interpretation of literature is impossible. Poets, to put it bluntly, are now left holding the whole cultural bag; even religion has deserted its post on the cultural front. But poetry cannot, in spite of Arnold's expectations, substitute for religion, except in so far as religious experience is also aesthetic. What it can do to take the place vacated by religion, it has done; and it has in consequence been receiving the exegesis formerly applied to the Scriptures.

The task of the arts is to treat of the actual in their day in the light of the pitifully slight available tradition. For criticism, the task is to bridge the gap between society and the arts. It must train readers in the nearly forgotten practice of symbolic thinking; it must show artists how to follow old practices under new conditions. For the multiform current needs, the linguistic emphasis of the New Criticism is not enough. Its service is only preliminary to filling the needs of the time. In our age, without knowledge or standards of art, ignorant of aesthetic experience, and lacking a religious tradition, one must look to the critics for analysis and exposition as well as for comparison and judgment.

In the same vein, Blackmur in 1950 called upon the New Critics to cease to rest upon their laurels. They must not let their method harden into methodology, but must include more attention to scholarly research. Criticism and scholarship are go-betweens for artist and reader; if they will not attempt to become more than this, they will bring artist and reader into profitable relation; and having accomplished this service, they should both retire to the background. In preparation the better to perform their service, the New Critics should delve prayerfully into the critical theories of Aristotle and Coleridge. Their previous misconceptions of these two authorities have been harmful to their thinking. Both have written sacred books for criticism, which have been buried under unwieldly masses of often obscuring commentary. The time is ripe for a reformation in which every critic reads these scriptures for himself. The future of American criticism, Blackmur believes, is bound up in the success with which critics pursue this study.

Yvor Winters

On the periphery of the New Criticism is Yvor Winters, who for fifteen years has disagreed violently with Ransom and in only less degree with Brooks. Between Winters and Ransom the bone of contention is the content and purpose of poetry. Winters elevates the logical structure, which to Ransom is of minimal significance, to an importance equal with the texture of the poem. He believes that an aesthetic may be created by analysis of the ethical significance of poems, and unlike Brooks he considers a poem defective if not readily susceptible of paraphrase. His concern with moral values and abstract statement severs him from close relations with others in the movement.

To Ransom's strictures upon Winters' moral approach to literature, which have already been mentioned, Winters responds by charging Ransom with too restricted a conception of moral judgment as merely the classifying of an act as morally good or bad. To Winters, morals are closely akin to mores. Ethical interest, so defined, is the only poetical interest that concerns Winters. Poetry has value as it correctly evaluates experience. The poet's training is designed to give him an ever sounder attitude toward his experience and to extend its range. This purpose places such a premium upon knowledge and achievement that the most valuable poem in Winters' eyes is that which achieves formal perfection under the greatest difficulty. Contemporary poets, Winters declares, for the most part ignore this requisite to greatness. In harmony with his conception of values, he describes poetry as a means of enriching one's awareness of human experience and of strengthening one's moral temper. His point of view here, he asserts, simply restates ideas current in English poetic theory since Sir Philip Sidney's day.

Winters' skepticism of critical definition equals Blackmur's. One can merely indicate the unique experience which is poetry; and surely it is more important to discover the precise nature of that experience than to reduce it to generalization and thereby for poetical purposes demolish it. Unlike weights and measures, critical standards are feelings of rightness and completeness formed and refined in some measure by study of the masters. They closely resemble Addison's conception of good taste. Though values therefore cannot be accurately measured in literature, they can, as near unanimity about great poets proves, be gauged with fair accuracy.

As this attitude implies, Winters admires traditional poetry; it is economically and firmly constructed to produce its effect. It balances feeling and motivation; it admits a wide range of feeling; and its conventional modes release the mind from concern with them to concentrate fully upon its denotative and connotative meanings. Though not hostile to experiment and innovation, Winters feels that recent poetry has been rash in letting go of tradition and convention.

In *Maule's Curse* (1938), Winters defends his heretical attitude toward Hawthorne, Melville, Poe, and Emerson. The artist, he insists, needs moral standards; Emerson's "sentiment divine / Against the being of a line," if accepted, renders poetry impossible. Hawthorne, in abandoning the ordered world of his Puritan ancestors, gave up the only systematic concept he knew; when he temporarily adopted Puritan principles for *The Scarlet Letter,* he composed merely a dramatic allegory. In spite of his manifold faults, James Fenimore Cooper wrote successfully because he possessed an ordered concept of life that made his Indian pictures artistically credible.

Poe, however, receives the full broadside of Winters' attack upon American obscurantism. Poe is "a bad writer accidentally and temporarily popular," whose impressionistic admirers have awed scholars into amassing a large body of imposing editions, commentaries, and criticism about him. Objective examination of his works, Winters believes, explodes the Poe bubble by exposing their badness. He goes beyond W. C. Brownell and Norman Foerster in denying to Poe even the reputation of a stylist, almost the only merit they had left him. Poe was too contemporaneous in his literary knowledge; his declaration that no age probably ever thought before his own betrays his crass ignorance of the long literary and scholarly tradition.

Mechanical rules, Winters continues, govern Poe's conception of literature. He attends constantly to devices designed to produce impressions; to Poe, artistic unity is simply totality of effect. The probability that in the reading of longer poems interruptions will break the psychological continuity of effect leads him to rule out as poetry whatever work cannot be read at a single sitting, just as he prefers the short story to the novel. Winters joins the line of American defenders of the epic from Henry Timrod to the present who can see how the reader retains the whole of *Paradise Lost* in his mind in order to relate his enjoyment of a passage to his inclusive response to the whole. In defining poetry to his own satisfaction, Poe ruthlessly excludes nearly all the great masters from Homer to his own day—a defect, one may add, found in many of Winters' own contemporaries.

Ransom's strictures upon Winters probably contributed to his dilating upon Poe's reaction to didactic poetry. Poe's charges against some of Longfellow's and Lowell's poetry would have been justified if he had simply condemned them for writing badly. This fault, not their didacticism, deserved censure. They failed to articulate the lesson with the object, dragging in arbitrarily a meaning that did not inhere in the object. Merely tagging a moral to the end of a poem —like a Q. E. D., as Stedman remarked of Longfellow—is not faulty when, as in Bryant's "To a Waterfowl," the lesson in spite of being articulated to the object needs clarification. Poe's discarding of truth and retention of beauty as the sole matter of poetry proves his failure to grasp the nature of beauty, which is in fact not the matter of poetry but a quality of style. Complete communication of a moral or humane truth requires beauty of expression; it is truth understood primarily in conceptual terms. Truth is not poetry, but poetry is truth plus something more, a complete experience. Poe is again wrong in requiring strangeness as a quality of beauty; this is the demand of a romantic journalist. The root of Poe's trouble, as Winters sees it, lies in his failure to realize that truth, like any other idea, may be contemplated poetically without any desire to propagandize in its favor.

Poe's tales are mechanical contrivances to create an emotion, to contrive a puzzle, not to understand an experience. He fails to see that human experience when understood arouses emotional response. In all Poe's work, Winters declares, his absorption in mechanical devices is caused by his lack of theme. Having few ideas to express, he naturally belittles their importance; and he cannot see that all experience is moral experience. By this whole attack upon Poe, which to many seems excessively severe, Winters bolsters his own preoccupation with morals as he defines them.

In *The Anatomy of Nonsense* (1943), Winters attacks the romantic literary tradition. The romantic theorist, being usually deficient in reason and either without talent or untrained or both, leaves reason out of his poetic theory and sets up a mechanism to defend his deficiencies. Poetry, however, is composed by and for the intelligent. By words the poet communicates his rational understanding of his subject together with the feeling it generates. The poem's value resides in the relation between its rational core and its feeling. Ransom and

Tate are too fearful of abstract statement, which is integral to poetry. Since poetry is for the intelligent, the critic must add to his poetic capacity scholarly discipline. The romantic critic's avoidance of scholarly training leaves him incompetent to judge poetry.

Later essays by Winters emphasize his steadfast support of the close relation between beauty and moral truth in poetry. This position contradicts Ransom's preference for texture above structure and adds another basic principle to the New Critics' preoccupation with words. His critique of Robert Frost (1948) finds this poet valuable, as he can apprehend certain kinds of objective truth, and asserts that the great poet resembles what man ought to be—an idea stemming from Emerson and found also in the later Van Wyck Brooks. A spiritual drifter, as he conceives Frost to be, cannot be a major poet. An important topic of nineteenth-century debate is thus tossed again into the critical arena.

Definitive evaluation of the considerable contribution made by the New Critics must await the passage of time. It is already evident that their concentration upon linguistic expression has benefited the study of poetry. Readers needed to realize that "the poem's the thing." By this redirection of poetic study and by the publicity they have given to poetic problems, they have increased the number of readers of poetry. Even their too sweeping assertions, by stirring opponents to combat them, have injected new life into the study of literature. The self-evaluation of the New Critics during the past seven years, and the indications that they are increasingly ready to widen their study, are encouraging signs. Whether this expansion indicates their further development or their disappearance as a school, no one can now say. They remain, however, one of the most important and colorful schools of criticism which the century has yet produced.

Chapter 12

Recent Practicing Critics

WHILE THE NEW CRITICS were marching and counter-marching, other writers, inspired by the stimulating early essays of Van Wyck Brooks in the years following World War I, were examining America's usable past and pregnant present. Though not guiltless of literary theories, they were engaged primarily in criticism of books, and as a rule they kept in view the American average reader instead of the fit though few. Of the many who contributed to this important activity during the past quarter-century, T. K. Whipple, Edmund Wilson, and the later Van Wyck Brooks are perhaps especially significant.

T. K. WHIPPLE

In two volumes of collected essays, *Spokesmen* (1928) and *Study out the Land* (1943), Thomas K. Whipple passed judgment upon contemporary writers. The earlier volume attacks sentimentalism in the vein of James Russell Lowell. The sentimentalist, shutting his eyes to the emotional stimulus of real objects, tries instead to react conventionally to the class of objects without looking at them; the poet sees things as they are, whether fair or foul, and responds to them. The creative artist must from experience or imagination obtain materials before he can transmute them into poetry.

His mind needs sensuous, emotional, intellectual food and exercise. Such pabulum the United States supplies not only in tradition but also in its practical present.

Whipple impatiently dismisses those critics who harp on the hardships of the American writer. We lack tradition, we devote our best efforts to money-making, we puritanically look askance at art, we seek a "democratic" standardization or leveling-off. American writers have nevertheless since World War I successfully been opposing the weak sensuousness of thought, the deficient concept of the human drama, the weak criticism, the immature sentimentalism and romanticism, and the moralism that such a society breeds in literature.

Practical forces in America, he admits, have prevented American writers from achieving greater success. E. A. Robinson lacks sensuousness, opulent imagery, and variety. Robert Frost succumbs at times to the belief that "the fact is the sweetest dream that labor knows"; at such times he regards poetry in the same glance with an axe-helve. Carl Sandburg sees poetry as little more than a running commentary on the poet's daily life. His lax taste fails to discipline his undoubted power, and he does not see that thought and judgment are legitimate ingredients of poetry. Vachel Lindsay looks on poetry as a weapon for saving the world. His moralism is that of the pulpit exhorter, not that poetic moralism which seeks the more abundant life. All four find the practical side of America cramping.

Among the novelists, Dreiser suffers from similar faults, at times weakening almost to the error of expressive form. Willa Cather, however, supports Whipple's belief in the usableness of the American scene. She proves that the American writer may represent American life without becoming bogged down in it or assuming any invidious relation to it. Difficult though times are for the writer, Whipple insists that what Miss Cather has accomplished with her materials others also can accomplish.

Whipple's second volume opens with a highly provocative essay, "Machinery, Magic, and Art" (1931). Artists, he charges, are chiefly responsible for the crassness of the age in which they dwell, because they have neglected their service to their age. By asserting a distinction between fine and useful art, artists have relinquished their sole claim upon the average man's attention. All art ought to be useful to man as it formerly was among the Greeks, who—as Howells had earlier remarked—had no notion of art for art's sake. Amid warring theories of art, the so-called practical arts, like engineering, have prospered because the public mind feels assured of their use and realizes the power which they transmit and regulate. "What men crave is power," and unless an art can show power, men will ignore it.

In the fine arts there resides a nonphysical power known to the ancients as magic, a psychological machinery by which men can augment their power over the mind and emotions of others. Its principal means are images and rhythm. Whipple is of course aware of the double meaning in the Latin *carmen* as both song and charm or spell, and of the long-established ambiguity of *vates* as both poet and prophet. From ancient spell and charm developed ritual, which in turn became drama and choral singing, while sacred myth developed into fiction. From these impulses toward that power which underlies magic sprang both art and science. But while science has remained true to the acquisition of power, the fine arts have drifted away until nowadays many artists, especially the imagists, have totally divorced art from power. Critics who deny social function to art emasculate it. By the "magic" of his art—the power of image and rhythm—the artist transmits a power to us. Rhythm is order and harmony, which proceed from the work of art into our seldom ordered lives and effect a catharsis of disorder. The image is the potent transmitter of this power. Too many artists, abetted by critics, by making their images impotent, lose public interest; art is consequently ignored in the common man's scheme of things in favor of science with its demonstrated power. Unless the American artist quickly returns to the sources and means of power, his days in the land are numbered.

Tradition also plays a large part in transmitting artistic power; but for the average American tradition is sadly broken. A man from a fairly advanced culture, he was suddenly plunged into primitive living conditions, only to find before becoming adjusted to these that civilization has overtaken him, with hitherto unknown additions. For the Western settler this development has been even more chaotically speeded up than for the first colonists. In Oklahoma, for example—though Whipple named no specific cases—where the process has been most syncopated, a man's normal life spans the 1889 land rush through the era of the fringed surrey into the age of jet propulsion, with all the corresponding cultural developments foreshortened in time, so that in such an instance at least nature has actually proceeded by jumps. Americans who have thus been rushing headling through cultural stages, Whipple finds, have quite lost the sense of orderly tradition. Worse off than the people of Arnold's day in this respect, they are dwellers in three worlds: a dead past, which still speaks; a recent past, whose echoes still ring in their ears; and a kaleidoscopically changing present. Like dissolving views on a cinema screen, they can hardly be distinguished and severally evaluated, much less built into a structural development.

Quite in harmony with his belief in the significance in the American scene, Whipple insisted in 1937 that the so-called renaissance of the postwar era had been rather a death struggle. He charged the writers of these decades with refusal to face the situation, to make use of the present forces in the world for their art. Their insistence upon divorcing art from the sources of power had, he declared, almost fatally weakened art in America. The Marxist radicals, who were trying their best to harness the new forces, had great advantages over other writers. Their defects indeed prevented the literary capitalizing upon their position; their strong enthusiasm and energy were counterbalanced by their inexperience as writers, and they lacked matter. If the conservatives would, with their superior knowledge of literary practice and their available matter in the American tradition, connect their work to the source of power, they could wrest the literary initiative from the radicals. His demand for a literature of power brings vigorously to the fore a concept of literature quite alien to that of the New Critics.

EDMUND WILSON

A reviewer whose activity reaches into the present literary scene is Edmund Wilson. His essays and reviews have for nearly four decades dotted the pages of periodicals and have been collected into several volumes. His early literary relations were diverse. A graduate of Princeton, he was an admirer of Babbitt's and More's scholarship who refused to be restricted to their academicism. He delighted in Huneker's gusto, which in his pages has been transformed into nostalgia, and in Mencken's debunking of Puritanism. He admired Whipple's attempts as a midwesterner to understand and appraise Midwestern novelists. He was an associate of Max Eastman and an admirer, with reservations, of Leon Trotsky. Knowledge of various sources figures in his papers: American burlesque, the New York of Ring Lardner and Burton Rascoe, Greenwich Village, the New Humanists, Marxism and Russian Communism, and the Greek tragedies, enter into the products of his fertile mind. Few men are better equipped to discuss twentieth-century trends than Wilson, who has himself been no small part of them.

Wilson's pre-depression reviews indicate his awareness of the literary weaknesses in the postwar decade. His friend Fitzgerald, he wrote, had imagination uncontrolled by intellect, a flair for expression without ideas. A native of the Middle West, he should have written of it as the milieu he actually understood. Though Wilson thought Ezra Pound's poetry contained good lines, he felt that it failed to hang together. The numerous American revivals of art for art's sake were in his eyes detrimental to American letters. Without equaling Whipple in condemning the disconnection of American poetry from the sources of power, he decried the poets' deliberate appeal to the eye and deafness to the sound of great poetry. Their worship of Whitman overlooked Whitman's extraordinary musical gift, and their merely intellectual appeal failed to attract readers. Since they lived without engaging in the important or interesting affairs that great poets always have engaged in, they had nothing significant to convey. Tone-deaf poets with nothing of interest to say rely perforce upon manner, which produces poetry of the surface, without depth. Imperfect diction, too, was a shortcoming of this decade. Even when, as in Eugene O'Neill's plays, dramatic ideas appeared, they were inadequately clad in words; and an idea, however excellent, cannot become literature until suitably expressed.

Critics fared no better at his hands. They were badly educated

or had never learned to write, or both. His contempt for these criticasters equaled that of Babbitt and More. These two belonged to
an age which, though less lively and emancipated than the present,
possessed a sounder culture; and they were sounder craftsmen.
Stephen Crane, who passed with them for a mere journalist, could
not write carelessly. Mencken, for all his proneness to paradox and
vulgarity, succeeded in making his opinions into literature of a certain distinction, though after frequent repetition it was by 1926 beginning to pall. The exception was T. S. Eliot, who, in spite of his
bookishness and despondent outlook, was the most important critic
of the English-speaking world. The ignorance of even the best current critics, however, appeared in their admiration of past poetry
for only those qualities which seemed to them modern and like what
they themselves cultivated.

In summarizing the pre-depression decade, Wilson found four
powerful literary parties and a school. The parties were, first, that
of H. L. Mencken and the *American Mercury;* second, that of T. S.
Eliot and those American writers who were loyal to the leader over
the water; third, a noncritical group loosely named neoromantics,
among whom Edna Millay and Scott Fitzgerald were prominent;
and finally, the social revolutionists, led by John Dos Passos and
Michael Gold. The school comprised the "psychologico-sociological
critics," among whom were Van Wyck Brooks, Lewis Mumford, and
Joseph Wood Krutch. Amid all these writers, however, no serious
criticism was being produced. Unlike the French, whose literary
parties clash to their mutual advantage, the Americans were content
to write apologies for or expositions of whatever each was doing,
existing the while in groups almost completely insulated from each
other. (This situation was soon to alter considerably.) Without daily
conflict, the American critics were almost devoid of that maturity
which comes from the clash of opposing minds.

Their immaturity showed itself in the lack of specialists in literary criticism. While scientific and technical books found competent reviewers, a volume of poetry or a novel could not find in
America a reviewer trained for the task. The critics too lacked competent criticism of their work. Mencken and Eliot both showed the
need of reviewers capable of pointing out their strength and weak-

ness. The lack of adequate judgment of our earlier literature was crippling to current criticism. Although there were good biographies of several American authors in 1928, critical assessments of these writers were a pressing need.

Wilson's most influential work dates from the thirties; though he continues active, his critical lines were pretty accurately run by the beginning of World War II. His attention was devoted chiefly to the Marxist view of literature and to defining his position with reference to Eliot, the New Humanists, and the psychoanalytical critics.

On Marxist literature Wilson's earliest significant comment appeared in an unsigned editorial in the 1930 *New Republic* about a month after it had printed a violent attack by Michael Gold on Thornton Wilder. Wilson contended that the Marxist critical view deserved attention if only for the ineffectualness of the retorts to Gold's review; amid the pointlessness and insipidity of most current criticism such a document could not fail to attract notice. Reviewers in the main, he declared, merely sample books prior to jotting down whatever thoughts these books suggest to them. Wilson did not defend as final evaluation of literature Gold's economic interpretation. Economic forces do much to form an author's thought; at the same time, writers tend to form their own group, which cuts across social and economic strata and thus sets the author's position outside of any one class. Moreover, the literary traditions and the author's craftsmanship play a more important part in his work than does its social significance. The contribution of Marxism to literary study, Wilson concluded, lies in its awareness of origins and social significance; it can tell nothing about the greatness of a work.

In 1935, Wilson lived for five months in the Soviet Union. While he was there, the Communists discovered his former association with Max Eastman, an admirer of Trotsky; and when Wilson declined to repudiate Eastman at their invitation, their cordiality to him perceptibly cooled. Commenting in 1952 on the Russian situation, he referred ironically to his touching conviction in 1935 that Leninist thought could reign in Stalinist Russia, and that the Russian people would be given unrestricted access to the books and cultures of the past. To the Marxist temptation to use art as propaganda, he found the unscrupulous Stalinist regime adding a callous prostitution of literature solely for their political advantage. As a Princeton undergraduate he had been excited by the exertions of Mencken and Huneker to enlighten America by their defense of unpopular, unconventional causes. Upon entering the literary fray, he found as current causes the interpretation of Joyce, Eliot, and Proust to America, and the informing of the American "bourgeoisie" about the latest developments in Marxist Russia. Stalin's treaty with Hitler in 1939 completed the disillusionment which his visit to the Soviet Union had fostered. Assessing the Marxist Russians in 1941, he declared that state socialism could insure happiness only for the dictators who administered it; and although he cherished the dream of Marx and Engels of a homogeneous society directed by the creative minds of its members, he felt assured that Communism did not open the road to its attainment.

Wilson's examination of his critical contemporaries is always enlightening. He combines deep respect for Eliot's attainments with alertness to what seem to him Eliot's defects. Eliot's criticism springs, he believes, from a distrust of impressionist criticism which has moved him to undertake a systematic study of aesthetic values, in the course of which he has effected a revaluation of English literature. Being an American, he approaches English literature with an enthusiasm and detachment which a British scholar could with difficulty attain. To the rationalism of the eighteenth century he couples far broader appreciation than that century possessed. His dramatic imagination, which makes him a more successful poet than Ezra Pound, contributes also to his success as a critic. He arouses in his readers a desire to read for themselves—a prime quality of good criticism.

But Wilson finds flaws in Eliot's critical method. His concept of tradition is indeed essentially sound. His viewing literature as a whole and his comparing different periods and countries produce valuable generalizations as to what literature should be. His method, however, is nonhistorical, in Wilson's eyes a serious defect. Though Eliot realizes the effects of time and social forces upon literature, he discounts their importance. His method tends toward a pedantic, futile aestheticism, lacking the values for man that Ruskin, Renan,

[273]

Sainte-Beuve, and Taine possessed. Wilson in this substantially ac-
cords with T. K. Whipple in demanding that criticism, like literature, connect itself with the sources of power. Moreover, in considering what literature should be, Eliot loses sight of what it is.
He is still the New Englander, fearful of vulgarity, yet fascinated
by it, and vaguely regretful of opportunities in life which his fastidiousness has denied him.

Toward the New Humanists, Wilson's emotions have been
mixed. He does not apparently care greatly for Babbitt. In describing an evening spent in More's company at his Princeton home,
though he points out with delicate irony More's amusing foibles, he
finds More's ideas stimulating and often close to his own. They share
their hostility to what they consider academic insincerity and in-
competence. Both demand moral insights of a writer, though Wilson
finds More's moral principles excessively narrow, even priggish. At
the same time, he admires More's capacity to grasp the work of
writers so uncongenial to him as Proust and Joyce. A critic who can
clearly formulate the case for a writer whose work he abhors possesses splendid critical parts. Wilson has a like capacity to include
in his criticism any view of literature which may illuminate it.

In *The Triple Thinkers* (1938, 1947) Wilson uses the essay on
More to introduce his own studies of those writers whom More
evaluated but could not enjoy. Vigorously defending prose writers,
he denies to the present minor poets the sole heritage of the great
epic and dramatic writers. Great works of art are composed in verse
or prose as the author's taste or the current fashion decides. The
beginnings of that modern prose which shares the poetic endowment
lie in the work of Flaubert and Ibsen, whose successors were Chek-
hov, Synge, and Shaw. In Wilson's own generation, James Joyce
has even combined the two techniques in *Ulysses* to produce a new
medium that merges the metrics of verse in a fabric essentially new.

The reader who has once learned to cut across genres, Wilson
proceeds, will not be led astray by literary kinds. He will compare
Pope with Thackery, who shares Pope's theme of the vanity of
the world, instead of with Shakespeare, who does not serve to bring
out Pope's peculiar quality. Similar emancipation will teach critics
of Whitman not to judge him by ordinary standards of verse. Wil-

[274]

son's argument here would have delighted James Huneker. The instructed reader will also readily accept the new art forms which modern journalism has produced to supply the demands of increasingly voracious readers. Since prose is in general easier to read than verse, readers demand prose; and in satisfying this demand writers have laid poetics under contribution, though not as Joyce has done. Whether verse will survive this invasion of its preserves, Wilson hesitates to state. But he emphasizes the fact that writers now regularly follow Flaubert, who added to prose that serious concern with "large questions" formerly in the poetic domain.

During World War II, Wilson considered with deep interest the psychoanalytical approach to literature. An admirer of Brooks's *Ordeal of Mark Twain*, he proceeded to examine Dickens, Kipling, and Henry James by the same means. Dickens' despairing six months in the blacking warehouse he presented as the cause of a psychic trauma which his entire career attempted to heal in depicting a world where such hardships could occur. Kipling's sufferings for six years as a child living with unsympathetic relatives developed that hatred which colored his work. Wilson's analysis of James's *The Turn of the Screw* has become almost as classic an instance of the psychoanalytic method as Brooks's life of Mark Twain. The short story, he contended, can show someone getting even with another; the novel, for which this spring of action is too trifling, depicts more elemental struggles. Because of the ruling hatred in his life, Kipling could not tap these deeper springs of action—a contention with which readers of his latest volume are likely to disagree. Wilson's use of the psychoanalytical method has drawn the fire of several critics, who charge him with carrying it too far. He has not, however, let it usurp the sole place in his critical method, but has resolutely defended the employment of any means that will illuminate the work.

Wilson's breadth of critical interests is in fact one of his chief assets. His psychoanalytical methods are kept from dominance by his deeply rooted liking for the historical approach; he remarks that George Saintsbury was probably the sole English critic at the turn of the century who approached first-rate stature. He insists that the New York literary tradition is as truly American as New England's; it attracts less notice, he mischievously remarks, because it is less provincial. Though he delights in the best that has been written, he admires also the stories of Sherlock Holmes: their level, though humble, is not ignoble, and vivid imagination counts for more in literature than fine execution. A practical critic whose interests embrace various interpretive methods to arrive at judgment is unlikely to be popular with any school; and it sometimes seems as if every man's hand is raised against Wilson. He survives, however, to be one of our most valuable contemporary critics.

VAN WYCK BROOKS—THE LATER PHASE

Since 1936, Van Wyck Brooks's reputation has widened among the reading public almost as much as it has fallen off among many critics. Like Browning's Lost Leader, he has been accused of deserting the critical ranks for handfuls of silver brought him by his somewhat florid accounts of the American literary scene. In the minds of many critics, a critic's rank is in inverse ratio to his popularity. It is therefore proper to examine his apology in *The Opinions of Oliver Allston* (1941) and *The Writer in America* (1953).

Brooks's strategy of defense includes vigorous sorties against his opponents. He first defends his surveys of the American literary scene as the logical development of his earlier demands for a usable American past and his prescriptions for a healthier American literary attitude. Since 1936 he had simply returned to the attack with heavier artillery; and though some of his earlier statements may have been inexact, they were mistakes of detail caused by inadequate knowledge or youthful lack of judgment. He had formerly seen the obverse of the coin; now he was contemplating its reverse as well. He was still what he always had been, an idealist, a believer in free will; and it was chiefly for these beliefs that his deterministic enemies constantly attacked him. Emersonian idealism has been, and will continue to be, the motive power of most American literature. It is not soft, as its enemies charge, but far more firm than Marxism, which produces men unable to stand alone; few beliefs have produced stronger men than those stern Americans Emerson, Thoreau, and John Brown of Osawatomie. Indeed, its force is patriotic, even international.

As the revolving years after World War I showed the United States forging to the lead in world affairs, Brooks became more and more doubtful that the nation was proving equal to the task. Obviously, examination of the springs of American culture should help to indicate our national strength and weakness. Believing also in the actuality of truth, he affirms the critic's duty as unresting search for this truth. Certain constant elements in man lead to his developing standards; and acceptance of these standards implies his belief that truth exists, for they are to him approximations to this truth. In any mental activity, these standards cannot be abandoned utterly; whenever a healthy, normal mind discovers itself, they are reborn, perhaps in a more nearly accurate statement than before. Brooks's support of standards for America could not escape censure in an age of critical relativism.

Brooks makes two suggestions to twentieth-century critics. First, beware of words ending in -ism: they stand for pigeonholes into which authors must be forcibly crammed, and the authors always suffer distortion in the cramming. General terms like classicism, romanticism, and naturalism are too indefinite to be useful. It may prove wiser to make new terms to name your critical ideas. Use every word according to sound etymology, with the exception that colloquialisms are permissible if accepted by men of respectable character and occupation. Secondly, abhor literary and critical theories. Brooks himself has no theories and wishes to have none. Not only are they divorced from literary life, they result in what Brooks calls "total definitions": definitions of literature and of the function of criticism fall especially under his censure. Any reader of Italian Renaissance criticism will recall that those periods promulgated errors not unlike those which Brooks sees in similar attempts by the New Critics.

Like many of his nineteenth-century predecessors, Brooks will erect no protective tariff around American literature. He baldly warns critics to make no literary generalizations about American literature that are inapplicable to all literatures. The true keynote of literature is genuineness. Authors become truly American when as great men writing in America they express by their lives their convictions and conceptions. In evaluating American literature, the critic is ruthlessly to take from the writer everything not rightly his. The patient who cannot survive such drastic surgery should be left to die unnoticed. Criticism exists to determine, cherish, and maintain values. It is a sober, calculating, intellectual process that cannot be pursued in the high-pitched, enthusiastic key of many of our critics. "No emphasis, no italics." Our critics are like Philip drunk who refuses to appeal to Philip sober; in their relativism all standards reel before their vision. Their drunken enthusiasms stampede them after new gods en masse, and their lack of general reading causes them repeatedly to "discover" anew principles long known. Though better than their predecessors of the twenties, they still lack a sense of the past and consequently cannot relate their objects to the stream of tradition. Accordingly they resort to discussions of technique, and demand of authors only technical novelty. Such criticism quickly becomes dated and meaningless.

Agreeing with Tolstoy that literature transmits the highest feelings of man, Brooks declares that the writer's strength derives from his consciousness of human needs and longings. The quality of his response determines its value. Although his statement here agrees with Eliot, he complains that Eliot has seen what are indeed religious values in merely sectarian terms; looking for Anglican orthodoxy, he strains at gnats while swallowing camels. By erecting personal impressions into laws and thus trying to elevate dogma into doctrine, Eliot makes a tradition to suit himself.

But what, Brooks inquires, have one's personal impressions to do with tradition? Tradition includes all that man has kept alive for his own advancement and perfecting; it unites mankind by providing stability and direction. Eliot's phantasmal tradition does more to destroy genuine tradition than to support it. He likes Joyce and proclaims him a defender of tradition, though in all Joyce's work the past "went out in a bad smell." Joyce administers an insulin shock that rubs down the mental grooves formed by conventional thinking; but like all shock treatments, it is a means, not an end; and it may kill the patient. Along with Ezra Pound, Marcel Proust, Paul Valéry, and Gertrude Stein, Eliot represents not tradition but the dead clutching hand of the *fin de siècle*. He lacks the soul of his age which he claims to express, whereas the nineteenth-century writers whom he condemns possessed theirs.

Brooks turns next upon the New Critics, who share Eliot's withdrawal from the fullest life of their time. They are Southerners who have reacted against Southern ways and, having nowhere else to go, have taken refuge in a world of abstraction. They swarm over literature like entomologists or geometricians until they have pre-empted whatever chairs the old academic scholars have vacated. Brooks wryly accepts Ransom's claim that their literary criticism is "unprecedented," but questions its right to the terms "literary" or "criticism." Such scientific investigation of poetry, as he slyly calls it, naturally amuses the undergraduate minds to whom the coterie address themselves; but Brooks gravely doubts the results of their instruction. In reducing criticism to mechanics, the New Critics present their students with a concept of literature seldom realized in the greatest works: *Hamlet*, says Eliot, is a failure, yet remains one of the greatest poems. A critic attracted to literature for its mechanical structure is likely to be disappointed and, upon finding his preference for structure more nearly satisfied in the sciences, will revert to them or to engineering. Poetry being what it is, the New Critics are reasoning *in vacuo*. Moreover, in their revolt from the romantic poetry of their predecessors, their poets write without reference to feeling or interest in the world of men. The real depths of literature are vital, not metaphysical. Under the misdirected dissection by these critics, poetry disintegrates and disappears.

Brooks, in fine, looks upon literature much as did Carlyle and Tolstoy, as the product of a great man writing, not of a rhetorician. The New Criticism ignores the public as a whole, and overlooks authors like James Fenimore Cooper, who have exerted tremendous influence upon that public. It has ushered in a new scholasticism as arid as any that has preceded it. Literature is more than art; its greatness consists in its subject matter, which the New Critic is prone to depreciate if not actually to remove. The evident spleen of Brooks's attack upon the New Criticism renders him a far less formidable opponent to it than Ronald Crane, thought-provoking though many of his strictures are.

[279]

The issues between the theoretical critic, as exemplified by the New Critics, and the practitioners who abhor theory have not been resolved. They parallel in part the quarrel between literary critic and literary historian, and are probably to be settled by some such compromise as that advocated by R. P. Blackmur, who is receptive to many modes of literary interpretation. Ransom, too, has indicated a willingness to expand his approach. It is not too much to hope that coming years will witness further amalgamation of the two groups.

The Chicago Critics

The amalgamation anticipated in the previous paragraph has been to some extent a project of the developing group at the University of Chicago of which Ronald Crane is the center. There is, however, a heavy scholarship in the writings of its members that may weaken its influence by severely limiting its readers. It has collected its ideas into a volume of essays, *Critics and Criticism* (1952), and other volumes are beginning to appear. The general agreement among its members, who have perhaps not worked together long enough for such violent disagreements as divided the New Critics, renders unnecessary detailed discussion of individual critics in the group.

The Chicago Critics study literature as part of a larger problem connected with the well-known concern of their university in humane education for the present age. They concentrate upon literary criticism as one of the four humanistic arts: linguistics, analysis of ideas, literary and artistic criticism, and history. In higher education, they believe that all four should have adequate representation. Although they do not lose sight of the other three arts, the business of the Chicago Critics is literary criticism.

The study of criticism as they envisage it is not designed to develop any new or peculiar critical method, but to examine and evaluate those approaches to literature which have been or currently are being used for its interpretation and judgment. Their work includes therefore the criticism of criticism. As Elder Olson and others of their group have stated, they stand opposed to the dogmatic assumption by any critic that his position and method are alone correct. Crane's attack upon Cleanth Brooks as a stalking-horse for the New Critics is an onslaught upon critical monism quite in harmony with the pluralistic approach of these critics. Criticism being a branch of philosophy, Olson writes, the number of possible critical positions is determined by the number of possible philosophical positions; and these latter are determined by the number of aspects of a subject capable of being brought into a discussion, and by the kinds of basic dialectic which may be brought to bear upon the subject matter. Criticisms differ according as they center upon one or another facet of art: its medium, its productive cause, its end, or as they focus upon several of these facets at once. They differ also as they proceed integrally in the manner of Plato, or differentially in the manner of Aristotle. Each criticism, however, is valid within its limits.

Since criticism is to the Chicago Critics reasoned discourse, the Aristotelian approach to literature is basic to their method. They work inductively and concentrate upon the structure of the object under consideration. From the internal nature of the poem they seek to discover whether it is a finely constructed whole, and they judge each poem upon its intrinsic merits. So far, they conform closely to the New Critics' procedure; they recognize the value of concentration upon the poem as a poem and not another thing, just as they alertly oppose what appear to them to be faults in that criticism. They do not, however, willingly accept the label of "Neo-Aristotelian," which has been affixed to them, for it carries connotations which they do not approve. In particular, they oppose the practice of earlier Aristotelians who extend Aristotle's words on tragedy to other literary genres. The search, for example, for some quality in lyric poetry analogous to plot in tragedy seems to them based upon a mistaken assumption that it must exist. Each literary genre has its own principles of construction, and poems achieve wholeness by conforming to the principles of their genres. It is Aristotelian method, not perverted use of Aristotelian principles, which they consider basic to their work.

Far from proclaiming any new critical panacea, the Chicago Critics urge the application to literature of varied critical pro-

[281]

cedures. Their purpose being to understand the work of art, they bring to bear upon it whatever they believe will serve to elucidate it, no matter whence it may be derived. Critical principles, Crane observes, are neither doctrinal absolutes not historically necessitated shibboleths; they are simply instruments of inquiry and analysis.

Since they are concerned to explore all practicable avenues to literary understanding, the Chicago Critics are concerned with those formerly traveled as well as with those still in use. They therefore study the literary tradition. The very ponderousness of their erudition, it may be, will hinder their effectiveness. In *Critics and Criticism*, which marshals their work under three heads, after five essays dealing with contemporary approaches to literature, the second and third sections deal respectively with classical or Renaissance ways of viewing literature and with the philosophy of criticism. Some of the essays in these two sections—Richard McKeon's "Literary Criticism and the Concept of Imitation in Antiquity" (1936) and Elder Olson's "An Outline of Poetic Theory" (1948), with its modernization of Aristotle's *Poetics*—are already landmarks of critical study, while Olson's explication of Yeats' "Sailing to Byzantium" is equally celebrated in critical practice.

In one notable respect the Chicago Critics differ from the groups which have been attacked as academic. Instead of being bound by tradition, their employment of previous standards as means for inquiry frees them to improve on convention or find better whenever they can. They are truly Aristotelian in their distinction between means and ends and in regarding as an end the illumination of the object under analysis. With all their investigation into classical and Renaissance literary theory, they have kept free from that excessive deference to authority which has so hampered free investigation; and they welcome new approaches to literature with the same interest they feel in those of old. What the future course of these critics will produce, it is impossible to say; but they are undoubtedly one of the most interesting groups at present occupying the attention of literary men.

During the past six years it has become increasingly evident that American literary and critical opinion has reached a stage in its development which it is using to take stock of itself. The arrival at mid-century no doubt had something to do with this pause, just as the turn of the preceding century gave rise to much speculation about the same subject. The expanding concept of criticism in the words of prominent New Critics—the most noticed of the current schools—no doubt was the chief reason for this stock-taking.

These New Critics, especially Ransom and Blackmur, declare that their method, having made its initial, linguistic contribution to the study of literature, must now expand to embrace other interpretative modes as well. Indicative of the feeling that they must survey their position and attainments is the publication of anthologies of the New Criticism, Robert Wooster Stallman's *Critiques and Essays in Criticism, 1920–1948* (1949) and Ray West's *Essays in Modern Literary Criticism* (1952), in both of which the editors have attempted to present a rounded picture of the New Criticism. A work of greater inclusiveness, Morton Zabel's *Literary Opinion in the United States* (1951, first edition, 1937) sets the New Critics amid the work of other significant American critics from the beginning of the century in order to give some perspective to their contribution.

Although these volumes were doubtless prepared to satisfy the interest in current literary opinion, their number is significant of their author's awareness that the time was ripe for evaluation; and they would scarcely have approximated a rounded picture if criticism had not arrived at some significant stage whence the authors could see the course of criticism as a whole. These anthologies are far more unified in concept and execution than the almost casual assemblies of critical essays published two or three decades ago.

Further indications exist that the time is ripe for evaluation of American literary and critical accomplishment. Comparison of the encyclopaedic *Literary History of the United States* (1948) with its predecessor, *The Cambridge History of American Literature*, shows an awareness of the significance of criticism in the writers of the later work that apparently did not exist three decades ago. Perhaps the most significant symptom of all is the publication of René Wellek and Austin Warren's *Theory of Literature* (1949), in which the authors have earnestly tried, with a measure of success, to weld poetics, scholarship, literary history, and criticism into a coherent literary theory. Though they make no secret of their preference for the intrinsic approach to literature which has characterized the efforts of the New Critics, their combination of it with the various extrinsic approaches has been received with an interest that betrays the awareness of readers that Americans must now pause to synthesize what has been attained in letters as preparation for further progress.

This inclusion into one study of various sorts of literary interpretation and criticism causes one to suspect that T. S. Eliot's metaphor of the stream of literary tradition includes the course of criticism too. Even his paradox that authors contribute most to the stream when they most closely resemble their predecessors seems to be valid for the critics. The concern with Dryden at the beginning of the nineteenth century, though cut off by the incursion of romantic ideas, revived in the New Humanists and in Eliot and his followers. Ideas of Kant and the German romanticists, with Coleridge as partial transmitter and interpreter, contributed not only to romantic theory in America but, with changes in emphasis, to I. A. Richards and the New Critics. The way in which Mme de Staël and later Taine related literature to race and milieu appealed to nineteenth-century critics, was violently distorted by Marxist critics, and has been restored to more rational form by Edmund Wilson and Van Wyck Brooks. And the significance of the individual's response to literature, which formed part of Lowell's criticism, though overstated by the impressionists, has constituted part of the ammunition used to combat theorists who would restrict the evaluation of literature to a single set of criteria. In short, whatever belongs to the critical tradition has a way of turning up repeatedly, sometimes in surprising circumstances.

Although America has bred doctrinaire critics throughout the period under consideration, the tendency has been to absorb into the critical stream whatever each has had to contribute to the development of literary thinking. Monist interpretations of literature, whether they have tried to limit poetry to rhythmical creations of beauty restricted in length, to some linguistic or rhetorical principle, or to the rise of the proletariat, have each been fitted into the whole picture as partial contributions to the greater, over-all problem. And all attempts in America to divorce literature from life have failed. The critic has found it necessary to know not only literary history and the history of ideas, but political, social, economic, and religious history as well. Though the well-intentioned seekers in the 1840's after a democratic literature were emphasizing an absurd literary criterion, they were not far off the right trail. In the United States pre-eminently, literature and society are inextricably interlaced. One may remodel to fit the critic Goethe's questions about the intent and attainment of the author; having ascertained how fully the critic has made literature accessible, the encyclopedic critic adds to his view the arc of the individual's contribution in the endeavor to complete the circle.

Lack of space prevents adequate presentation of the critical contribution by the unjustly attacked professorial critics. If the numerous references to them as academic and pedantic made by their enemies have made their work appear negligible or deleterious, the impression is wrong. Besides the professors who have been noted here as setting their obvious imprint upon American criticism, there have been a long line of distinguished men who with little fanfare have done yeoman service to American literary thinking. Among these benefactors, to name a few of the many, were and are Thomas Sergeant Perry, Albert Stanburrough Cook, John Livingston Lowes, Charles G. Osgood, and Lane Cooper, against whose solid contribution the Hyman Kaplans of criticism vainly cast their pebbles.

More than a decade ago, in attempting to show the relation of some fifteen American critics to the classical founders of criticism, the writer used Cyprian's similitude of the perennial need to return to the fountains of the stream. The present study attempts to show how from the small yet vigorously flowing early reaches of the stream, amplified by new rills from time to time, have come new emphases and deeper knowledge of literature in America. Although American critics, like their brethren abroad, cannot claim to have discovered new critical principles, they have done valuable service in adapting literary theory to fit changing American situations and needs, and in illuminating older principles. This book can provide little more than prolegomena to detailed study of American literary and critical thought; it has attempted, however, to indicate some of

[285]

the principal levels through which the stream has flowed. "Still glides the stream, and shall for ever glide"; and it is hoped that this general survey of its course will help others to map it in greater detail to its better understanding.

Bibliographical Notes

Periodicals listed in these notes bear the following code references:

AL: *American Literature*
AM: *Atlantic Monthly*
AMM: *American Monthly Magazine*
AR: *American Review*
AS: *American Scholar*
B: *Bookman*
C: *Century Magazine*
CE: *College English*
CJ: *Classical Journal*
CL: *Comparative Literature*
CW: *Classical Weekly*
D: *The Dial*
DR: *Democratic Review*
EJ: *English Journal*
F: *Forum*
H: *Harper's Magazine*
K: *Knickerbocker Magazine*
KR: *Kenyon Review*
MA: *Monthly Anthology*
MLN: *Modern Language Notes*
MP: *Modern Philology*
MQR: *Massachusetts Quarterly Review*

N: *Nation*
NAR: *North American Review*
NE: *New Englander*
NEQ: *New England Quarterly*
NR: *New Republic*
NYM: *New York Mirror*
NYQ: *New York Quarterly*
NYR: *New York Review*
P: *Portico*
PF: *Port Folio*
Po: *Poetry*
PMLA: *Publications of the Modern Language Association of America*
Poly.: *Polyanthus*
PM: *Putnam's Magazine*
PQ: *Philological Quarterly*
PR: *Partisan Review*
R: *Russell's Magazine*
S: *Scribner's Magazine*
SAQ: *South Atlantic Quarterly*
SewR: *Sewanee Review*
SLM: *Southern Literary Messenger*

SP: *Studies in Philology*
SLQ: *Southern Literary Quarterly*
SQR: *Southern Quarterly Review*
SR: *Southern Review*
SRL: *Saturday Review of Literature* (now *Saturday Review*)
SwR: *Southwest Review*
TAPhA: *Transactions of the American Philological Association*
UKCQ: *University of Kansas City Quarterly*
UTQR: *University of Toronto Quarterly Review*
WR: *Whig Review*
WMQ: *William and Mary Quarterly*
YR: *Yale Review*

CHAPTER I

ON THE CULTURAL SITUATION IN THE UNITED STATES: Van Wyck Brooks, *The Flowering of New England* (New York, 1936); Merle Curti, *The Growth of American Thought* (New York, 1943); M. F. Heiser, "The Decline of Neoclassicism," *Transitions in American Literary History* (Durham, 1954), 91–159; R. W. Horton and H. W. Edwards, *Backgrounds of American Literary Thought* (New York, 1952), 7–107; Orie W. Long, *Literary Pioneers* (Cambridge, 1935); G. H. Orians, "The Rise of Romanticism," *Transitions in American Literary History*, 161–244; Vernon L. Parrington, *Main Currents in American Thought* (3 vols., New York, 1927–30), I.

SOURCE MATERIALS: Review of William Tudor's *Letters on the Eastern States* (Boston, 1820), PF, Vol. IX (1820), 461–74; Solyman Brown, *An Essay on American Poetry* (New Haven, 1818); review of Irving's *The Sketch Book*, NAR, Vol. IX (1819), 333; Joel Barlow, *The Columbiad* (Paris, 1813), vii–viii, xii; James Savage, review of Webster's *Dictionary*, MA, Vol. VII (1809), 246–64; review of George Crabb's *English Synonyms*, P, Vol. III (1817), 99; Walter Channing, "On American Language and Literature," NAR, Vol. I (1815), 307–14; review of Eustaphieve's *Demetrius*, P. Vol. V (1818), 397–98; E. T. Channing, "On Models in Literature," NAR, Vol. III (1816), 208; John Knapp, "National Poetry," NAR, Vol. VIII (1818), 170; Willard Phillips, "Bryant's *Poems*," NAR, Vol. XIII (1821), 380; W. C. Bryant, "Lectures on Poetry," in Parke Godwin, *Prose Writings of William Cullen Bryant* (2 vols., New York, 1884), I, 23–35; "Cooper's novels," NAR, Vol. XXIII (1826), 151–52; "Prince Pückler Muscau and Mrs. Trollope," NAR, Vol. XXXVI (1833), 20; "English and American Literature," PF, Ser. III, Vol. V (1815), 191; Walter Channing, "Reflections on the Literary Delinquency of America," NAR, Vol. II (1815), 38; Samuel Knapp, *Lectures on American Literature* (New York, 1829).

ON MME DE STAEL'S INFLUENCE IN AMERICA: R. C. Whitford, "Mme de Staël's Literary Reputation in America," MLN, Vol. XXXIII (1918), 476–80; R. L. Hawkins, *Mme de Staël and the United States* (Cambridge, 1930).

An indispensable guide to periodical literature is Frank Luther Mott, *A History of American Magazines* (3 vols., Cambridge, 1938).

CHAPTER II

STUDIES OF THE PERIOD: R. W. Bolwell, "Concerning National-ism in American Literature," AL, Vol. VII (1935), 405–16; W. B. Cairns, *On the Development of American Literature from 1815 to 1833* (Madison, 1898); William Charvat, *Origins of American Critical Thought* (Philadelphia, 1936); H. H. Clark, "Literary Criticism in the *North American Review,* 1815–1835," *Transactions of the Wisconsin Academy of Science, Art, and Letters,* Vol. XXX (1940), 299–350; H. H. Clark, "Nationalism in American Literature," UTQ, Vol. II (1933), 491–519; M. W. Fishwick, "*The Portico* and Literary Na-tionalism after the War of 1812," WMQ, Vol. VIII (1951), 238–45; C. T. Hazelrigg, *American Literary Pioneer: . . . James A. Hillhouse* (New York, 1953); Heiser, "The Decline of Neoclassicism," *Trans-itions in American Literary History,* 91–159; A. L. Herold, *James Kirk Paulding: Versatile American* (New York, 1926); *Journal of the Pro-ceedings of the Society which Conducts the Monthly Anthology and Boston Review* (Boston, 1910); Albert Keiser, *The Indian in American Literature* (New York, 1933); J. C. McCloskey, "The Campaign of the Periodicals after the War of 1812 for National American Literature," PMLA, Vol. L (1935), 262–73; J. C. McCloskey, "A Note on *The Portico,*" AL, Vol. VIII (1936), 300–304; Tremaine McDowell, *William Cullen Bryant: Representative Selections* (New York, 1930), xxxix–lxviii; Annabel Newton, *Wordsworth in Early American Criti-cism* (Chicago, 1928); G. H. Orians, "The Romance Ferment after Waverley," AL, Vol. III (1932), 418–31; Orians, "The Rise of Ro-manticism," *Transitions in American Literary History,* 161–244; E. W. Parks, *Southern Poets: Representative Selections* (New York, 1936); J. P. Pritchard, *Return to the Fountains* (Durham, 1942), 13–25; W. E. Sedgwick, *The Problem of American Literature as Seen by Contemporary Critics in 1815–1830* (unpublished Harvard dissertation, 1934); A. M. Sibley, *Pope's Prestige in America* (New York, 1949);

R. E. Riegel, *Young America: 1830–1840* (Norman, 1949); R. E. Streeter, "Association Psychology and Literary Nationalism in the North American Review, 1815–1825," AL, Vol XVII (1945), 243–54; K. B. Taft, *Minor Knickerbockers: Representative Selections* (New York, 1947), 15–19.

SOURCE MATERIALS: A. M. Walter, "On Pope," MA, Vol. II (1805), 234–36; E. T. Dana, review of J. B. Linn's *The Power of Genius,* MA, Vol. II (1805), 530–38; P. Allen, "Imitation," MA, Vol. VI (1809), 242–45; W. C. Bryant, review of Solyman Brown's *An Essay on American Poetry,* in Godwin, *Prose Writings of William Cullen Bryant,* I; J. S. J. Gardiner, "The Remarker," MA, Vol. V (1808), 599; James Savage, "Perversion of Language," MA, Vol. VI (1809), 162–63; E. T. Channing, *Lectures Read to the Seniors in Harvard College* (Boston, 1856), 559–60, 565–66.

ON THE ROMANTIC POETS: Review of *Rokeby,* PF, Vol. XVI (1813), 14–15; review of *Lara,* PF, Ser. III, Vol. VI (1815), 35; review of *Harold the Dauntless,* AMM, Vol. I (1817), 161–62; review of Moore's *Lalla Rookh,* AMM, Vol. I (1817), 342, 348–49; "Lord Byron," NAR, Vol. XX (1825), 33; "Lord Byron's Character and Writings," NAR Vol. XXI (1825), 324–25; W. E. Channing, "National Literature" (1823), *Works* (new and complete ed., Boston, 1896), 502; E. T. Channing, review of Moore's *Lalla Rookh,* NAR, Vol. VI (1817), 1–25.

ON WORDSWORTH AND COLERIDGE: Review of *Biographia Literaria,* AMM, Vol. II (1817), 105; review of *Rokeby,* PF, Vol. XXI (1821), 13–14; R. H. Dana, Sr., "Preface to *The Idle Man*" (1833), *Poems and Prose Writings* (2 vols., New York, 1850), I, 147–52; F. W. P. Greenwood, review of Wordsworth's *Poems,* NAR, Vol. XVIII (1824), 356–71; "Lord Byron's Character and Writings," NAR, Vol. XXI (1825), 349; "The Decline of Poetry," NAR, Vol. XXVIII (1829), 15–16; "English Poetry of the Nineteenth Century," NAR, Vol. XXXV (1832), 174; review of *Kubla Khan,* AMM, Vol. I (1817), 12; "Coleridge," NAR, Vol. XL (1835), 301.

ON TRADITION IN LITERATURE: J. S. J. Gardiner, "The Remarker," MA, Vol. II (1805), 518; J. S. Buckminster, "The Remarker," MA Vol. III (1806), 19–20, Vol. IV (1807), 85; Allen, "Imitation," MA, Vol. VI (1809), 244–45; "Burns," MA, Vol. III (1806), 303; Channing, "On Models in Literature," NAR, Vol. III (1816), 202–208; Dana, review of *The Sketch Book* (1819), in *Poems and Prose Writings,* II, 268–313; J. K. Paulding, "National Literature"

(1820), in Taft, *Minor Knickerbockers,* 15–19; John Neal, *American Writers,* ed. by F. L. Pattee (Durham, 1937), 76; Knapp, *Lectures on American Literature.*

ON ORIGINALITY: Willard Phillips, review of Byron's *Childe Harold,* III, NAR, Vol. V (1817), 98–110; Channing, "National Literature," *Works,* 124–37; Knapp, *Lectures on American Literature,* 186; Paulding, "National Literature," in Taft, *Minor Knickerbockers,* 15–19; E. T. Channing, review of *The Battle of Niagara,* NAR, Vol. VIII (1818), 142–56; Bryant, "Lectures on Poetry," in Godwin, *Prose Writings of William Cullen Bryant,* I, 23–44; Bryant, review of Solyman Brown, *ibid.* 45–66; Channing, *Lectures Read to the Seniors in Harvard College,* 272–73.

ON NATURE: "The American Drama," P, Vol. III (1817), 370–73; "Observations on Taste," P, Vol. V (1818), 340–47; "On the Rules of Poetry," P, Vol. III (1817), 461–75; J. G. Palfrey, review of *Tales of My Landlord,* NAR, Vol. V (1817), 257–86; Dana, review of Allston's *Sylphs of the Seasons* (1817), in *Poems and Prose Writings,* II, 101–31; E. T. Dana, review of *Rob Roy,* NAR, Vol. VII (1818), 149–84; Paulding, "National Literature," in Taft, *Minor Knickerbockers,* 15–19; A. H. Everett, "The Life and Writings of Schiller" (1823), *Critical and Miscellaneous Writings* (Boston, 1845), 102–38; Greenwood, review of Wordsworth's *Poems,* NAR, Vol. XVIII (1824), 356–71; "The Decline of Poetry," NAR, Vol. XXIV (1827), 443–63; Neal, *American Writers,* 213.

ON IMAGINATON: Review of *The Village: A Poem,* P, Vol. III (1817), 167–92; "View of the Present State of Polite Learning," P, Vol. I (1816), 202–14; Channing, review of Moore's *Lalla Rookh,* NAR, Vol. VI (1817), 1–25; Willard Phillips, review of Godwin's *Mandeville,* NAR, Vol. VII (1818), 92–105; "Hogg's Works," NAR, Vol. IX (1819), 1–23; Jared Sparks, review of Brainard's *Poems,* NAR, Vol. XXI (1825), 217–24; "Lord Byron's Character and Writings," NAR, Vol. XXI (1825), 300–59; Bryant, "Lectures on Poetry," in Godwin, *Prose Writings of William Cullen Bryant,* I, 3–14; Dana, review of Pollok's *Course of Time* (1828), in *Poems and Prose Writings,* 344–79; C. S. Hillard, review of Catharine Sedgwick's *Clarence,* NAR, Vol. XXXII (1831), 73–95; "Writings of Bulwer," NAR, Vol. XLIV (1837), 426–34.

ON DIDACTICISM: Bryant, "Lectures on Poetry," in Godwin, *Prose Writings of William Cullen Bryant,* I, 3–14, 30–31; Knapp, *Lectures on American Literature,* 187; Channing, "John Milton," *Works,* 499;

W. C. Bryant, review of J. A. Hillhouse, *Hadad: A Dramatic Poem*, NYR, Vol. I (1825), 1–13; Review of Southey's *Curse of Kehama*, PF, n. s., Vol. VI (1811), 513–38; E. A. Poe, "Sonnet—To Science"; Channing, "National Literature," *Works*, 124–26; "Remarks on Fielding's Novels," P, Vol. IV (1817), 460–70.

ON FEMALE AUTHORS: "Novels Defended," PF, Vol. XXXV, 221–40; "Female Authors," Poly., Vol. IX (1814), 99–101; review of Maria Edgeworth's *Harrington* and *Ormond*, AMM, Vol. I (1817), 414; "Works of Mrs. Barbauld," NAR, Vol. XXIII (1826), 368–85; "Mrs. Hemans's Poems," NAR, Vol. XXIV (1827), 443–63; review of *Hope Leslie*, NAR, Vol. XXVI (1828), 403–20; review of Catharine Sedgwick's *The Linwoods*, NAR, Vol. XLII (1836), 160–95.

ON THE GOTHIC NOVEL: Review of J. Eliot's *Self-Indulgence*, Poly., Vol. VIII (1812), 203–206; E. T. Channing, review of Dunlap's *Life of Charles Brockden Brown*, NAR, Vol. IX (1819), 58–77; review of *The Wilderness* and *The Spectre of the Forest*, NAR, Vol. XIX (1824), 209–23; review of *Rokeby*, PF, Vol. XX (1813), 557–66; review of *Harold the Dauntless*, AMM, Vol. I (1817), 161–62; review of *The Bridal of Vaumond*, AMM, Vol. II (1818), 254; "The Character of Walter Scott," P, Vol. I (1816), 331–38; review of Godwin's *Fleetwood*, MA, Vol. III (1806), 159.

ON AMERICAN THEMES IN LITERATURE: William Tudor, review of Lydia Huntley's *Moral Pieces*, NAR, Vol. I (1815), 120–21; Knapp, "National Poetry," NAR, Vol. VIII (1818), 169–76; Channing, review of Dunlap's *Life of Charles Brockden Brown*, NAR, Vol. IX (1819), 58–77; J. K. Paulding, "National Literature," *Salmagundi*, Ser. II (August 19, 1820), reprinted in Taft, *Minor Knickerbockers*, 15–19; W. H. Gardiner, review of *The Spy*, NAR, Vol. XV (1822), 250–82; review of *The Wilderness* and *The Spectre of the Forest*, NAR, Vol. XIX (1824), 209–23; Neal, *American Writers*, 205–206; review of *Escalala: An Indian Tale*, NAR, Vol. XX (1825), 210–14; "Cooper's Novels," NAR, Vol. XXIII (1826), 150–97; review of *The Red Rover*, NAR, Vol. XXVII (1828), 139–54.

CRITICAL ATTITUDES TOWARD AMERICAN WORKS: MA, Vol. I, (1804), 455–56; "Patronage of Genius," Poly., Vol. II (1806), 113–17; review of *The Poems of Philip Freneau*, MA, Vol. IX (1810), 198–203; Gardiner, "The Remarker," MA, Vol. II (1805), 630–31; William Tudor, review of Irving's *Knickerbocker's History of New York*, MA, Vol. VIII (1810), 123–28; Bryant, review of Solyman Brown, in Godwin, *Prose Writings of William Cullen Bryant*, I, 45–56;

[292]

"Literary Intelligence," PF, Vol. XXXIV (1820), 503; Dana, review of *The Sketch Book*, in *Poems and Prose Writings*, II, 272; Gardiner, "The Remarker," MA, Vol. III (1806), 19.

On Anglo-American Literary Relations: Dana, review of Allston's *Sylphs of the Seasons*, in *Poems and Prose Writings*, II, 101–102, 129–30; review of William Tudor's *Letters on the Eastern States*, NAR, Vol. XI (1820), 68–103.

On a National Literature: "Willis's Writings," NAR, Vol. XLIII (1836), 384–412; review of Paulding's *The Backwoodsman*, AMM, Vol. IV (1819), 162–63; Dana, review of *The Sketch Book*, in *Poems and Prose Writings*, II, 269–70; Edward Everett, review of Percival's *Poems*, NAR, Vol. XIV (1822), 1–15.

Other Significant Critical Writings: Gilbert Wakefield, "On the Characteristicks of Poetry," MA, Vol. II (1805), 279–82; "Criticks," Poly., Vol. II (1806), 32–33; "Moore's Poems," Poly., Vol. III (1806), 252–55; review of *The Poems of Philip Freneau*, MA, Vol. IX (1810), 198–203; "Observations on the Poetry of Southey and Walter Scott," MA, Vol. IX (1810), 392–400; "New Art of Criticism," Poly., Vol. IX (1813), 251–57; "On a Fragment of Ancient Poetry," Poly., Ser. II, Vol. IX (1814), 247–54; William Tudor, "An Address Delivered to the Phi Beta Kappa Society," NAR, Vol. II (1815), 14; "The American Drama," P, Vol. III (1817), 370–73; "The State of Learning in the United States," NAR, Vol. IX (1819), 240–59; "Mr. Ingersoll's Discourse," NAR, Vol. XVIII (1824), 157–78; R. C. Sands, "Domestic Literature," *Writings in Prose and Verse* (2 vols., New York, 1835), I, 103–15; "Boccaccio's *Decameron*," NAR, Vol. XIX (1824), 68–86; "The Wise Men of Gotham," NAR, Vol. XXIV (1827), 37–55; "American Poems," NAR, Vol. XXIX (1829), 220–41; review of *The Last Days of Pompeii*, NAR, Vol. XL (1835), 447–57; Samuel Knapp, "Reminiscences of Ballston and Saratoga Springs," K, Vol. VI (1835), 96–106; review of Bulwer's *Devereux*, SR, Vol. IV (1829), 369–405; review of *Anne of Geierstein*, SR, Vol. IV (1829), 498–522; review of Bryant's *Poems*, SR, Vol. VIII (1832), 443–62; "English Language in America," SLM, Vol. II (1836), 10–11; review of Sedgwick's *The Linwoods*, NAR, Vol. XLII (1836), 160–95.

Chapter III

Lives of Emerson: By Oliver Wendell Holmes (Boston, 1885); Richard Garnett (New York, 1888); G. E. Woodberry (New York,

1907); O. W. Firkins (Boston, 1915); Van·Wyck Brooks (New York, 1932); R. L. Rusk (New York, 1949).

WORKS OF EMERSON: *Complete Works* (12 vols., Boston, 1903–1904); *The Journals* (10 vols., Boston, 1909–14); *Uncollected Writings* (New York, 1912); *The Letters,* ed. by R. L. Rusk (6 vols., New York, 1939).

ON EMERSON: Walter Blair and Clarence Faust, "Emerson's Literary Method," MP, Vol. XLII (1944–45), 79–95; N. A. Brittin, "Emerson and the Metaphysical Poets," AL, Vol. VIII (1936), 1–21; Van Wyck Brooks, *Emerson and Others* (New York, 1927), 1–106; S. G. Brown, "American Literature Re-examined: Emerson," UKCQ, Vol. XV (1948), 27–37; W. C. Brownell, *American Prose Masters* (New York, 1909), 133–204; J. T. Flanagan, "Emerson as a Critic of Fiction," PQ, Vol. XV (1936), 30–45; V. C. Hopkins, "Emerson and Cudworth: Plastic Nature and Transcendental Art," AL, Vol. XXIII (1951), 80–98; V. C. Hopkins, "The Influence of Goethe on Emerson's Aesthetic Theory," PQ, Vol. XXVII (1948), 325–44; V. C. Hopkins, *Spires of Form: A Study of Emerson's Aesthetic Theory* (Cambridge, 1951); Joseph Jones, "Emerson and Bergson on the Comic," CL, Vol. I (1949), 63–72; Ernest Marchand, "Emerson and the Frontier," AL, Vol. IX (1937), 149–74; J. B. Moore, "Emerson on Wordsworth," PMLA, Vol. XLI (1926), 179–92; R. C. Pettigrew, "Emerson and Milton," AL, Vol. III (1931), 45–59; Pritchard, "Ralph Waldo Emerson," *Return to the Fountains,* 44–60; E. G. Sutcliffe, *Emerson's Theories of Literary Expression* (Urbana, 1923); F. T. Thompson, "Emerson's Indebtedness to Coleridge," SP, Vol. XXIII (1926), 55–76; F. T. Thompson, "Emerson and Carlyle," SP, Vol. XXIV (1927), 438–50; F. T. Thompson, "Emerson's Theory and Practice of Poetry," PMLA, Vol. XLIII (1928), 1170–84.

LIVES OF THOREAU: By H. S. Salt (London, 1896); Mark van Doren (Boston, 1916); H. S. Canby (Boston, 1939).

WORKS OF THOREAU: *Collected Works* (20 vols., Boston, 1906).

ON THOREAU: Raymond Adams, "Thoreau's Literary Apprenticeship," SP, Vol. XIX (1932), 617–39; Bartholow Crawford, *Henry David Thoreau: Representative Selections* (New York, 1934); Norman Foerster, "The Intellectual Heritage of Thoreau," *Texas Review,* Vol. II (1917), 192–212; Norman Foerster, "Thoreau as Artist," SR, Vol. XXXIX (1921), 2–13; C. L. Gohdes, "Henry Thoreau, Bachelor of Arts," CJ, Vol. XXIII (1928), 323–36; F. W. Lorch, "Thoreau and the Organic Principle in Poetry," PMLA, Vol. LIII (1938), 286–302; P. E. More, "Thoreau's Journal," *Shelburne Essays,* Ser. V (Boston, 1908), 106–31; Pritchard, "Henry David Thoreau," *Return to the Fountains,* 61–67; J. P. Pritchard, "Cato in Concord," CW, Vol. XXVI (1924), 3–5; Ethel Seybold, *Thoreau: The Quest and the Classics* (New Haven, 1951); Randall Stewart, "The Concord Group: A Study in Relationships," SewR, Vol. XLIV (1936), 434–46.

On MARGARET FULLER: S. M. Fuller, *Papers on Literature and Art* (New York, 1846); S. M. Fuller, *Memoirs of Margaret Fuller Ossoli* (2 vols., Boston, 1852); S. M. Fuller, *Life Without and Life Within,* ed. by A. B. Fuller (Boston, 1859); "Margaret Fuller," N, Vol. XXXIX (1884), 268–69; G. E. DeMille, "Emerson and Margaret Fuller," *Literary Criticism in America* (New York, 1931), 118–32; Madeleine Stern, *The Life of Margaret Fuller* (New York, 1942); Mason Wade, *Margaret Fuller: Whetstone of Genius* (New York, 1940); J. W. Thomas, *James Freeman Clarke: Apostle of German Culture to America* (Boston, 1949).

LIVES OF ORESTES BROWNSON: By A. M. Schlesinger, Jr. (Boston, 1939); Theodore Maynard (New York, 1943).

WORKS OF BROWNSON: *Works,* collected by Henry F. Brownson (20 vols., Detroit, 1885). Brownson's principal critical essays, all in Vol. XIX, are: "American Literature" (1839), "Modern French Literature" (1842), "Modern Idolatry" (1845), "Schiller's Aesthetic Theory" (1846), "American Literature" (1847), "A Review of Lowell's Vision of Sir Launfal" (1849), and "Literature, Love, and Marriage" (1864).

CHAPTER IV

LIVES OF POE: By G. E. Woodberry (2 vols., Boston, 1909); Edward Shanks (New York, 1917); Hervey Allen (2 vols., New York, 1926); A. H. Quinn (New York, 1941).

WORKS OF POE: *The Complete Works,* ed. by J. A. Harrison (17 vols., New York, 1902); *The Works,* ed. by E. C. Stedman and G. E. Woodberry (10 vols., Chicago, 1895); *Politian: An Unfinished Tragedy,* ed. by T. O. Mabbott (Richmond, 1923); *The Doings of Gotham,* ed. by J. E. Spannuth (Pottsville, 1929).

On POE: Margaret Alterton, *Origins of Poe's Critical Theory* (Iowa City, 1925); Margaret Alterton and Hardin Craig, *Edgar Allan*

Poe: Representative Selections (New York, 1935); H. T. Baker, "Coleridge's Influence on Poe's Poetry," MLN, Vol. XXV (1910), 94–95; J. O. Beaty, *John Esten Cooke, Virginian* (New York, 1922); Brownell, "Poe," *American Prose Masters*, 207–67; Killis Campbell, *The Mind of Poe* (Cambridge, 1933); A. L. Cooke, "Edgar Allan Poe— Critic," *The Cornhill Magazine*, Vol. CV (1934), 588–97; J. E. Cooke, *Poe as a Literary Critic*, ed. by N. B. Fagin (Baltimore, 1946); DeMille, "Poe," *Literary Criticism in America*, 86–117; T. S. Eliot, *From Poe to Valery* (New York, 1948); N. B. Fagin, *The Histrionic Mr. Poe* (Baltimore, 1949); Norman Foerster, "Poe," *American Literature* (Boston, 1928), 1–51; L. E. Gates, *Studies and Appreciations* (New York, 1900), 110–28; D. K. Jackson, *Poe and the Southern Literary Messenger* (Richmond, 1934); P. E. More, "The Origins of Hawthorne and Poe," *Shelburne Essays*, I, 51–70; P. E. More, "A Note on Poe's Method," SP, Vol. XX (1923), 302–309; J. P. Pritchard, "Aristotle's *Poetics* and Certain American Literary Critics," CW, Vol. XXVII (1934), 81–85; J. P. Pritchard, "Horace and Edgar Allan Poe," CW, Vol. XXVI (1933), 129–33; Pritchard, "Edgar Allan Poe," *Return to the Fountains*, 26–44; J. M. Robertson, *New Essays towards a Critical Method* (London, 1897), 55–130; E. C. Stedman, *Poets of America* (Boston, 1885), 225–72; Yvor Winters, "Edgar Allan Poe: A Crisis in the History of American Obscurantism," *Maule's Curse* (Norfolk, Conn., 1938), 93–122.

CHAPTER V

GENERAL STUDIES: H. F. Barnes, *Charles Fenno Hoffman* (New York, 1930); I. G. Everson, *George Henry Calvert: American Literary Pioneer* (New York, 1944); R. W. Griswold, *The Prose Writers of America* (revised and enlarged ed., Philadelphia, 1870); R. W. Griswold, *The Poets and Poetry of America* (Philadelphia, 1842); R. W. Griswold, *The Female Poets of America* (Philadelphia, 1848); Heiser, "The Decline of Neoclassicism," *Transitions in American Literary History*, 91–159; G. S. Hillard, *The Relation of the Poet to His Age* (Boston, 1843); D. K. Jackson, ed., *American Studies in Honor of William Kenneth Boyd* (Durham, 1940); W. A. Jones, *Characters and Criticisms* (2 vols., New York, 1857); R. W. July, *The Essential New Yorker: Gulian Crommelin Verplanck* (Durham, 1951); H. S. Legaré, *Writings* (2 vols., Charleston, 1845); E. W. Parks, *Segments of Southern Thought* (Athens, Ga., 1938); E. W. Parks, *Southern Poets: Representative Selections* (New York, 1936); F. L. Pattee, *The Feminine Fifties* (New York, 1940); James Reese, *The Dramatic Authors of*

America (Philadelphia, 1845); Linda Rhea, *Hugh Swinton Legaré: A Charleston Intellectual* (Chapel Hill, 1934); Riegel, *Young America*; A. M. Schlesinger, Jr., *The Age of Jackson* (Boston, 1945); B. T. Spencer, "A National Literature, 1837–1855," AL, Vol. VIII (1936), 125–59; John Stafford, *The Literary Criticism of "Young America"* (Berkeley and Los Angeles, 1952); Taft, *Minor Knickerbockers.*

ON A NATIONAL LITERATURE: (For many of the following references to New York periodicals, I am indebted to Stafford, cited above; for references to some southern periodicals, to Jackson and Parks. Most references I have collected myself.) Review of Béranger's poems, SR, Vol. VII (1831), 42–67; "American Literature," SR, Vol. VII (1831), 437–38; "Rights of Authors," SLM, Vol. III (1837), 37–39; Malcolm Cowie, preface to William Gilmore Simms, *The Yemassee* (New York, 1937), xxi; E. A. Duyckinck, review of Cornelius Mathews, NYR, Vol. VII (1840), 430–39; review of Longfellow's *Voices of the Night* and *Ballads and other Poems*, SQR, Vol. I (1842), 493–506; William Gilmore Simms, *Views and Reviews* (New York, 1845), 36–40; SLM, Vol. XI (1845), 395; Griswold, *The Prose Writers of America*, 14; notice of Longfellow's *Belfry of Bruges*, SLQ, Vol. IX (1846), 524–25; E. A. Duyckinck, "Nationality in Literature," DR, Vol. XX (1847), 264–72; J. S. Dwight, *Christian Examiner*, Vol. XXXIII (1842), 32; Horace Binney Wallace, review of Griswold's *The Prose Writers of America*, in *Literary Criticisms: and Other Papers* (Philadelphia, 1856), 5, 46–47; "Fugitive Poetry of America," SQR, Vol. XIV (1848), 101–31; "American Literature and Charleston Society," SQR, Vol. XXIII (1853), 402–403; William Gilmore Simms, review of later poems of Henry Taylor, SQR, Vol. XV (1849), 485; "Lowell, the Poet," PM, Vol. I (1853), 547–48; Herman Melville, "Hawthorne and His *Mosses*," *Literary World*, Vol. VII (1850), 145–46; "American Literature," H, Vol. I (1850), 37.

ON REGIONAL SENTIMENT: Review of Mrs. Welby's poems, SQR, Vol. VIII (1845), 407–408; "Southern Literature," SLM, Vol. I (1834), 1–3; M. R. H. Garnett, "An Address Delivered before the . . . Alumni of the University of Virginia," in Jackson, *Studies*, 215; "Editor's Table," SLM, Vol. XVIII (1852), 756; G. N. Sanders, "Fogy Literature," DR, Vol. XXX (1852), 396–97.

ON NATIONAL LITERATURE: "Historical Romance in Italy," NAR, Vol. XLVI (1838), 325–40; Simms, *Views and Reviews*, 42–59; Griswold, *The Prose Writers of America, 16*; P. P. Cooke, "Old Books and New Authors," SLM, Vol. XII (1846), 55; "American Epics," *Putnam's Monthly*, Vol. III (1854), 639–48; Wallace, review of Griswold's *The Prose Writers of America,* in *Literary Criticisms,* 47; review of *Margaret,* SLQ, Vol. IX (1846), 507–22; "The Late Reverend Sylvester Judd," NYQ, Vol. II (1853), 278–312.

ON DEMOCRATIC LITERATURE: For a summary of Jones's papers in DR (1842–43), see Stafford, *The Literary Criticism of "Young America,"* 67–70; see also Daniel Whitaker, SQR, Vol. I (1842), 496; Griswold, *The Prose Writers of America,* 5, 47–48; E. W. Johnson, "The Progress and Disorganization," WR, Vol. II (1845), 90–99; C. W. Webber, "Hawthorne," WR, Vol. IV (1846), 296–316; G. W. Peck, "Omoo," WR, Vol. VI (1847), 45; H. N. Hudson, "Whipple's *Essays and Reviews,*" WR, Vol. IX (1849), 266; "Democracy and Literature," DR, Vol. XI (1842), 196–200; review of Bulwer's *Devereux,* SR, Vol. IV (1829), 369–405; review of Béranger's poems, SR, Vol. VII (1831), 42–67; review of Talfourd's *Letters of Charles Lamb,* NAR, Vol. XLVI (1838), 55–71; George Holmes, review of Sue's *The Wandering Jew,* SQR, Vol. IX (1846), 73–114; "Modern Fiction," SLM, Vol. VIII (1842), 342–48; *Christian Parlor Magazine,* Vol. I (1844), 21–22; "The Confessions of a Novel Reader," SLM, Vol. V (1839), 179–93; K, Vol. V (1835), 320, 322; DR, Vol. XX (1847), 462; "Infirmities of Genius," H, Vol. III (1851), 327–29; "Wordsworth, Byron, Scott, and Shelley," H, Vol. III (1851), 502–505; Wallace, "Washington Irving," *Literary Criticisms,* 74; W. A. Jones, "Children's Books," DR, Vol. XV (1844), 537–38; Simms, *Views and Reviews,* 37, 216; "Innovations in Style," SLM, Vol. IV (1838), 322–27, 344; John Neal, *Brother Jonathan,* Vol. VI (1843), 322; "American Authorship—Hawthorne," SQR, Vol. XXIII (1853), 486–508; "The Inferiority of American Literature," SLM, Vol. VI (1840), 707–10; review of Hillhouse's *Poems and Discourses,* NAR, Vol. L (1840), 231–62; "H. W. Longfellow," SLM, Vol. VIII (1842), 150–54; review of *Ahasuerus, A Poem,* SQR, Vol. II (1842), 312–21; "Fugitive Poetry of America," SQR, Vol. XIV (1848), 101–31; "Nathaniel Hawthorne," *New Englander,* Vol. V (1847), 56–69; Wallace, review of Griswold, *The Female Poets of America,* in *Literary Criticisms,* 94.

ON FEMALE AUTHORSHIP: "The Woman Question," *Western Messenger,* Vol. VI (1838),15–19; F. W. P. Greenwood, "Female Literature," *Miscellaneous Writings* (Boston, 1846), 240–55; Wallace, review of Griswold's *The Female Poets of America,* in *Literary Criticisms,* 94–95; SLM, Vol. XIX (1853), 660.

ON THE THEORY OF THE NOVEL: "Cooper's Novels," NAR, Vol. XLVI (1838), 1–19; *Columbian Magazine,* Vol. VI (1846),

213–14; for Simms's ideas on the novel, see Cowie's preface to *The Yemassee; Simms, Views and Reviews,* 23, 25, 26–27, 30–32, 215–16; SQR, Vol. XV (1849), 45; "Novels: Their Meaning and Mission," PM, Vol. IV (1854), 389–96; "The Genius of Charles Dickens," PM, Vol. V (1855), 263–72; Daniel Whitaker, SQR, Vol. II (1842), 437; review of Cranch's poems, SQR, Vol. VI (1844), 259–61; R. P. Hall, *Poems, by a South Carolinian* (1841), iv, v; W. A. Jones, "Unitarian Portraits," DR, Vol. XV (1844), 389–96; "New Poetry in New England," DR, Vol. XX (1847), 392–98.

On Critical Theory: P. P. Cooke, SLM, Vol. I (1835), 388; "Nature—A Prose Poem," DR, Vol. I, 18, 319–20; "Criticisms on Painting," K, Vol. XVI (1840), 230–33; "Miss Fuller's *Papers on Literature and Art,*" DR, Vol. XIX (1846), 198–202; W. A. Jones, "Critics and Criticism of the Nineteenth Century," DR, Vol. XV (1844), 153–62; W. A. Jones, "Criticism in America," DR, Vol. XV (1844), 241–49; "Modern English Poets," DR, Vol. XIX (1846), 316–20; review of *Margaret,* SLQ, Vol. IX (1846), 507–22; Amory D. Mayo, "The Poetry of Keats," MQR, Vol. II (1848), 414–28; Simms, review of later poems of Henry Taylor, SQR, Vol. XV (1849), 484–526; "Lowell, the Poet," PM, Vol. I (1853) 547–58; "Wordsworth," NYR, Vol. IV (1839), 1–70; E. S. Gould, "American Criticism on American Authors," NYM, Vol. XIII (1836), 321; "American Literature," K, Vol. V (1835), 317–26, 378–84, 473–80; "Chateaubriand's Sketches of English Literature," NAR, Vol. XLIX (1839), 317–48; "The Yucatan Ruins," DR, Vol. XII (1843), 391; Wallace, review of Griswold's *The Prose Writers of America,* in *Literary Criticisms,* 37–38; "Cooper's Works," DR, Vol. XXV (1849), 52; "Mr. Forrest's Oration," DR, Vol. III (1838), 37–38, 54.

Chapter VI

Works of Whitman: *Complete Prose Works* (New York, 1914); *Complete Poems and Prose* (Philadelphia, 1892); *Uncollected Poetry and Prose* (2 vols., New York, 1921); *Poetry and Selected Prose and Letters,* ed. by Emory Holloway (2 vols., London, 1938); see also H. L. Traubel, *With Walt Whitman in Camden* (3 vols.: Vol. I, Boston, 1906; Vols. II and III, New York, 1908, 1914).

On Whitman: G. W. Allen, *American Prosody* (New York, 1935), 217–43; G. W. Allen, *Whitman Handbook* (Chicago, 1946); Harold Blodgett, *The Best of Whitman* (New York, 1953), 3–36; H. S.

Canby, *Walt Whitman, An American: A Study in Biography* (Boston, 1943); S. K. Coffman, " 'Crossing Brooklyn Ferry': A Note on the Catalogue Technique in Whitman's Poetry," MP, Vol. LI (1954), 225–32; Norman Foerster, "Whitman," *Nature in American Literature* (New York, 1923), 176–220; Foerster, "Whitman," *American Criticism*, 157–222; David Goodale, "Some of Whitman's Borrowings," AL, Vol. X (1938), 202–13; Henry James, *Views and Reviews* (Boston, 1908), 101–10; M. O. Johnson, *Walt Whitman as a Critic of Literature* (Lincoln, 1938); Sidney Lanier, *Lectures on the English Novel*, in *Works*, IV, 39–54; Amy Lowell, "Whitman and the New Poetry," YR, Vol. XVI (1927), 502–19; F. O. Matthiessen, *American Renaissance* (New York, 1941), 517–656; Harriet Monroe, "Walt Whitman," *Poets and Their Art* (New York, 1926), 179–84; More, "Walt Whitman," *Shelburne Essays*, IV, 180–211; S. P. Sherman, "Walt Whitman," *Americans* (New York, 1922), 153–85; Stedman, "Walt Whitman," *Poets of America*, 349–95; Floyd Stovall, *Walt Whitman: Representative Selections* (New York, 1939).

CHAPTER VII

LIVES OF LONGFELLOW: By Samuel Longfellow, *Life of Henry Wadsworth Longfellow* (3 vols., Boston,1891); H. S. Gorman, *A Victorian American: Henry Wadsworth Longfellow* (New York, 1926); Lawrance Thompson, *Young Longfellow* (New York, 1938).

WORKS OF LONGFELLOW: *Prose Works* (2 vols., Boston, 1857).

ON LONGFELLOW: J. C. Austin, "J. T. Fields and the Revision of Longfellow's Poems," NEQ, Vol. XXIV (1951), 239–50; W. A. Chamberlain, "Longfellow's Attitude toward Goethe," MP, Vol. XVI (1918), 57ff.; Arthur Colton, "Longfellow: An Essay in Reputations," B, Vol. LXXVI (1933), 128–33; G. R. Elliott, "The Gentle Shades of Longfellow," *The Cycle of Modern Poetry* (Princeton, 1929), 64–82; Francis Gribble, "H. W. Longfellow," *Fortnightly Review*, Vol. LXXXI (1907), 241–50; J. T. Hatfield, "The Longfellow-Freiligrath Correspondence," PMLA, Vol. XLVIII (1933), 1223–91; J. T. Hatfield, *New Light on Longfellow* (Boston, 1933); W. D. Howells, "The White Mr. Longfellow," *Literary Friends and Acquaintance* (New York, 1901), 178–211; H. M. Jones, "Longfellow," *American Writers on American Literature* (New York, 1934), 105–24; H. M. Jones, "The Longfellow Nobody Knows," *Outlook*, Vol. CLIX (1928), 577–79; Long, *Literary Pioneers*; J. P. Pritchard, "The Horatian Influence upon Longfellow," AL, Vol. IV (1932), 22–38; Pritchard, "Henry Wadsworth Longfellow," *Return to the Fountains,* 79–89; Odell Shepard, *Henry Wadsworth Longfellow: Representative Selections* (New York, 1934); Stedman, "Henry Wadsworth Longfellow," *Poets of America,* 180–224; G. E. Woodberry, "Longfellow," *Literary Memoirs of the Nineteenth Century* (New York, 1921), 215–26.

LIVES OF HOLMES: J. T. Morse, *Life and Letters of Oliver Wendell Holmes* (2 vols., Boston, 1896); M. A. D. Howe, *Holmes of the Breakfast-Table* (New York, 1939); E. M. Tilton, *Amiable Autocrat* (New York, 1947).

WORKS OF HOLMES: *Works,* Riverside ed. (11 vols., Boston, 1891–1906).

ON HOLMES: W. G. Ballantine, "Oliver Wendell Holmes," NAR, Vol. CXC (1909), 178–93; Van Wyck Brooks, "Dr. Holmes: Forerunner of the Moderns," SRL, Vol. XIV (1936), 13–15, 34; H. H. Clark, "Oliver Wendell Holmes: A Reinterpretation," NEQ, Vol. XII (1939), 19–34; E. W. Emerson, *The Early Years of the Saturday Club* (Boston, 1918); H. D. Fuller, "Holmes," *American Writers on American Literature* (New York, 1931), 153–63; C. H. Grattan, "O. W. Holmes," *American Mercury,* Vol. IV (1925), 37–41; E. E. Hale, "Oliver Wendell Holmes," *Review of Reviews,* Vol. X (1894), 495–501; S. I. Hayakawa, "Holmes's Lowell Institute Lectures," AL, Vol. VIII (1936), 281–90; S. I. Hayakawa and H. M. Jones, *Oliver Wendell Holmes: Representative Selections* (New York, 1939); Howells "Oliver Wendell Holmes," *Literary Friends and Acquaintance,* 146–77; W. S. Knickerbocker, "His Own Boswell," SewR, Vol. XLI (1933), 454–66; J. R. Lowell, review of *Elsie Venner,* AM, Vol. VII (1861), 509–11; John Macy, "Holmes," *The Spirit of American Literature* (New York, 1913), 155–71; J. P. Pritchard, "The Autocrat and Horace," CW, Vol. XXV (1932), 217–23; Pritchard, "Oliver Wendell Holmes," *Return to the Fountains,* 90–98; W. L. Schroeder, *Oliver Wendell Holmes, An Appreciation* (London, 1909); Stedman, "Oliver Wendell Holmes," *Poets of America,* 273–303; J. T. Trowbridge, "My Own Story: Recollections of Holmes and Longfellow," AM, Vol. XCI (1903), 600–15.

LIVES OF LOWELL: H. E. Scudder, *James Russell Lowell* (2 vols., Boston, 1901); R. C. Beatty, *James Russell Lowell* (Nashville, 1942); Leon Howard, *Victorian Knight-Errant* (Berkeley and Los Angeles, 1952).

WORKS OF LOWELL: *Works,* Elmwood ed. (16 vols., Boston, 1904); *The Round Table* (Boston, 1913); *The Function of the Poet,* ed. by Albert Mordell (Boston, 1920); *New Letters,* ed. by M. A. D. Howe (New York, 1932).

ON LOWELL: "Mr. Russell Lowell," *Blackwood's,* Vol. CL (1891), 454–60; Brownell, "Lowell," *American Prose Masters,* 271–335; H. H. Clark, "Lowell's Criticism of Romantic Literature," PMLA, Vol. XLI (1926), 209–28; H. H. Clark and Norman Foerster, *James Russell Lowell: Representative Selections* (New York, 1947); DeMille, "Lowell," *Literary Criticism in America,* 49–85; F. W. Farrar, "An English Estimate of Lowell," F, Vol. XII (1891), 141–52; Foerster, "Lowell," *American Criticism,* 111–56; Norman Foerster, "Lowell's Criticism of Romantic Literature," PMLA, Vol. XLI (1926), 209–28; Grattan, "Lowell," *American Mercury,* 63–69; E. E. Hale, *James Russell Lowell and His Friends* (Boston, 1899); J. M. Hart, "James Russell Lowell," PMLA, Vol. VII (1892), 25–31; Howells, "Studies of Lowell," *Literary Friends and Acquaintance,* 212–50; Ferris Lockwood, "Mr. Lowell on Art-Principles," S, Vol. XV (1894), 186–89; R. M. Lovett, "Lowell," *American Writers on American Literature* (1934), 177–89; Rollo Ogden, *Life and Letters of Edwin Lawrence Godkin* (2 vols., New York, 1907); J. P. Pritchard, "Lowell's Debt to Horace's *Ars Poetica,*" AL, Vol. III (1931), 259–76; Pritchard, "Aristotle's *Poetics* and Certain American Literary Critics," CW, Vol. XXVII (1934), 89–93; J. P. Pritchard, "Lowell and Longinus," TAPhA, Vol. LXXVI (1945), 358–76; J. P. Pritchard, "A Glance at Lowell's Classical Reading," AL, Vol. XXI (1950), 442–55; Pritchard, "James Russell Lowell," *Return to the Fountains,* 99–118; J. J. Reilly, *James Russell Lowell as a Critic* (New York, 1915); G. B. Smith, "James Russell Lowell," *Nineteenth Century,* Vol. XVII (1885), 988–1008; Stedman, "James Russell Lowell," *Poets of America,* 304–48; F. H. Underwood, "James Russell Lowell," *Contemporary Review,* Vol. LX (1891), 477–98; W. C. Wilkinson, *A Free Lance in the Field of Life and Letters* (New York, 1874), 50–183; George Wurfl, "Lowell's Debt to Goethe," *Pennsylvania State College Studies,* Vol. I (1936).

WORKS OF WHIPPLE: *Lectures on Subjects Connected with Literature and Life* (Boston, 1850); "Nathaniel Hawthorne," AM, Vol. V (1860), 614–22; *Essays and Reviews* (2 vols., New York, 1848–49); *Character and Characteristics Men* (Boston, 1866); *Literature of the Age of Elizabeth* (Boston, 1876); *Charles Dickens* (2 vols.); *American Literature, and Other Papers* (Boston, 1887).

ON WHIPPLE: T. W. Higginson, "Edwin Percy Whipple," AM,

Vol. LVIII (1886), 345–48; Denham Sutcliffe, " 'Our Young American Macaulay': Edwin Percy Whipple," NEQ, Vol. XIX (1946), 3–18; Bliss Perry, "Edwin Percy Whipple," in Emerson, *Early Years of the Saturday Club.*

WORKS OF STEDMAN: *Victorian Poets* (Boston, 1875); *Poets of America* (Boston, 1885); *The Nature and Elements of Poetry* (Boston, 1892); *Genius: and Other Essays* (New York, 1911).

ON STEDMAN: Laura Stedman and G. M. Gould, *Life and Letters of Edmund Clarence Stedman* (2 vols., New York, 1910); DeMille, "Stedman," *Literary Criticism in America,* 133–57; J. P. Pritchard, "Stedman and Horatian Criticism," AL, Vol. V (1933), 166–69; Pritchard, "Aristotle's *Poetics* and Certain American Literary Critics," CW, Vol. XXVII (1934), 97–99; Pritchard, "Edmund Clarence Stedman," *Return to the Fountains,* 119–34.

WORKS OF WOODBERRY: *Appreciation of Literature* (New York, 1921); *Heart of Man* (New York, 1920); *Literary Essays* (New York, 1920); *Literary Memoirs of the Nineteenth Century; Literature and Life* (New York, 1921); *Nathaniel Hawthorne* (Boston, 1902); *Selected Letters* (Boston, 1933); *Studies of a Litterateur* (New York, 1921); *The Torch: and Other Lectures and Addresses* (New York, 1920).

ON WOODBERRY: John Erskine, "George Edward Woodberry," SRL, Vol. I (1925), 761; John Erskine, "The Human Spirit," SRL, Vol. X (1933), 25–26; G. S. Hellman, "Men of Letters at Columbia," *The Critic,* Vol. XLIII (1903), 321–27; Harold Kellock, "Woodberry—A Great Teacher," N, Vol. CXXX (1930), 120–22; L. V. Ledoux, *George Edward Woodberry: A Study of His Poetry* (Cambridge, 1917); J. P. Pritchard, "Horace's Influence upon American Criticism," TAPhA, Vol. LXVIII (1937) 228–63; J. P. Pritchard, "Aristotle's Influence upon American Criticism," TAPhA, Vol. LXVII (1936), 341–62; Pritchard, "George Edward Woodberry," *Return to the Fountains,* 148–58; M. H. Shackford, "George Edward Woodberry as Critic," NEQ, Vol. XXIV (1951), 510–27; J. E. Spingarn, "George Edward Woodberry," DAB, Vol. XX, 478–81; C. F. Thwing, "George Edward Woodberry," *Harvard Graduates Magazine,* Vol. XXXVIII (1930), 433–43.

CHAPTER VIII

LIFE OF HOWELLS: O. W. Firkins, *William Dean Howells: A Study* (Cambridge, 1924).

WORKS OF HOWELLS: *Criticism and Fiction* (New York, 1891); *My Literary Passions* (New York, 1895); *Literary Friends and Acquaintance; Literature and Life* (New York, 1902); *My Mark Twain* (New York, 1910); *Life in Letters of William Dean Howells,* ed. by Mildred Howells (2 vols., New York, 1928); "The Editor's Study," *Harper's Magazine* (1886–91); "The Editor's Easy Chair," *Harper's Magazine* (1900–20). See also Clifton J. Malone, *The Hitherto Uncollected Critical Opinions of William Dean Howells ... Appearing in the "Editor's Study" and the "Editor's Easy Chair" of Harper's Monthly Magazine* (unpublished University of Oklahoma thesis, 1946).

ON HOWELLS: H. H. Boyesen, "The Progressive Realism of American Fiction," *Literary and Social Silhouettes* (New York, 1894), 58–78; S. L. Clemens, "William Dean Howells," H, Vol. CXIII (1906), 221–25; Van Wyck Brooks, *New England: Indian Summer* (New York, 1940), 204–49, 373–94; DeMille, "Howells," *Literary Criticism in America,* 182–205; Hamlin Garland, "Howells," *American Writers on American Literature* (1934), 285–97; Grattan, "Howells: Ten Years After," *American Mercury,* Vol. XX (1930), 42–50; Alexander Harvey, *William Dean Howells: A Study of the Achievement of a Literary Artist* (New York, 1917); Macy, "Howells," *The Spirit of American Literature,* 278–95; Brander Matthews, "Mr. Howells as a Critic," F, Vol. XXXII (1902), 629–38; H. L. Mencken, *Prejudices,* Ser. I (New York, 1919), 52–58; Carl Van Doren, "Howells: May 1920," *The Roving Critic* (New York, 1923), 72–73; W. L. Phelps, *Howells, James, Bryant, and Other Essays* (New York, 1924); Robertson, "Mr. Howells' Novels," *Essays towards a Critical Method* (1889), 149–99; Bernard Smith, *Forces in American Criticism* (New York, 1939), 158–75; W. F. Taylor, "William Dean Howells," SewR, Vol. XLVI (1938), 288–303; Pritchard, "William Dean Howells," *Return to the Fountains,* 135–47; Lionel Trilling, "William Dean Howells and the Roots of Modern Taste," PR, Vol. XVIII (1951), 516–36.

WORKS OF JAMES: *French Poets and Novelists* (New York, 1878); *Hawthorne* (New York, 1879); *Partial Portraits* (New York, 1888); *Essays in London and Elsewhere* (New York, 1893); *Views and Reviews* (1908); *Notes on Novelists* (New York, 1914); *Notes and Reviews by Henry James,* ed by Pierre de Chaignon la Rose (Cambridge, 1921); *The Art of the Novel: Critical Prefaces,* ed. by R. P. Blackmur (New York, 1934).

ON JAMES: R. P. Blackmur, "The Critical Prefaces of Henry James," *The Double Agent: Essays in Craft and Elucidation* (New York,

1934), 234–68; Brooks, *New England: Indian Summer,* 224–49, 276–95, 395–408; Brownell, "Henry James," *American Prose Masters,* 339–400; W. D. Howells, "Henry James, Jr.," C, n. s., Vol. III (1882) 25–29; W. D. Howells, "Mr. Henry James's Later Work," NAR, Vol. CLXXVI (1903), 125–37; Lyon Richardson, *Henry James: Representative Selections* (New York, 1941); S. P. Sherman, "The Aesthetic Idealism of Henry James," *On Contemporary Literature* (New York, 1917), 226–55; S. P. Sherman, "The Special Case of Henry James," *The Emotional Discovery of America* (New York, 1932), 35–47; Edmund Wilson, "The Ambiguity of Henry James," *The Triple Thinkers* (New York, 1948), 88–132; Yvor Winters, "Maule's Well: or, Henry James and the Relation of Morals to Manners," *Maule's Curse,* 169–216; Mayo Hazeltine, "Henry James, Jr.," *Chats about Books . . .* (New York, 1883), 347–60.

MINOR REALISTS: Review of Brown's "Sixty Years Gleanings from Life's Harvest," A, Vol. III (1859), 770; review of Miss Cummins's *El Fureidis,* AM, Vol. VI (1860), 119; review of Trowbridge's *The Old Battle-Ground,* AM, Vol. VI (1860), 376–77; review of Whittier's *Home Ballads and Other Poems,* AM, Vol. VI (1860), 638; J. E. Cabot, "On the Relation of Art to Nature," AM, Vol. XIII (1864), 183–99, 313–29; review of Longfellow's translation of the *Divine Comedy,* NAR, Vol. CV (1867), 124–48; "Mr. Trollope's Last Novel," N, Vol. XXXI (1880), 138–39; O. B. Frothingham, "The Morally Objectionable in Literature," NAR, Vol. CXXXV (1882), 323–38; C. D. Warner, "Modern Fiction," AM, Vol. LI (1883), 464–74; John Burroughs, "The True Realism," *Indoor Studies* (Boston, 1904), 252–56; H. W. Mabie, "The Significance of Modern Criticism," *Essays in Literary Interpretation* (New York, 1892), 46–70; Boyesen, "The Progressive Realism of American Fiction," *Literary and Social Silhouettes,* 58–78; Hamlin Garland, *Crumbling Idols* (Chicago, 1894); "Hamlin Garland," AM, Vol. LXXVI (1895), 840–44; Hiram Corson, *The Aims of Literary Study* (New York, 1894); Paul Shorey, "Present Conditions of Literary Production," AM, Vol. LXXVIII (1896), 156–68; Frank Norris, *The Responsibilities of the Novelist* (New York, 1903), 1, 8–9, 15–16; P. H. Frye, "George Sand," *Literary Reviews and Criticisms* (New York, 1908), 56; Frye, "Zola," *ibid.,* 74–75; *"Indecent Publications"* (review of Swinburne's *Laus Veneris),* NQR, Vol. XIV (1866), 150–58; notice of Swinburne's *Laus Veneris,* NAR, Vol. CIV (1867), 287–92, Sidney Lanier, *Lectures on the English Novel,* in Centennial Edition, IV, 4, 26, 55–60; review of *Le Roman Experimental,* AM, Vol. XLVII (1881), 116–19; T. S. Perry, "Zola's Last Novel" *(Nana),* AM, Vol. XLV (1880), 693–99; C. B. Martin, "Zola as a Critic," AM, Vol. XLIII (1879), 650–56;

W. R. Thayer, "The New Story-Tellers and the Doom of Realism," F, Vol. XVIII (1894), 470–80. See also B. J. Bowron, "Realism in America," CL, Vol. III (1951), 268–85; Herbert Edwards, "Zola and the American Critics," AL, Vol. IV (1932), 114–29; Hazeltine, "Zola," *Chats about Books*, 188–211; Harry Levin, "What is Realism?" CL, Vol. III (1951), 193–99; Harold Strauss, "Realism in the Proletarian Novel," YR, Vol. XXVIII (1938), 360–74; Lionel Trilling, "Reality in America," *The Liberal Imagination* (London, 1951), 3–21.

CHAPTER IX

ON IMPRESSIONISM: "The Renaissance," N, Vol. XVII (1873), 243–44; "Carr's *Essays on Art*," N, Vol. XXVIII (1879), 437–38; Agnes Repplier, "Curiosities of Criticism," AM, Vol. LIX (1887), 314–23; W. P. Trent, "The Authority of Criticism," F, Vol. XXVII (1899), 243–56; John Burroughs, "Criticism and the Man," *Literary Values* (Boston, 1902), 94–97; L. E. Gates, "Impressionism and Appreciation," AM, Vol. LXXVI (1900), 73–84; "Swinburne's New Volume," N, Vol. XXVII (1878), 45–46; Grant Allen, "Novels with a Purpose," NAR, Vol. CLXIII (1896), 223–35; Gates, *Studies and Appreciations*, 92–93; Burroughs, "Thou Shalt Not Preach," *Literary Values*, 155–56; Henry Timrod, "Literature in the South," R, Vol. V (1859), 385–95; Norman Hapgood, "A Theory of Dramatic Criticism," F, Vol. XXVII (1899), 121–22; Norris, "The Novel with a Purpose," *The Responsibilities of the Novelist* (1928), 21–28.

ON REGIONALISM AND NATIONALISM: "Editor's Table," R, Vol. I (1859), 82; "DeForest's *Overland*," C, Vol. III (1872), 505–506; "Howells's *Foregone Conclusion*," N, Vol. XX (1875), 12–13; "*The Europeans*, and Other Novels," AM, Vol. XLIII (1879), 167–73; G. E. Waring, Jr., "George W. Cable," C, Vol. XXIII (1882), 602–605; P. H. Hayne to M. C. Tyler, in *A Collection of Hayne Letters*, ed. by D. M. McKeithan (Austin, 1944), 320, 352, 378; Sidney Lanier to Bayard Taylor, in *Letters of Sidney Lanier*, ed. by H. W. Lanier (New York, 1902), 121; J. C. Harris, in Julia C. Harris, *Joel Chandler Harris: Editor and Essayist* (Chapel Hill, 1931), 45–47; J. S. Bassett, "The Problems of the Author in the South," SAQ, Vol. I (1902), 201–208; E. W. Parks, *Charles Egbert Craddock* (Chapel Hill, 1941), 177–222; Carey McWilliams, "Localism in American Criticism," SwR, Vol. XIX (1934), 410–28; J. L. Allen, "Local Color," *The Critic*, Vol. VIII (1886), 13ff. See also G. C. Knight, *James Lane Allen and the Genteel Tradition* (Chapel Hill, 1935), 59; Boyesen, "The Progressive Realism of American Fiction," *Literary and Social Silhouettes*, 58–78;

Hamlin Garland, "The Literary Emancipation of the West," F, Vol. XVI (1893), 157–66; R. G. White, "Americanisms," AM, Vol. XLI (1878), 495–502; "Margaret Fuller," N, Vol. XXXIX (1884), 268–69; H. E. Scudder, "American Classics in School," AM, Vol. LX (1887), 85–91; S. G. Fisher, "Has Immigration Dried up Our Literature?," F, Vol. XVI (1894), 560–67; H. W. Mabie, "American Literature and American Nationality," F, Vol. XXVI (1899), 633–40; *The Independent,* Vol. LIV (1902), 2784–86; Norris, "The Great American Novel," *The Responsibilities of the Novelist,* 66.

GENERAL: G. W. Allen, "Sidney Lanier as a Literary Critic," PQ, Vol. XVII (1938), 121–38; J. L. Allen, "Caterpillar Critics," F, Vol. IV (1889), 527–36; J. L. Allen, "Two Principles in Recent American Fiction," AM, Vol. LXXX (1897), 433–41; B. A. Botkin, "Regionalism: Cult or Culture?," EJ, Vol. XXV (1936), 181–85; Gamaliel Bradford, Jr., "The Mission of the Literary Critic," AM, Vol. XCIV (1904), 537–44; H. R. Brown, "The Great American Novel," AL, Vol. VII (1935), 1–14; H. S. Canby, "Essays in Criticism," *Seven Years' Harvest* (New York, 1936), 97–132; P. L. Ford, "The American Historical Novel," AM, Vol. LXXX (1897), 721–28; Mayo Hazeltine, "As to Age-End Literature," NAR, Vol. CLX (1895), 743–52; H. C. Howe, "The Contradictions of Literary Criticism, NAR, Vol. CLXXV (1902), 399–408; J. B. Hubbell, *The Last Years of Henry Timrod* (Durham, 1941); H. M. Jones, *Ideas in America* (Cambridge, 1944); H. M. Jones, *The Theory of American Literature* (Ithaca, 1948); Mabie, "The Significance of Modern Criticism," *Essays in Literary Interpretation,* 46–70; Brander Matthews, "The Study of Fiction," *The Historical Novel* (New York, 1901), 75–108; Brander Matthews, "Romance against Romanticism," *ibid.,* 31–48; Brander Matthews, "American Literature," *Aspects of Fiction* (New York, 1902), 3–24; Gregory Paine, *Southern Prose Writers: Representative Selections* (New York, 1947); E. W. Parks, *The Essays of Henry Timrod* (Athens, Ga., 1942); Parks, *Segments of Southern Thought;* Parks, *Southern Poets;* F. A. Porcher, "The New World and the New Man," R, Vol. IV (1858), 195ff.; Philip Rahv, "On the Decline of Naturalism," PR, Vol. IX (1942), 482–93; Agnes Repplier, "Fiction in the Pulpit," AM, Vol. LXIV (1889), 527–36; Agnes Repplier, "Literary Shibboleths," AM, Vol. LXV (1890), 631–38; Agnes Repplier, "Pleasure: A Heresy," AM, Vol. LXVII (1891), 393–402; W. G. Simms, "Literary Prospects of the South," R, Vol. III (1858), 193–206; H. N. Snyder, "The Reconstruction of Southern Thought," SAQ, Vol. I (1902), 145–55; W. R. Thayer, "The Pause in Criticism —and After," AM, Vol. LXXX (1897), 227–32; Calvin Thomas, "Have We Still Need of Poetry?," F, Vol. XXV (1898), 502–12; W.

P. Trent, *William Gilmore Simms* (Boston, 1892); G. P. Voigt, "Timrod's Essays in Literary Criticism," AL, Vol. VI (1934), 163–67; R. P. Warren, "Some Don'ts for Literary Regionalists," AR, Vol. VIII (1936), 142–50; G. E. Woodberry, *Two Phases of Criticism: Historical and Aesthetic* (1914).

CHAPTER X

SOURCE MATERIALS: "The New Criticism," in J. E. Spingarn, *Creative Criticism* (New York, 1925), 3–46.

WORKS OF HUNEKER: *Iconoclasts* (New York, 1905); *Egoists* (New York, 1909); *Promenades of an Impressionist* (New York, 1910); *The Pathos of Distance* (New York, 1913); *Ivory, Apes, and Peacocks* (New York, 1915); *Unicorns* (New York, 1917); *Steeplejack* (New York, 1920); *Letters of James Gibbons Huneker* and *Intimate Letters of James Gibbons Huneker*, ed. by Josephine Huneker (New York, 1922).

ON HUNEKER: DeMille, "Huneker," *Literary Criticism in America*; Alfred Kazin, *On Native Grounds: An Interpretation of Modern American Prose Literature* (New York, 1942), 62–66; H. L. Mencken, "James Huneker," *A Book of Prefaces* (New York, 1917), 151–94; Mencken, "James Huneker," *Prejudices*, Ser. III (New York, 1922), 65–84; J. P. Pritchard and J. M. Raines, "James Gibbons Huneker: Critic of the Seven Arts," *American Quarterly*, Vol. II (1950), 53–61; Bernard Smith, "Huneker and the Tribe," *Proletarian Literature in the United States*, ed. by Granville Hicks (New York, 1935), 373–79.

WORKS OF BROWNELL: "The Academy and the Language," *Academy Papers* (New York, 1925), 39–59; *American Prose Masters* (New York, 1909); *French Art* (New York, 1892); *French Traits* (New York, 1888); *The Genius of Style* (New York, 1924); *Standards* (New York, 1917); *Victorian Prose Masters* (New York, 1901).

ON BROWNELL: G. M. Harper, "An American Critic: W. C. Brownell," *John Morley and Other Essays* (Princeton, 1920), 93–110; R. M. Lovett, "William Crary Brownell," NR, Vol. LVI (1928), 204–206; L. J. A. Mercier, "W. C. Brownell and Our Neo-Barbarism," F, Vol. LXXXI (1929), 376–81; Pritchard, "William Crary Brownell," *Return to the Fountains*, 159–69; S. P. Sherman, "William Crary Brownell," *Points of View* (New York, 1924), 89–126; S. P. Sherman, "Mr. Brownell and the Quest for Perfection," *Critical Woodcuts* (New York, 1926), 111–21.

Works of Babbitt: *Literature and the American College* (Boston, 1908); *The New Laokoön* (Boston, 1910); *The Masters of Modern French Criticism* (Boston, 1912); *Rousseau and Romanticism* (Boston, 1919); "Humanist and Specialist," *Brown University Papers*, Vol. III (1926); "Humanism: An Essay at Definitions," *Humanism and America: Essays on the Outlook of Modern Civilisation*, ed. by Norman Foerster (New York, 1929); "President Eliot and American Education," F, Vol. LXXXI (1929), 1–10; *On Being Creative: and Other Essays* (Boston, 1932); "Style in a Democracy," SRL, Vol. IX (1932), 325–36; *Spanish Character: and Other Essays* (Boston, 1940).

On Babbitt: M. M. Colum, "Literature, Ethics, and the Knights of Good Sense," S, Vol. LXXXVII (1930), 599–608; M. M. Colum, "Self-Critical America," S, Vol. LXXXVII (1930), 197–206; S. E. Dubbel, "He Searched the Past," SAQ, Vol. XXXV (1936), 50–61; T. S. Eliot, "The Humanism of Irving Babbitt" (1927), *Selected Essays: 1917–1932* (New York, 1932), 383–92; G. R. Elliott, "Irving Babbitt as I Knew Him," AR, Vol. VIII (1936), 36–60; G. R. Elliott, "T. S. Eliot and Irving Babbitt," AR, Vol. VII (1936), 442–54; P. E. More, "Irving Babbitt," UTQ, Vol. III (1934), 129–45; G. B. Munson, "An Introduction to Irving Babbitt," *Destinations: A Canvass of American Literature Since 1900* (New York, 1928), 24–40; Hoffman Nickerson, "Irving Babbitt," AR, Vol. II (1934), 385–404; J. P. Pritchard, "Aristotle's Influence upon American Criticism," TAPhA, Vol. LXVII (1936), 341–62; J. P. Pritchard, "Horace's Influence upon American Criticism," TAPhA, Vol. LXVIII (1937), 228–63; Pritchard, "Irving Babbitt," *Return to the Fountains*, 170–79; Edmund Wilson, "Sophocles, Babbitt, and Freud," NR, Vol. LXV (1930), 68–70; Edmund Wilson, "Notes on Babbitt and More," NR, Vol. LXII (1930), 115–20.

Works of More: *Shelburne Essays* (11 vols., Boston, 1904–21); *New Shelburne Essays* (3 vols., Princeton, 1928–36); *A Paul Elmer More Miscellany*, ed. by A. H. Dakin (Portland, Me., 1950).

On More: G. S. Brett, "Paul Elmer More: A Study," UTQR, Vol. IV (1935), 279–95; G. R. Elliott, "Mr. More and the Gentle Reader," B, Vol. LXIX (1929), 143–51; Pritchard, "Aristotle's Influence upon American Criticism," TAPhA, Vol. LXVII (1936), 341–62; Pritchard, "Horace's Influence upon American Criticism," TAPhA, Vol. LXVIII (1937), 228–63; Pritchard, *Return to the Fountains*, 180–90; P. S. Richards, "An American Platonist," *The Nineteenth Century*, Vol. CV (1929), 479–89; Robert Shafer, *Paul Elmer More and American Criticism* (New Haven, 1935); S. P. Sherman, "An Imaginary Conversation with Mr. P. E. More," *Americans,* 316–36; Wilson, "Mr. More and the Mithraic Bull," *The Triple Thinkers,* 3–19; Wilson, "Notes on Babbitt and More," NR, Vol. LXII (1930), 115–20.

WORKS OF SHERMAN: *Matthew Arnold: How to Know Him* (Indianapolis, 1917); *On Contemporary Literature; Americans; The Genius of America: Studies in Behalf of the Younger Generation* (New York, 1923); *Points of View; Critical Woodcuts; The Main Stream* (New York, 1927); *Shaping Men and Women* (New York, 1928); *The Emotional Discovery of America; Life and Letters of Stuart P. Sherman,* ed. by Jacob Zeitlin and Homer Woodbridge (2 vols., New York, 1929).

ON SHERMAN: Anon., "The Life and Times of Stuart Sherman," B, Vol. LXX (1929), 289–304; P. H. Boynton, *The Challenge of Modern Criticism* (Chicago, 1931), 54–66; G. E. DeMille, "Stuart Pratt Sherman: The Illinois Arnold," SewR, Vol. XXXV (1927), 79–83; H. E. Luccock, *Contemporary American Literature and Religion* (Chicago, 1934); F. W. P. McDowell, "Stuart P. Sherman: The Evolution of His Critical Philosophy and Method," SP, Vol. L (1953), 540–57; Pritchard, "Aristotle's Influence upon American Criticism," TAPhA, Vol. LXVII (1936), 341–62; Pritchard, "Horace's Influence upon American Criticism," TAPhA, Vol. LXVIII (1937), 228–63; Pritchard, "Stuart Pratt Sherman," *Return to the Fountains,* 191–99; Burton Rascoe, *Theodore Dreiser* (New York, 1925); Carl Van Doren, "The Great and Good Tradition: Stuart P. Sherman, Scourge of Sophomores," C, Vol. CVI (1923), 631–36.

GENERAL: Munson, *Destinations;* G. R. Elliott, *The Cycle of Modern Poetry* (Princeton, 1929); G. R. Elliott, *Humanism and Imagination* (Chapel Hill, 1938).

ON HUMANISM: Boynton, *The Challenge of Modern Criticism;* Seward Collins, "Criticism in America," B, Vol. LXXI (1930), 241–56, 353–64, 400–15, and Vol. LXXII (1930), 145–64, 209–28; Mary Colum, "On Thinking Critically," F, Vol. XCI (1934),76–82; John Farrar, "The American Tradition," B, Vol. LVIII (1924), 609–14; Henry Hazlitt, "All Too Humanism," N, Vol. CXXX (1930), 181–82; *The Critique of Humanism: A Symposium,* ed. by C. H. Grattan (New York, 1930).

ON IMAGISM: O. W. Firkins, "The New Movement in Poetry," N, Vol. CI (1915), 458–60; *Some Imagist Poets* (Boston, 1916);

Conrad Aiken, "The Place of Imagism," NR, Vol. III (1915), 75–76; L. W. Smith, "The New Naïveté" AM, Vol. CXVII (1916), 487–92; Amy Lowell, *Six French Poets: Studies in Contemporary Literature* (Boston, 1915); Amy Lowell, *Tendencies in Modern Poetry* (New York, 1917); Amy Lowell, *Poetry and Poets* (Boston, 1930); S. K. Coffman, *Imagism: A Chapter for the History of Modern Poetry* (Norman, 1951); Glenn Hughes, *Imagism and the Imagists* (Palo Alto, 1931).

WORKS OF MENCKEN: *A Book of Prefaces* (New York, 1917); *Prejudices,* Ser. I–VI (1919–26).

ON MENCKEN: Sherman, "Mr. Mencken, the Jeune Fille, and the New Spirit in Letters," *Americans,* 1–12; V. F. Calverton, "The Vaudeville Critic: H. L. Mencken," *The Newer Spirit* (New York, 1925), 102–106; Sherman, "Mr. Mencken as Liberator," *Critical Woodcuts,* 235–43; Irving Babbitt, "The Critic and American Life," F, Vol. LXXIX (1928), 161–76; Van Wyck Brooks, "Mr. Mencken and the Prophets," *Sketches in Criticism* (New York, 1932).

OTHER STUDIES: J. E. Spingarn, *Creative Criticism and Other Essays* (New York, 1931); H. S. Canby, "Barbarians à la Mode," *Definitions* (New York, 1922), 174–82; *The Critique of Humanism,* ed. by Grattan; *Humanism and America: Essays in the Outlook of Modern Civilisation,* ed. by Norman Foerster (New York, 1930).

ON THE SEARCH FOR A USABLE PAST: Van Wyck Brooks, "America's Coming of Age" (1915), *Three Essays on America* (New York, 1934), 13–112; Brooks, "Letters and Leadership" (1918), *ibid.,* 113–90; Van Wyck Brooks, "On Creating a Usable Past," D, Vol. LXIV (1918), 337–41; Waldo Frank, *The Rediscovery of America* (New York, 1940), 74–75; Canby, "Back to Nature," *Definitions,* 79–85, 98–110; Norman Foerster, "Introduction," *The Reinterpretation of American Literature* (New York, 1928), vii–xv; Farrar, "The American Tradition," B, LVIII (1924), 609–14; Boynton, *The Challenge of Modern Criticism,* 17–27, 110–13; Colum, "On Thinking Critically," F, Vol. XCI (1934), 76–82; Canby, "Essays in Criticism," *Seven Years' Harvest,* 98–132.

ON PSYCHOANALYTICAL CRITICISM: Wilson, "The Historical Interpretation of Literature," *The Triple Thinkers,* 265–66; Conrad Aiken, "The Mechanism of Poetic Inspiration," *Scepticisms* (New York, 1919), 32–47; Canby, "Back to Nature," *Definitions,* 92–108; F. C. Prescott, *The Poetic Mind* (New York, 1922); Maxwell Bodenheim,

"Psychoanalysis and American Fiction," N, Vol. CXIV (1922), 683–84; Waldo Frank, *The Rediscovery of America* (New York, 1929), 126; J. W. Krutch, "Beauty's Rose," N, Vol. CXLV (1937), 132–33; Bernard De Voto, "Freud's Influence on Literature," SRL, Vol. XX (1939), 10–11; Lionel Trilling, "The Legacy of Sigmund Freud: Literary and Aesthetic," KR, Vol. II (1940), 152–73; Kenneth Burke, "Freud and the Analysis of Poetry," *The Philosophy of Literary Form* (Baton Rouge, 1941), 261, 266–67; F. J. Hoffman, *Freudianism and the Literary Mind* (Baton Rouge, 1945); F. J. Hoffman, "Psychoanalysis and Literary Criticism," *American Quarterly*, Vol. II (1950).

ON MARXISM: R. W. Horton and H. W. Edwards, "Marxism," *Backgrounds of American Literature* (New York, 1952), 203–45; Canby, "To-Day in American Literature," *Definitions*, 113–26; Aiken, "The Ivory Tower: Louis Untermeyer as a Critic," *Scepticisms*, 258–67; Heywood Broun, "The Elder Critic and the Young Enthusiast," B, Vol. LIII (1921), 1–4; Stanley Burnshaw, "A New Direction for Criticism," *The New Masses*, Vol. XIV (1935), 23–24; V. F. Calverton, *The Newer Spirit: A Sociological Criticism of Literature* (New York, 1925); Michael Gold, "Out of the Fascist Unconscious," NR, Vol. LXXV (1933), 295–96; *Proletarian Literature in the United States*, ed. by Granville Hicks (New York, 1935); Granville Hicks, *The Great Tradition* (New York, 1933); J. T. Farrell, *A Note on Literary Criticism* (New York, 1936); J. T. Farrell, *The League of Frightened Philistines: and Other Papers* (New York, 1945); J. T. Farrell, *Literature and Morality* (New York, 1947); Wilson, "Marxism and Literature," *The Triple Thinkers*, 197–213; Edmund Wilson, "Dos Passos and the Social Revolution" (1929), *The Shores of Light: A Literary Chronicle of the Twenties and Thirties* (New York, 1952), 429–35; Wilson, "The Economic Interpretation of Wilder" (1930), *ibid.*, 500–503; Wilson, "An Apeal to Progressives" (1931), *ibid.*, 518–33; Wilson, "The Literary Class War" (1932), *ibid.*, 534–39; Wilson, "Letter to the Russians about Hemmingway" (1935, 1952), *ibid.*, 616–29; Wilson, "Communist Criticism" (1937), *ibid.*, 640–50; Wilson, "Shut Up That Russian Novel" (1938), *ibid.*, 722–31; Wilson, "Marxism at the Crossroads" (1941), *ibid.*, 732–43.

See also *The American Writers' Congress*, ed. by Henry Hart (New York, 1935); C. I. Glicksberg, "Proletarian Literature in the United States," *Dalhousie Review*, Vol. XVII (1937), 22–32; C. I. Glicksberg, "The Criticism of James T. Farrell," SwR, Vol. XXXV (1950), 189–96; Ludwig Lewisohn, *Expression in America* (New York, 1932); Bernard Smith, *Forces in American Criticism* (New York, 1939).

CHAPTER XI

GENERAL: Harriet Monroe, *Poets and Their Art* (New York, 1926), xi; R. W. Stallman, "The New Criticism and the Southern Critics," *A Southern Vanguard,* ed. by Allen Tate (New York, 1947), 28–51.

WORKS OF T. S. ELIOT: *The Sacred Wood* (London, 1920); "Experiment in Criticism," B, Vol. LXX (1929), 225–33; *For Lancelot Andrewes* (London, 1928); *Selected Essays: 1917–1923; The Use of Poetry and the Use of Criticism* (London, 1933); *After Strange Gods* (New York, 1934); *Essays Ancient and Modern* (London, 1936); "The Social Function of Poetry," in R. W. Stallman, *Critiques and Essays in Criticism: 1920–1948* (New York, 1949), 105–16; *From Poe to Valery; Notes towards the Definition of Culture* (New York, 1949); *Poetry and Drama* (New York, 1951).

ON ELIOT: W. J. Bate, "T. S. Eliot," *Criticism: The Major Texts* (New York, 1952), 519–25; Horace Gregory, "A Defense of Poetry," NR, Vol. LXXVI (1933), 235–38; Horace Gregory, "The Man of Feeling," NR, Vol. LXXIX (1934), 23–24; Heiser, "The Decline of Neoclassicism," *Transitions in American Literary History,* 152; F. O. Matthiessen, *The Achievement of T. S. Eliot* (Boston, 1935); Delmore Schwartz, "The Literary Dictatorship of T. S. Eliot," PR, Vol. XVI (1949), 119–37; Edmund Wilson, "T. S. Eliot," *Axel's Castle: A Study in the Imaginative Literature of 1870–1930* (New York, 1931), 93–131; Eliseo Vivas, "The Objective Correlative of T. S. Eliot," *American Bookman,* Vol. I (1944), 7–18.

WORKS OF KENNETH BURKE: *Counter-Statement* (New York, 1931); *The Philosophy of Literary Form;* "The Five Master Terms," *Twentieth Century English,* ed. by W. S. Knickerbocker (New York, 1946), 272–88.

WORKS OF JOHN CROWE RANSOM: *God Without Thunder: An Unorthodox Defense of Orthodoxy* (New York, 1930); *The World's Body* (New York, 1938); "The Formal Bases of Criticism," SewR, Vol. LII (1944), 556–71; *The New Criticism* (Norfolk, 1941); "Poetry: I. The Formal Analysis" and "Poetry: II. The Final Cause," KR, Vol. IX (1947), 436–56, 640–58; "The Literary Criticism of Aristotle," *Lectures in Criticism* (New York, 1949), 15–43; "The Understanding of Fiction," KR, Vol. XII (1950), 189–218; "William Wordsworth: Notes toward an Understanding of His Poetry," KR,

Vol. XII (1950), 498–519; "The Poetry of 1900–1950," KR, Vol. XIII (1951), 445–54; *The Kenyon Critics: Studies in Modern Literature from the Kenyon Review* (New York, 1951).

WORKS OF ALLEN TATE: *Reactionary Essays on Poetry and Ideas* (New York, 1936); *Reason in Madness: Critical Essays* (New York, 1941); *On the Limits of Poetry: Selected Essays, 1928–1948* (New York, 1948); "To Whom Is the Poet Responsible?," *Hudson Review*, Vol. IV (1951), 325–34; *The Forlorn Demon: Didactic and Critical Essays* (Chicago, 1953).

WORKS OF CLEANTH BROOKS: *Understanding Poetry: An Anthology for College Students*, with R. P. Warren (New York, 1938); *Modern Poetry and the Tradition* (Chapel Hill, 1939); "The New Criticism and Scholarship," *Twentieth Century English*, ed. by Knickerbocker, 371–83; *The Well Wrought Urn: Studies in the Structure of Poetry* (New York, 1947); "Irony as a Principle of Structure," in M. D. Zabel, *Literary Opinion in America*, revised ed. (New York, 1951), 729–41; "The Formalist Critics," KR, Vol. XIII (1952), 72–81.

ON BROOKS: R. S. Crane, "Cleanth Brooks: or, The Bankruptcy of Critical Monism," MP, Vol. XLV (1948), 226–45.

WORKS OF R. P. BLACKMUR: *The Dougle Agent; The Expense of Greatness* (New York, 1940); "The Enabling Act of Criticism," *American Issues*, ed. by Willard Thorp (Philadelphia, 1941); "The Lion and the Honeycomb," *Hudson Review*, Vol. III (1951), 487–507.

WORKS OF YVOR WINTERS: "Poetry, Morality, and Criticism," *The Critique of Humanism*, ed. by Grattan, 301–33; *Primitivism and Decadence: A Study of American Experimental Poetry* (New York, 1937); *Maule's Curse; The Anatomy of Nonsense* (Norfolk, 1943); *In Defense of Reason* (New York, 1947); "Robert Frost; or, The Spiritual Drifter as Poet," SewR, Vol. LVI (1948), 564–96; "Robinson Jeffers," Po, Vol. XXXV (1930), 279–86.

ANTHOLOGIES OF THE NEW CRITICISM: Stallman, *Critiques and Essays in Criticism: 1920–1948*; M. D. Zabel, *Literary Opinion in America*, revised ed. (New York, 1951); R. B. West, Jr., *Essays in Modern Literary Criticism* (New York, 1952).

ON THE NEW CRITICISM: Conrad Aiken, "Back to Poetry," AM, Vol. CLXVI (1940), 217–23; Van Wyck Brooks, "What Is Primary

[314]

Literature?" YR, Vol. XXXI (1941), 24–37; Van Wyck Brooks, *The Opinions of Oliver Allston* (New York, 1941); Van Wyck Brooks, *The Writer in America* (New York, 1953); Canby, "Prophecies and Speculations," *Seven Years' Harvest*, 276–304; R. S. Crane, "Two Essays in Practical Criticism," *University Review*, Vol. VIII (1942), 199–202; R. G. Davis, "The New Criticism and the Democratic Tradition," AS, Vol. XIX (1949–50), 9–19; Leo Gurko, *The Angry Decade* (New York, 1947); W. J. Handy, *Poetry as Knowledge* (unpublished University of Oklahoma doctoral thesis, 1954); Kazin, *On Native Grounds;* Alfred Kazin, *Literary Scholarship: Its Aims and Methods* (Chapel Hill, 1941); H. J. Muller, "The New Criticism in Poetry," SR, Vol. VI (1941), 811–39; H. J. Muller, *Science and Criticism: The Humanistic Tradition in Contemporary Thought* (New Haven, 1943); Hoyt Trowbridge, "Aristotle and the 'New Criticism,'" SewR, Vol. LII (1944), 537–55; H. J. Muller and Cleanth Brooks, "The Relative and the Absolute: An Exchange of Views," SewR, Vol. LVII (1949), 357–77; Elder Olson, "Recent Literary Criticism," MP, Vol. XL (1943), 275–83; Elder Olson, "William Empson, Contemporary Criticism, and Poetic Diction," MP, Vol. XLVII (1950), 222–52; W. J. Ong, "The Meaning of the 'New Criticism,'" *Twentieth Century English*, ed. by Knickerbocker, 344–70; Ezra Pound, *Make It New* (New Haven, 1935); Theodore Spencer, "The Critic's Function," SewR, Vol. XLVII (1939), 552–58; Randall Stewart, "New Critic and Old Scholar," CE, Vol. XV (1953), 105–10; Mark Van Doren, "Achievements of Intellectualist Poetry," *The Private Reader* (New York, 1942); Van Doren, "Seventeenth Century Poets and Twentieth Century Critics," *ibid.;* Van Doren, "Poetry and Subject Matter," *ibid.;* Stanley Hyman, *The Armed Vision* (New York, 1948); Austin Warren, "Literary Criticism," *Literary Scholarship: Its Aims and Methods* (Chapel Hill, 1941), 131–74; Austin Warren, *Rage for Order* (Chicago, 1948); René Wellek and Austin Warren, *Theory of Literature* (New York, 1948); Hyatt Howe Waggoner, *The Heel of Elohim: Science and Values in Modern American Poetry* (Norman, 1950).

Chapter XII

General: T. K. Whipple, *Spokesmen: Modern Writers and American Life* (New York, 1928); T. K. Whipple, *Study Out the Land* (Berkeley, 1943); Wilson, *Axel's Castle;* Wilson, *The Triple Thinkers;* Edmund Wilson, *The Wound and the Bow: Seven Studies* (Boston, 1941); Edmund Wilson, *Classics and Commercials: A Literary Chron-*

icle of the Forties (New York, 1950); Wilson, *The Shores of Light;* Brooks, *The Opinions of Oliver Allston;* Brooks, *The Writer in America; Critics and Criticism: Ancient and Modern,* ed. by R. S. Crane (Chicago, 1952). On the Chicago Critics, see W. K. Wimsatt, Jr., "The Chicago Critics," CL, Vol. V (1953), 50–74.

Index

43, 45, 47, 49, 50, 57, 59–60, 64, 73, 77, 97, 101, 111, 112, 119, 120, 122–23, 129, 130, 132, 134, 141, 158, 188, 197, 233, 245–46, 251; *Lyrical Ballads,* 17, 78; Preface of 1815, 25

Yeats, William Butler: 233, 259, 282

Young, Edward: 14–15, 90, 130, 150, 234
"Young Americans": 91, 93–94, 97, 108, 112, 120

Zabel, Morton: 179, 207, 283
Zola, Émile: 30, 46, 125, 166–67, 180, 189, 207, 215, 244–45; *Le roman experimental,* 189; *Nana,* 189

This book on *Criticism in America* has been set in the types first conceived by the English type founder, William Caslon, whose great specimen sheet was issued in 1734, fourteen years after he began his labors on these now classic fonts. Based upon Dutch types of the seventeenth and eighteenth centuries, they are, however, greatly superior. They possess, in the Linotype versions used for the text of this book and in the American Type Founders' display sizes used for headings, splendid qualities both in individual letters and in the mass. In other words, they are highly readable without being obtrusive. Greatly favored in American printing during the period covered by John Paul Pritchard's account, they were an obvious choice for it.